ADAM ROBERTS

SUPERFAST PRIMETIME ULTIMATE NATION

THE RELENTLESS INVENTION OF MODERN INDIA

PublicAffairs
New York

Published by PublicAffairs™, an imprint of Perseus Books, LLC, a subsidiary of Hachette Book Group, Inc.

PublicAffairs books are available at special discounts for bulk purchases in the United States by corporations, institutions, and other organizations. For more information, please contact the Special Markets Department at Perseus Books, 2300 Chestnut Street, Suite 200, Philadelphia, PA 19103, call (800) 810-4145, ext. 5000, or e-mail special.markets@perseusbooks.com.

BOOK DESIGN BY LINDA MARK

A CIP catalog record for this book is available from the Library of Congress.
ISBN 978-1-61039-669-1 (hardcover)
ISBN 978-1-61039-670-7 (ebook)
LCCN: 2017006077

First Edition

10 9 8 7 6 5 4 3 2 1

For Sigyn and Glyn, with love

CONTENTS

THE WISDOM OF PARROTS

GOVIND PURI, IN SOUTH DELHI, IS HOME TO THE MODESTLY aspirational. People move through its alleys with a sense of purpose. Young men press by on motorbikes; screechy horns announce their arrival. Acrid fumes linger. Uniformed children bustle past. Houses are neat but ramshackle, their ceilings low. In the tiny, single-roomed home of Bhim Joshi, one's eyes need a moment to adjust after the bright sunshine outside. It contains one bed, one chair, and one low-energy bulb dangling from a cord. A fan blows hot dust onto blue walls.

Mr. Joshi, in a pressed white shirt and trousers, has been a fortune teller for thirty of his forty-five years. It is the family trade. He gestures to two cages each containing a parrot, explaining that "only one is effective," then places a green bird on his bed. I pass him a bundle of rupees as Indrani, my assistant and translator, immediately points out I have overpaid, as ever. The bird's work is disappointing and brief. In a blur it pecks at something among twenty playing cards spread on the bed.

"What does he say about India's future?" I ask. Unhappily, the bird has picked a scrap of paper, not a card. Worse, Mr. Joshi explains, Saturn is stubbornly unhelpful. He foresees "a little trouble, but India will get support. The economy is in difficulties but will revive." He cheers up: "Then India's place in the world will be number one." He switches from Hindi to English, repeating himself with a smile: "Number One!"

Mr. Joshi says the stars ordain that India will become the greatest power on Earth. In national affairs, a drama is looming: the death of an elderly leader, the assassination of another, and the marriage of an important dynastic figure. Then India will emerge stronger, with sporting triumph and great riches. One of the birds begins to sing boldly. I ask about individual political leaders. Will Narendra Modi—at the time an ambitious regional politician—grow more powerful? Mr. Joshi takes out a tatty almanac, with columns of dates, squiggles, and details of planetary comings and goings. He furrows his brow, purses his lips, and pretends to make a series of difficult calculations. Then a smile spreads. "He can become prime minister," he assures me, spinning a yarn about Modi's family business and great wealth. An hour later, wondering how different a reading by the defective bird might have been, we zigzag back through alleys, passing a stall with a griddle of sizzling meat.

Could Mr. Joshi and his feathered assistant foresee the future by drawing on ancient wisdom, Vedic history, a spiritual understanding, and knowledge of the stars? Were their premonitions of fate divined from something rich and powerful, an astrological force that can be tapped in the sub-continent but lies beyond the reach of closed Western minds? Not at all. They were jovial entertainers who scratched a living by spinning plausible stories. Mr. Joshi was a benign con-artist and charlatan, as likely to be right as anyone else, or as the flip of a coin.

Those who claim to intuit the future from reading the stars nonetheless get a respectful hearing in South Asia (and far beyond), including from the most powerful leaders. I once spent an entertaining morning in Galle, Sri Lanka, in a mansion with white marble floors whose owner was chief astrologer to Sri Lanka's president. We munched on a breakfast of treacle pudding, the astrologer's plate balanced on a bulging potbelly, and he foretold for me the president's lucky numbers. He also guaranteed the president a smashing victory in an election a few weeks away. It was a virtuoso performance in every respect but one: the president lost.

Looking back at Mr. Joshi's predictions, I find that most of them proved comically wrong. Perhaps he'd used the defective parrot. His promise that India, whose national football team was ranked 162nd in the world (behind tiny Barbados), would win the soccer World Cup turned out to be somewhat ambitious. India has never yet even attended the World Cup finals. He was wrong, too, to say that Mitt Romney would become America's president. But the art of reading the future is to make many specific predictions, hope one turns out to be correct, and then celebrate it. Mr. Joshi was spot on, for example, to say Modi would become prime minister. And his prediction that India would be big and powerful, "Number One," was not entirely fanciful. By the 2020s it will indeed be the most populous country on Earth. It has long been the largest democracy, and it is also gaining as an economic and military power. What would it take for India to prove Mr. Joshi right? What is keeping his prophesy from coming true?

I want India to succeed—not least because of the fun I have had, and the genuine welcome from Indians, during my several years as *The Economist*'s bureau chief in the country. Once I wrote a column for the *Times of India,* admitting that as a foreign writer in India I had the "best job in journalism," with freedom to explore a stimulating, thrilling, warm—if sometimes exasperating—country, to throw myself into conversation with bright, friendly, and demanding people, and to witness a giant beginning to shake off at least some of its worst problems. I even relished joining television debate programs, usually with Karan Thapar, a master of current affairs discussion, or hosting and speaking at conferences, and admired how most Indians tolerate a foreigner who shares in discussions about their future. It felt—and it feels—as if India is moving through a period historians will judge as a time of substantial progress, on most scores, however frustrating it is that many problems linger. The thrill I have had from traveling, reporting, reading about, and discussing India is immense. The challenge of progressing faster and improving millions of lives is just as big.

Introduction

SUPERFAST PRIMETIME ULTIMATE NATION

U NDERSTATEMENT GETS YOU NOWHERE IN CROWDED, NOISY, easily distracted India. Even overstatement often falls short. In India, a land of bombastic claims, you must be bold. It is not enough, for example, to promise to build a shiny new electricity plant. Instead you should brag about your forthcoming "Ultra Mega Power Project." Want to advertise a hospital? Then call it a "Max clinic" or "Max Super Speciality" and slap up the name in neon lights. If your daughter is to marry, then spend a fortune on a lavish week-long party for thousands, including strangers, so you can brag about your grand status. And if you ride a long-distance train, take a Shatabdi Superfast Express—or, better still, wait for India's super-duper bullet train, which is due to run on a Diamond Quadrilateral route.

On television, even on the dullest day, channels—"India's Best! India's Favourite! The Super Primetime Show!"—offer a guaranteed stream of Breaking News in flashing red-and-white block letters. More Latest Breaking News is scheduled for after the commercial break. It might concern "India's First 24x7 Primetime Prime Minister," or a Supercop, a Superduper Hit Hindi song, perhaps gossip about a Bollywood Megastar and her SuperHit film. News will break in a MegaCity about a Mega Factory or a politician's Mega Rally. A journalist who has chatted to someone interesting will naturally brag of her World Exclusive. And as private universities blossom, outfits vie for attention with superlative names. My favorite: "The Lovely Professional University" in Punjab, India's "Largest Best Private University," offers those who enroll a "mammoth ultra-modern high-tech campus sprawling over high-tech gigantic campus on the National Highway No. 1." No self-respecting student would settle for less.

India similarly sells itself as an "Incredible" tourist destination. Individual states brag, too. Bihar calls itself "Blissful," Gujarat is "Vibrant," and Kerala lays claim to being "God's own country." A hard sell is not always worse than a soft one: a mineral-rich but mostly poor state in central India for a time tried luring outsiders with the underwhelming slogan of "Credible Chhattisgarh." Others failed to follow its modest example, though I yearned to find more states playing safe, dreaming up "Average Assam," "OK Odisha," or "Less-Backward-than-Before Bengal." But such caution is rare: bold and boastful are more often India's style.

The problem, inevitably, is when reality fails to match the boasts. Those superfast trains plod at fifty miles an hour, not bullet speed. The news turns out to have broken long before. Super primetime television debate really means a gaggle of angry, middle-aged men with bushy mustaches shouting past each other—just as they did the night before. And along with politicians the world over, India's rulers struggle to live up to their showman promises. Talk of "good times" for all, a hundred new "smart cities," a manufacturing renaissance, and this becoming "India's century" can seem painfully misjudged amid desperate poverty or joblessness. Hot air rises. Sometimes the grandest swaggering belies a lack of confidence. Talk about politics, economics, and business and you'll hear a lot of belligerent claims, posturing, or bristling commentators. During social media or television debates, the open-minded are often crowded out by prickly nationalists who offer lectures on the greatness of their civilization and history, implying that a splendid future is India's by right. Many of the grandest claims, therefore, are best taken with a pinch of masala. But because India is growing, outsiders and Indians alike have to try to discern how bright its improving prospects really will be.

India can flourish. Its story, in the next few decades, should be the most cheerful period in its modern history. Demography—its size and youthfulness—gives it whopping potential advantages. The Indian economy can grow much faster than before and can grow more quickly than any other big economy in the next couple of decades. Villagers are moving into town and getting healthier, better educated, and less poor. Incomes are slowly rising, and consumer habits are changing. Bright people can find it easier than ever to inform themselves about the world. More are forming new companies, using new technology. More will—I hope—demand to live in a humane, liberal, and open society. These threads, woven together, can produce better lives and a stronger country—a rising, Asian, democratic giant. But first India has a lot of simple catching up to do: it must travel far simply to match basic standards already found elsewhere in Asia. The choices and policies the country's leaders should take are not too difficult to imagine. The uncertainty lies in whether they get around to taking and implementing them.

The crop of leaders who came to power in 2014 represented a decisive break from previous decades. Narendra Modi and those under him vowed to reshape the material prospects of roughly one-fifth of the planet's population. Potential gains were tremendous, an immense opportunity to be grabbed. Yet India's golden chance could also be lost, as previous chances had been. In the late twentieth century, economies in East Asia raced to be global manufacturing hubs, drawing hundreds of millions of people off fields and away from peasant work, creating a massive, new, Asian middle class. Those other countries invested early in schools and hospitals, improved conditions for women, lowered economic barriers, put their businesses and labor force into global supply chains, and so raised incomes fast. India, inward-looking and proud, kept aloof in not-so-splendid isolation, shunning trade and foreigners. As a result it remained mostly poor and rural. That began to change only when the country was forced, by an economic crisis, to begin opening to foreign trade, investment, and competition in the early 1990s.

To flourish in the twenty-first century, India needs its leaders to get four broad things right—the four broad themes and the sections of this book: Superfast, Primetime, Ultimate, and Nation. First, and the basis of almost everything, India needs to get conditions right for the economy to grow fast and for a long time. This means, especially, fostering better-functioning markets and generating tens of millions of jobs. If you traveled around India in the mid-2010s, ranging from its most backward, pre-industrial corners in the northeast to its booming megacities, you found a lopsided giant. The country was changing but remained divided, with big barriers between states, typified by long lines of parked lorries waiting at every state border so officials could shake down drivers for bribes or paperwork. Enormous patches of territory looked almost medieval, yet they were only a short distance from cities where life was modern and relatively comfortable.

In some states, such as Gujarat, Maharashtra, or Tamil Nadu, India flexed growing industrial muscle and demonstrated modernity—like reliable power and smooth roads—that cheered corporate leaders. Some Indian companies, operating at home and abroad, were bulking up. Especially in the south, where schools and hospitals were better, and increasingly along its coastal states, India developed human capital—healthy and bright workers, entrepreneurs, teachers—essential for widespread prosperity. In some states, the services industry boomed. But India in all had a desperately long way to go to turn its economy—over $2 trillion strong in 2016 but still with a modest share of the world economy—into a big global actor. Becoming Superfast, meaning a growing country with a powerful economy, will underpin almost everything else as India tries to improve its prospects. Getting less poor, as quickly as possible, is the basis for other progress such as building a welfare system, funding a greater military force, and strengthening foreign policy.

The world's biggest democracy also needs political parties, parliament, courts, and other actors to deliver better outcomes for people. By the late 2010s more educated, better-informed voters are impatient in the face of misrule, and fewer tolerate corruption and failure by their politicians. As a result, protests and public anger will be likely to get harder to manage. Those elected will have to do more than promise to help favored caste, religious, or other groups and learn how to deliver jobs and good economic times that will bring wider gains.

In the first seven decades or so of Indian democracy, that barely happened. Instead many politicians were rewarded for other reasons. The near-feudal powers of some big families—dynasties—let them dominate large populations of voters and also areas of business. But dynasts will not remain so powerful forever, even if they will not disappear entirely. By 2014, a more mobile, informed, and demanding electorate had the ability to make Indian democracy work better and politicians more responsive. Voters, especially those in town, were also getting more impatient, nationalist, furious over inequality, and perhaps more prone to bullying minorities. Today, two enormous domestic political issues loom. Indian rulers and voters have to manage and encourage a changing role of women in society. They will also have to respond to growing—potentially catastrophic—threats to India's environment, exemplified by the choking and poisonous smog that hangs over Delhi for much of the year. Demographic, economic, and other trends will give Indian politicians a rare opportunity to exploit: a young, large population getting wealthier and more urban, but also more demanding. If done right, in the political realm, India will enter its Primetime period, the second theme of the book.

The third broad area concerns India's growing role abroad. From being a bit player globally, India is sure to grow in the twenty-first century to be a more influential actor, shaping more events beyond its immediate region. A massive diaspora, a growing economy, increasing military and diplomatic might, a big and growing budget as a donor, nuclear weapons, and forms of soft power will all make India count in ways it has not before. (And as a democracy, unlike China, it is better placed to build supportive networks internationally and win sympathy from others.) Few people within India, even as late as the 2010s, took a strong interest in international affairs, beyond obsessing over Pakistan. This will change.

Three big relationships will probably dominate foreign affairs in the coming decades. Most pressing, and nearest to home, India needs to settle (where it can) old animosities with Pakistan. It can try to do that first by developing its economic strength as fast as possible and getting its internal politics to function much better—for example, in Kashmir. It needs, too, to tame the excessively nationalist posturing of its television broadcasters. But it will also have to engage Pakistan's civilian leaders and encourage moderates within its neighbors' armed forces. Perhaps even more importantly, India will have to find ways to better manage its relationship with China. Again, India first needs greater capacity at home—economic, infrastructure, diplomatic, military—and stronger relationships with more friends in the world. Finally, India's already improving relations with America will be a key to help with other relationships and could help to unlock faster economic growth. Cultural ties, especially given the 3 million or so people of Indian descent in America, could be especially significant. This third theme of foreign affairs, the "Ultimate" section of the book, has typically been neglected by most Indian politicians and voters. India's ultimate ambition, abroad, should be to gain much more influence and present itself as a rising great power. For that, an appetite inside India, to understand the outside world, will also grow.

The fourth and final broad area to get right—in this book summed up as "Nation"—concerns internal stability and the domestic, social aspects of the country. India's immense achievement in the seventy years after independence has been to remain stable and mostly peaceful. Much of Asia, the Middle East, and Africa escaped colonial rule at roughly the same time, only to fall into prolonged bouts of dictatorship, civil war, religious or ethnic massacres, proxy conflict as a part of the Cold War, and repression conducted by the state. Although South Asia suffered enormously at Partition in 1947, India afterward escaped the worst instability suffered elsewhere. India's democratic constitution, the religious moderation of its people, its political restraint, and the constant promotion of secular values are treasures to defend. But past success has been no guarantee of future performance. Indonesia aside, no other country has a larger Muslim population than India (Pakistan's Muslim population is roughly equal). Add in millions of Sikhs, Christians, Buddhists, and others inside India's borders, and the peaceful mixing of different religions with the majority Hindu population will always be a difficult process to get right.

How can India preserve this harmony in the face of rising Hindu nationalism, a form of Hindutva extremism asserting that India should be defined not by its secular tradition but explicitly by its majority Hindu culture and religion? Various politicians including Narendra Modi (as chief minister in Gujarat in 2002) have presided over, and later exploited for political gain, religious violence. Many liberals worry that intolerance is rising, especially after Modi's arrival to national office, warning that the space for secular, liberal debate and free speech is under threat. These fears could be overstated, but they also matter. Reasons to worry also exist when looking at hardening religious stances from others, especially the spread of Gulf-style, more fundamentalist, strains of Islam. A shift in behavior inside India threatens to produce more division between (and within) religious groups, less freedom for frank debate and discussion, and greater chances of violent confrontation. Again, such fears should not be exaggerated, but they are real.

The central figure to shape India's prospects, at least in the late 2010s and possibly for longer, is Narendra Modi, a prime example of a muscular, self-promoting figure with a nationalist-populist character. His profile fits a pattern of nationalist politicians who have risen to power in many countries at roughly the same time, in the years following a global financial crisis that began in 2008. Unbothered by any suggestion of being politically incorrect, a figure who champions himself as opposed to the elite or the establishment, Modi was happy to be counted as a voice of those with lower-to-middle incomes.

Modi is typical of a generation of leaders in several countries ready to whip up national grievances to strengthen their domestic control and popularity. In Japan Shinzo Abe promised voters economic revival and greater nationalist clout (after years of national pacifism and economic stagnation), just as in China Xi Jinping, its president, emerged as the most authoritarian leader of that country since Mao Zedong. Russia's president, Vladimir Putin, came to epitomize the idea of a strongman in international affairs. In Europe the rise of populist-nationalists was obvious in the mid-2010s, from Recep Tayyip Erdogan in Turkey to the far-right governments in Hungary and Poland, as well as movements that flared up within western European democracies—for example, as far-right parties reacted to inflows of migrants, or as British voters decided to withdraw from the European Union. In America, the president-elect, Donald Trump—cheered on from afar, by Hindu nationalists from India—also invoked nationalist slogans, lashed out against Muslims and other minorities, and promised to act tough against foreigners while offering vapid promises of future greatness.

The rise of muscular and majoritarian Modi in India can be seen as part of a global trend, as politicians of similar mold, such as Trump, Erdogan, Abe, Xi, and others, have come up. Yet India is exceptional. With a democracy and a fragile society where violence between members of different religious groups simmers, where old efforts have to be sustained to preserve calm between members of different religions, leaders must show that they can reduce tensions, not make them stronger.

Given these four themes, what are the chances that India will become a Superfast, Primetime, Ultimate Nation in the coming decades? Other countries, like China, are far more developed economically, but India has a political advantage as a democracy and is beginning to get its economic house, if slowly, into better order. Immense problems remain, and new ones erupt. Previous failures in India give skeptics plenty of reasons to doubt that it can really project itself successfully abroad. Yet even the most doubtful observers of India, those who worry that "neoliberal" policies are somehow the cause of more poverty, make no suggestion of taking India back to its most isolated and poverty-stricken days of earlier generations. India will improve in many ways in the coming decades, and anyone who has relished the chance to visit or live there will wish it well. How far and fast it now moves is the basic question of the book that follows.

FEBRUARY 2017

PART 1

SUPERFAST—ECONOMY

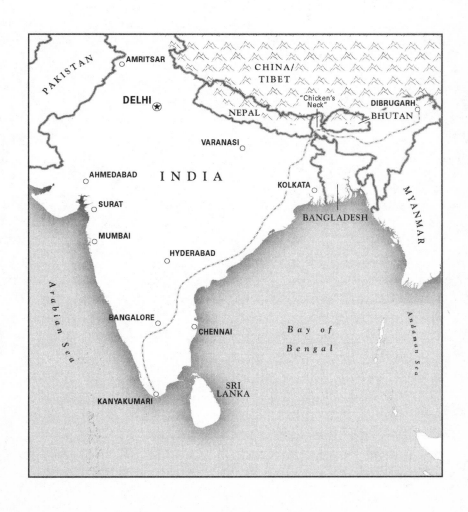

VIEW FROM A STOPPING TRAIN

THE AIR WAS CRISP IN DIBRUGARH, A TEA-PLANTATION TOWN high on the Brahmaputra River. The town offered modest sights: a colonial-era courthouse with elegant arches and a colonnade, streets lined with two-story concrete-and-glass boxes, shops stacked with imported Chinese plastic goods. "We are celebrating," said Ajit, a resident, though there were no fireworks, drums, religious processions, gaggles of families, or public boozing—the usual signs of merry-making. "Today is a festival for farmers, for cutting rice," he said. Locals would revel by feasting on sweet potatoes.

This land, at the end of a plain and below Himalayan foothills, was worth seeing as a vestige of an India that is fading away. The northeast, a region of paddy fields, terraced hills, beautifully crafted wooden homes—where lemongrass grew by the roadside and pigs plodded through villages—was far less heavily populated than much of the country. It was remote, more rural, notably poorer, and still heavily reliant on farming. Here nature could be wild: Cherrapunji, a small town in the tiny state of Meghalaya, bragged that it was the wettest place on Earth, where the monsoon might dump more than a thousand inches of rain in a year. Otherwise, the region could feel like a slow sort of place. No law in independent India prevented northeasterners from moving to more prosperous Delhi, or to southern India. (Citizens of China, by contrast, are restricted by its residency rule.) But years of poverty had much the same effect. Broken roads, a lack of phones, language differences, and cultural barriers long kept many Assamese, Nagas, Manipuris, Mizos, and others in their largely forgotten places. Only as generations of Indians grew more literate, and gathered a little wealth, did greater mobility begin.

This gradual historical development is a good jumping-off place for asking how India could get itself moving faster. Accordingly, the present chapter—and the rest of the section on Superfast India—is concerned with India's economy. If the country can get that rattling along more quickly, then much else will become easier to achieve. The idea of Superfast India means more than getting high rates of GDP growth, however. It means: getting structures, like good roads and a working state, set up for long-term, sustained growth; making sure that people get healthier and better educated as early as possible, in part so they can make India work better; spreading the gains of a bigger economy to far more people, especially by generating productive jobs; and using technology to give India a shortcut to meaningful economic development.

The isolation of some 50 million northeasterners, landlocked on the wrong side of Bangladesh, was an indication of the country's past failure to grow. But that isolation has been coming to an end: by the mid-2010s, for a little over $100, you could board one of many dozen flights each week from the region and leave for Kolkata or Delhi. Dibrugarh's fortune has been its shiny new airport served by a private airline, Indigo—India's largest airline and a model of corporate progress. Steadily profitable, Indigo has grown fast, is reliably on time, and has a young fleet. Its name and livery evoke something modern and mildly patriotic: historians say that the earliest trace of indigo dye is over five thousand years old, found at a site in western India. And like a dye staining a cloth, Indigo spread across the map of India. Along with other airlines, it has helped to change the country's sense of itself. Air routes have created a web of connections linking regions and towns, binding a continental-sized country. Each year some 85 million passengers flit through India's skies—fewer than the 394 million in China (or the 708 million in America), but enough to suggest a waking giant of a market. More crowded skies are a small sign of India becoming a new sort of place, of emerging prosperity, a country growing into its potential.

Another way from the northeast exists, if you can endure days on the road, or clattering on a train. In Dibrugarh after a weak winter sun has dropped, the Vivekananda Express, a continental stopping train, prepares to follow a route through the "chicken's neck," a twisting strip of land south of Bhutan and north of Bangladesh, then southward to India's distant southern tip. The service was launched to mark the 150th anniversary of the birth, in 1863, of Swami Vivekananda. A Bengali aristocrat revered by Hindu nationalists, Vivekananda did more than anyone to promote Hinduism globally in the nineteenth century. He famously addressed a gathering of "world religions" in Chicago, in 1893, speaking of India's main faith as the "mother of religions" and as "the most ancient order of monks in the world, the Vedic order of sannyasins." Hindus, he said, had taught the world tolerance. The crowd offered an ovation, and "the Hindu monk" went on to complete successful speaking tours of Britain and America. India remembers him with a memorial on a small island just off Kanyakumari, the southernmost point of the mainland. This weekly train trundles south to that spot.

The railways, however, are a relic of a run-down Indian past: overstaffed, under-funded, often dirty, rusting, with a design aesthetic unchanged since the 1940s. The national lifeline shifts at least 23 million passengers and 3 million metric tons of freight daily, which sounds like a lot. But it is too little and too slow for a massive, industrializing country. Goods and people move fitfully, at the wrong prices, often on tracks with no electricity. The railways ministry has for de-cades been a symbol of bureaucratic dysfunction. Having created paid posts—though not productive work—for some 1.3 million people, it is one of the largest employers in the world. But the railways themselves are a semi-modernized version of nineteenth-century infrastructure, a half-working institution that has helped limit India to mere wobbly, partial development. In fact, India's infrastructure more generally—bridges, roads, ports, powerlines—needs improving. Rail is a symbol of wider problems.

Traditions die hard on the rails. Well into the current century, rail-ways ministers dished out grace and favor, but made no serious effort to get trains moving. The aged network is almost a perverse source of democratic pride. Mussolini had made Italy's trains run on time, but he was a fascist. China has high-speed trains and 55,000 more miles of track than India, but China is authoritarian. India is chaotic and amia-bly slow—like its trains. Plus, it is a democracy. Ministers might bleed the railways, care only for the political short term, offer sops to voters in their home states, and oversee little investment, but for a long time crooked leaders have been tolerated as charismatic rogues, or as leaders who cared for the *aam aadmi*, the little guy. Failure on the rails has be-come emblematic of wider dysfunction—of a slow-trudging economy that fails to invest enough to develop. Since the British days, little new track has been laid. The Indian state has moved only slowly. The con-trast with the cheery private efficiency of Indigo is striking.

If you brave the stench of stations—where rails double as latrines—and ride the Vivek Express over 2,600 miles, you get an eighty-three-hour look at India, a glimpse of what needs fixing, and also, more brightly, some of what has begun to improve. The journey provides beginner facts: India is crowded, its people are young, much of its land is rich, well watered, and fertile. Along the way all your senses buzz at full tilt; absorbing strong colors and noise, you are jostled by crowds and confronted by heat and heady odors. Fellow passengers are drawn from a modestly rising middle class, those who have begun to prosper through travel. Northeasterners who moved away have won a chance to improve their lives materially. In Assam, the poorest of the Seven Sister states, incomes were just $860 in 2015, less than half the national average, little above subsistence level. For a day of back-bending toil, a tea-picker there might earn 50 rupees (less than a dollar), plus lodging in a shack and some food. That was near slave labor—conditions that tea companies preferred customers not to ponder over a cuppa. But if a worker got south to better-run Kerala, he could multiply his daily wage five-fold. The gap between northeast and south shows the distance that all of India hopes to travel to become a modestly well-off place.

"You are right to take the train, it is best way to see all India's beauties," Ajit said that evening in Dibrugarh, with the glib assurance of one who had never gone. The Express left on time without whistle or warning, and moved through one of the more neglected patches of territory on Earth. Whole books, often excellent ones, have been written on India with barely a passing mention of the northeast. Correspondents pass years in India without troubling to visit this region. Many Indians, even those familiar with London, New York, or Beijing, never set foot in Kohima or Guwahati. "Mainlanders," from the recognizably triangular Indian mass, talk of their eastern appendage with distant curiosity, as they might discuss Mongolia or Botswana. Some suggest it is somehow akin to China or East Asia, hardly proper India. Others speak of it as they do of the past—barely related to the booming upheaval in much of the rest of India. Northeasterners, they say, are eastern, "mongoloid." The thoughtless, or racist, call them "chinky eyes."

The northeast is poorer in part because of instability. Separatists had sought self-rule when Britain ruled India. They continued to seek it after 1947 and Indian independence. Naga separatist fighters and other rebels led guerrilla campaigns from the forests, winning foreign weapons and funding—early on, from China. Nagas, a broad term referring to at least seventeen tribal groups with many dozens of different languages and dialects, had declared themselves free from British rule a day before the rest of the country. Their leaders said they deserved recognition as a separate nation. Though the fighters did not come close to winning, they scrapped on for decades. Jawaharlal Nehru, India's first prime minister, professed his love for the wider region, but he also oversaw what amounted to a small civil war there, mostly ignored by the outside world. By the 1950s, the Naga National Council claimed that it would unite 800,000 Nagas across India and Burma, boycotted India's first general election, and fomented rebellion. India deployed its national army. Other rebellions flared. By the 1960s, with Indira Gandhi in charge, the national air force flew punitive raids against civilians, strafing and bombing villages in the Mizo hills. Years of sporadic violence, perpetrated both by the state and by the insurgents, helped to explain the northeast's lingering backwardness.

Northeasterners, even well into the current century, have had reasons to feel differently from the rest of India and not only for reasons of geography. An official from Kohima, the capital of Nagaland state, once grumbled to me that "we have had fifty years of insurgency basically because people here don't feel Indian." Food habits are a telling example. Christian and tribal northeasterners, influenced by Southeast Asian culture and Baptist missionaries, notably Americans, happily guzzle beef or pork—a diet alien to many Hindus and Muslims, nearly 95 percent of India's population. An obsession among Hindu nationalists to get the cow designated as a symbol of "mother India," and to ban the eating of beef, has left minorities, including those in the northeast, feeling excluded.

Economic activity began to pick up in the northeast over the past couple of decades, especially as the central government started paying almost $5 billion each year to buy off dissent. Rising incomes helped a little to reduce the idea of irredeemable differences. The spread of television brought further change. At the start of this century only 60 million households in India (out of about 192 million total), mostly in towns, and relatively few in the northeast, had a television set. By 2015, 175 million households had access to a TV (out of about 250 million total). Viewers could watch the same shows and ads at the same time. News channels broadcast common calamities and triumphs and stirred national debates. India's four great national obsessions—cricket, films, soap operas, and politics—offered a steady flow of material to chew over. Programs were often shouty or ridiculously confrontational, in some cases adding vim to the news with an animated ball of flame that exploded, for no obvious reason, every few seconds on-screen. Whatever the style, Indians for the first time reliably shared experiences simultaneously, allowing more to imagine their country as a single, national community.

The spread of cellphones did something similar. Only 25 million landlines existed in India as of this writing, in 2016, compared with more than 1 billion cellphones serving an estimated three-quarters of India's population. Within a few more years, half a billion Indians will have (mostly cheap) smartphones with Internet connections. On the train, most people send texts, instant messages, or e-mails. The spread of cellphones, more than any other technology, exemplifies dramatic—Superfast—development. These devices, as in other countries, have become ubiquitous. By making the spread of information almost free, they have unlocked profound (if sometimes hard-to-measure) changes in politics, the economy, and the wider society. Farmers and coastal fishermen, now equipped with phones, have better knowledge of weather to come and, crucially, of market prices for their goods. More information means power: the ability to choose where and when to bring goods for sale.

A great example comes from Kerala: after cellphones first appeared there in the late 1990s and early 2000s, fishermen could call ashore and find the best place to land their catches. They saw profits rise steadily, even as the average price of fish fell for customers—the result of less waste and more efficient markets. Similar gains spread throughout the country in the following decades. Equally important, those with cellphones could get a message from, say, a cousin in town, telling them of jobs available on a construction site and helping to smooth the flow of workers into urban jobs. The spread of such phones, largely driven by the increased activity of private firms, shows how infrastructure can improve dramatically: a small part of what should make the economy more successful, and lives better, in the long term.

Families in the northeast were helped by such phones. They kept in touch with migrant children, who increasingly went off to fill corners of Delhi, flourish at universities, and staff hotels and restaurants all over the country. Phones helped to enable migration, and more mobility helped to strengthen India. A graduate from Khonoma, a steep hillside Naga village of grey stone buildings perched above rice paddies, once the heartland of Naga separatism, said that he was leaving to teach at a mainland university after one-third of his fellow villagers had already migrated. Indians were growing readier than before to move about, and northeasterners appeared to believe less in separation and more in grabbing economic opportunity.

The Express did its own modest service, stitching the northeast a little more tightly to the rest of India. At one stop a man from Tripura, a tiny northeastern state, explained that he was traveling for hospital care to Vellore, in Tamil Nadu, over 2,000 miles away. A woman from Assam was taking her aged mother, who had a brain tumor, to a hospital in the same town. They discussed the south with admiration, because it was wealthier and better run than the north—a concrete example of what the rest of India might become. Aromas of spices and oil wafted from the last carriage, where a twenty-four-year-old from Manipur, Pentan Kshetu, presided over the train's kitchen. As he prepared rice, dal, and curry for passengers, he said earnestly that the railway "100 percent it is connecting India and everybody is proud." A Punjabi passenger called the service a "metaphor for uniting India" and admitted that "we didn't always think of the northeast being in India."

Kshetu's region was getting more stable. By the 2010s, those dozens of Assamese, Naga, Mizo, and other separatists had mostly fallen dormant, many having been bribed into quitting the forests. China long ago stopped supporting separatists. Governments of neighboring Bangladesh and Myanmar no longer gave rebels sanctuary. India's central government claimed it had struck a historic peace accord—in fact, one that had been under negotiation for decades—with the largest group of Naga separatists. "Unfortunately, the Naga problem has taken so long to resolve because we did not understand each other," said Narendra Modi, the prime minister, not long after coming to power. He blamed the British, in colonial days, for spreading "terrible myths" about Nagas as monsters or cannibals.

Even though much of the money the central government poured into the northeast was stolen, it probably helped the region to become more stable nonetheless. An American diplomat in Kolkata said that a "devil's bargain" let ex-insurgents and politicians take many funds to get themselves big cars, fancy houses, and private education for their children. But by doing so they also grew soft, smothered by the cash until unwilling to resume the hardships of rebel life. By the 2010s, shops in Dimapur, the dusty, low-rise main commercial town in Nagaland, had become crammed with pricey handbags, leather goods, and other accessories. The boss of one luxury-goods company once explained to me how sales there occasionally trumped revenues from much bigger towns, like Kolkata. And Monalisa, a poet-cum-journalist in Dimapur, called Nagaland "a wild world" where locals binged on others' money. Extra cash flowed when elections loomed: "This is the time to earn money from politics. We condemn this, but when we get the chance we take the money," she said, laughing. More potential existed for the region, including hydropower by tapping gushing rivers, natural gas deposits, tourism, construction of proper roads to the border with Myanmar, and trade with Southeast Asia or China. But these developments would not happen for years, despite India's long-standing claims to be "looking east and acting east."

As the train zigzagged south, pings and effusive greetings from cellphone companies marked India's progress. Time passed in happy conversation with gaggles of teachers and youngsters, soldiers and traders. Students crowded around laptops to watch films and explained that they were traveling to fill college classes in the south and find jobs in the booming tourism or restaurant trade. Civil servants headed to cities like Chennai and Bangalore for computer training. Petty entrepreneurs ran thriving business on board. Young men with steel urns shouted "chai chai" and poured shots of milky, sweet tea, filling tiny plastic cups for 5 rupees each. Small traders in the carriages exchanged stories of profits turned in far-flung corners of the country.

A middle-aged man in an orange lungi and a tatty white shirt said that he had spent twenty-seven years riding the trains, trading coconuts and goods such as paan—betel leaves chewed as a mild stimulant. He bragged about the natural wealth of his southern home, calling it a "small England" and describing it as a fertile region of international trade over the course of thousands of years. He introduced himself as "Mr. K" and proved to be a jovial companion. He swigged rum for breakfast, belched, and sounded satisfied with his mostly nomadic life: "I journey all over India. Goa, they have sea shore and many temples. Gujarat, for forest and lions. Srinagar, it is just like America! Madhya Pradesh, many palaces you will see. I am birthed in Tamil Nadu, so I like it most. I like, fully, India, for India has many types of man: Hindu, Muslim, Christian, Buddhist, even Britishers, Koreans, and Negroes. I will ask for them to send a photo!"

At times Mr. K and I stood in the open door, as he smoked and we watched the train creep through villages with tarmac roads. He pointed out improvements of the past few years. Here are signs of India beginning to change. Round haystacks encase the bases of new mobile-phone towers. Satellite dishes are balanced on corrugated metal roofs. Mr. K points out that smallholders have dug ponds in their fields to farm fish rather than grow crops, meeting soaring demand for protein as rural incomes have risen. Most houses now have concrete walls, no longer the hard-packed mud walls that were evident earlier in the journey: half of India's entire stock of concrete houses have been built in the decade after 2000. The train trundles past thousands of brick kilns, their chimneys spewing black smoke above paddy fields and casting shadows over the startlingly red earth.

These are signs that the most extreme poverty is slowly being overcome. Hunger and especially malnutrition persist: as recently as 2015, one in three Indians still got insufficient nutrients to live well. But thanks to the Green Revolution since the 1960s and 1970s, the use of higher-yield crops, fertilizer, and more irrigation, plus some basic welfare and nonfarm incomes, outright starvation is no longer a threat except in the most remote places. Paradoxically, present-day studies show that the daily quantity of calories consumed by Indians, on average, is drifting downward—though apparently for a welcome reason, because the demand for calories, among those who do less physical labor, is falling. How different this is from decades before. Under British rule the country, mostly agricultural, had suffered murderous famines, high taxes, and lack of investment, and later saw only modest industrial growth. British traders and rulers lacked the means or inclination to turn a massive nation of peasant farmers into a modern, industrial economy, even though some giants of Indian industry—such as Tata and Godrej—had come into existence then.

Colonial rule was a heavy burden on India. Although estimates are rough, the country's share of global income fell from roughly one-fifth to less than 5 percent in the broad span of the colonial era, an indictment of those who extracted much personal wealth along the way. Economic growth under the British was dismally low. Over the four decades between 1880 and 1920, for example, average annual economic expansion was just 1 percent, roughly the pace at which the population grew. Growth in incomes was dire or nonexistent for most, but this period at least saw investments in some hefty projects that brought long-term gains. Massive irrigation canals in Punjab allowed the creation of productive farms, notably of wheat, that today feed hundreds of millions in India and Pakistan. Railway lines—to extract coal, for example—were rolled out and helped to connect some well-planned new cities. But India at independence remained a predominantly peasant economy for most, with only a modest middle class and a tiny, prosperous urban elite.

Historic failures alone, however, cannot explain the economic disappointments and isolation that followed in the decades after independence. Under Nehru the economy largely remained in private hands, and Nehru himself demanded rapid industrialization. But his government believed in state-led development, publishing five-year plans for an economy directed primarily by civil servants who allocated resources and licenses to private actors, which inevitably meant favoring those with political ties. Nehru personally did not like the company of business leaders. Ramachandra Guha, a superb observer of Indian history, suggests that Nehru's Brahminical background and the influence on him of British socialists and aristocrats left him unable to trust capitalists, and he shunned them throughout his seventeen years as prime minister. The state-led model brought limited progress. Overall economic growth did nudge up and expansion occurred in some areas of heavy industry, such as steel-making. But imports were discouraged, and Indian firms were later told to make their own—often far lower standard—substitutes for foreign goods. Some industries were nationalized, and failing businesses were blocked from closing because of the loss of jobs. Nehru's turn toward closed borders and a state-led economy was not extreme in the context of the 1950s and early 1960s—the tragedy was that it was prolonged and deepened.

Where India really lost its way economically was in the later 1960s and 1970s under Nehru's daughter, Indira Gandhi, a driven political leader whose ambition was to centralize as much power as possible into her government. When politics demanded, she veered farther left than her father. She turned for support among radical students and left-leaning backers inside the Indian National Congress in the late 1960s, then nationalized India's banks and clamped strict bureaucratic limits on industrial and private growth. She ordered state-run companies, directed by officials, to take more control of the economy. India isolated itself ever further, with tariffs and other barriers discouraging trade and limiting who could access foreign currency. Efforts to boost small rural businesses achieved little. Under her, the powers of inspectors and other officials to lord it over private firms and individuals grew. The "license Raj" became a nightmare of bureaucratic bullying: firms had to deal with many dozen state authorities—by some estimates, as many as eighty different ones—to get a license to produce anything.

The rest of Asia began to liberalize economies from the 1970s onward, and incomes soon rose in the more open parts of East Asia as manufacturing grew. Yet India remained lumbered with the "Hindu rate of growth"—a term coined by an Indian economist, Raj Krishna, though some preferred to call it the "Nehruvian rate of growth"— meaning economic expansion only barely above population growth. Most people were stuck doing peasant labor. A consequence was that India's population grew far larger than it might have done. In the twentieth century, family sizes increased among poor, ill-educated, and rural people, whereas among urban people, and in much of the rest of Asia, family sizes shrank as incomes rose. That lingering poverty is the main reason why India's population will peak late in the twenty-first century at around 1.7 billion. Had India cut poverty earlier, its population might instead have been heading to a peak nearer 1.4 billion or 1.5 billion, roughly equal to China's.

India began to eliminate some of the worst of its economic policies from the mid-1980s and, especially, the 1990s. Even Indira Gandhi, belatedly, began to grasp the need for economic reforms, or at least more cautious spending, to control rampant price rises. Public spending and populist slogans had seemed beneficial at first, but they produced mostly shortages and inflation, and they did little to cut poverty. Efforts to liberalize financial parts of the economy began tentatively under Rajiv Gandhi, her son, in the 1980s and then intensified after a balance-of-payments crisis in 1991. Reforms were led by Narasimha Rao, a Congress prime minister, and his finance minister, Manmohan Singh. Rao ordered the scrapping of the worst elements of the "license Raj," thereby allowing more trade and financial flows and cutting some powers of bureaucrats. In doing so, he and Singh unleashed a new services economy in India—in call centers, business outsourcing, and more—the main driver of rising incomes ever since.

Looking out from the Vivek Express by night as it moves slowly south, one cannot always see the progress that has been achieved. Much of India still appears to be made up of darkened villages, and as recently as 2016 nearly two-thirds of Indians—officially—remained in the countryside. But their lives really are changing. Few villages are fully isolated. On most farms, average plots are too small to sustain families year-round, so most villagers supplement their harvests by collecting government welfare, running rural businesses such as tiny barber stalls or showrooms selling scooters and phones, trading goods in town, or receiving remittances from relatives working in cities. Even if many villages still fall dark after dusk, roughly three-quarters of Indians have some source of electricity at home. In the countryside many still cook their evening meal on smoky fires and charge their cellphones from car batteries. But this scenario is changing as well. Arun Jaitley, Modi's finance minister, vowed in 2015 that every Indian, by the early 2020s, would have a *pukka* house, electricity all day and night, clean drinking water, and sewerage. He conjured an image of India matching the basic achievements seen in the rest of Asia. It will probably take longer, until the 2030s, to reach his goal. But even if the economy plods along at roughly the pace of a stopping train, living standards will rise. The challenge, of course, is to move faster than that.

Traders pass through the rattling Vivek Express. Sellers of biscuits, tea, and samosas climb aboard, supplementing the stodgy fare from the train's kitchen. Mr. K munches on boiled eggs, giving an elaborate explanation of how they fend off the winter cold. Farther south, men arrive laden with biryanis, chicken, or vegetables. A steady flow of beggars follows. A transgender Hijra in a red-and-gold sari claps her hands and demands alms with just a little air of menace. A one-legged boy with a stick sweeps the floor for coins, followed by a beggar with no hands, a bag hung from his stumps. The train passes semi-urban areas, boys on bicycles, the odd station beautifully kept, brightly colored garments on clotheslines, small shrines. We move through an old mining district, skirting hills of black slag ringed with startlingly green palm trees. Nearby villages look grim, strewn with rubbish, blackened by dust. The thatched roofs on some houses are sagging. But webs of wires suggest that these at least have electricity. The Express nudges on at little more than walking pace.

India plans to fix its railways. The man in charge, Suresh Prabhu, the current railways minister, is probably the most effective figure in that post in decades. He has an admirable record from a previous ministerial stint in the early 2000s, when he reformed and liberalized India's power sector and refused to gather bribes for his party, Shiv Sena. Prabhu as railways minister says that India will learn from China's history on the rails, pointing out that Deng Xiaoping began fixing its train system in the 1980s even before reforming farms or industry. By 2015 China was investing three times more in its railways than India, as a share of its GDP, and charging its passengers higher prices. In India freight trains trundle without schedules; goods—even heavy products like steel—are diverted to lorries that pollute and jam already-crowded roads. Coal carried by trains at times fails to reach power plants, a reason for blackouts.

Prabhu further noted that "what matters is to be market friendly, completely transparent." Any move in that direction would help. Selling government-owned railway units is politically impossible, he conceded, but they can be made to behave more like private firms, compete, raise capital, and focus on what customers need. He wants to crush the power of the minister to meddle. "The whole idea is not to be ideological, but what makes it work better," he said. He spoke of spending $140 billion on the creation, by 2020, of new tracks, stations, trains, and more, with grand renovation a symbol of a changing, developing India.

This renovation is happening, but slowly. Unions have opposed reforms, especially any that would cut the number of workers. The railways have run schools, hospitals, and companies that make everything from engines to bottled water. Foreign firms like America's GE or Europe's Alstom have won contracts worth billions of dollars to produce new rolling stock from India's factories. Google has started equipping India's railway stations with high-speed Internet. And some of the new tracks are coming. For example, a long-promised Delhi–Mumbai freight corridor, some 1,000 miles long, is supposed to open by 2019 (it will probably come later), and another new rail corridor has begun unfurling eastward, toward Kolkata from Delhi. More dubious is Narendra Modi's vanity project—a $15 billion high-speed or "bullet" train from Mumbai to Ahmedabad—to be built largely by Japan as a tribute to the blossoming friendship between the two big Asian democracies. This pet scheme of Modi's is meant to symbolize progress, but funds would be better used to improve the rest of the railways network. Prabhu's basic, unglamorous projects—getting ordinary trains to trundle more quickly—will matter far more to most Indians.

Standing in the filthy corridors of the Vivek Express, more tortoise than bullet train, one realizes that there is much that could be improved quickly. A cleaner gathers a mound of plastic, cardboard, food scraps, bottles, tissues, and other mess, and hurls the trash through an open door and onto the tracks. Toilets are holes in the cubicle floor. Despite official talk of ending open defecation, the practice continues in most of India's 12,500 trains. A conductor who climbed aboard in Tamil Nadu called his train horrible, and was scathing about northern passengers. He described watching a man urinate from an open door, though an unoccupied toilet was beside him. He saw a woman hold her young daughter to piss in a sink. "It is the cow-belt population, a backward people, they hold India back," he complained. That train, by then, had the feel and smell of a refugee camp.

Outside, however, the air is fresh from the sea. Palm trees line the beaches of Kerala. There are backwater lakes, garish pink houses with bright murals on their walls, and roads that lead into neat towns. Eventually the Express empties. Mr. K, now dressed in a smart white shirt, disembarks, offering heartfelt good-byes. No new passengers bother to board, because travel here is far quicker on the well-built roads. Beyond the carriages, southern India is clean, warm, and well-ordered, relatively wealthy. Stations are quiet; the roads are straight. We have reached the most southerly point of India, Kanyakumari, only a few minutes behind schedule after a journey of several days. From the sea, a breeze wags the tips of branches, and a few passengers, Hindu pilgrims, shuffle off to visit the island shrine for Swami Vivekananda. The journey was not Superfast, but it revealed some significant changes unfolding across the length of India.

ARGUMENTATIVE INDIANS

SPARKS FLY EASILY IN INDIA. THE MOST AMIABLE DINNER GUEST from Mumbai, striking up a conversation with a counterpart from Delhi, will soon fall into an intense debate over the merits of each mega-city. If you are foolish enough to offer an opinion on Indian cricket—the game is taken more seriously than religion by many—then brace yourself for somebody within earshot to deliver authoritative statistics on batting and bowling, plus anecdotes aplenty, to correct your naive mistake. Venture into politics, let alone set out a view on some cultural matter, and you had better prepare for hours of closely argued and passionate history lessons, usually delivered as if from a well-rehearsed text.

Such debates may sometimes produce less light than heat, but they can also illuminate. Take the example of an erudite economist, Amartya Sen—appropriately, the author of *The Argumentative Indian,* among many excellent books. Sen has a sharp sense of humor and sustained energy and has never been shy about offering an opinion. In 1998 he won the Nobel memorial prize in economics for his writing about welfare and development. A Bengali, now a little gnarled and with a voice impediment, Sen has remained alert, traveling almost nonstop, well into his ninth decade. Until 2015, he led an ambitious project to relaunch an ancient university, Nalanda, in rural Bihar. And on frequent visits to India (he has long lived in Britain and America), he liked to chat over a glass of red Sula, an Indian wine, and discuss the fortunes of his motherland. Is the economy delivering gains for its people, and if so, how quickly and how equitably? How might progress come more quickly, and can it be sustained?

Sen, and his close collaborator, Jean Drèze, wrote at length about one issue in particular: the desperate need for much better "human capital," meaning people who are healthy, educated, able to work and live productively, sufficient to form a strong base for India's sustained growth. Sen had helped to draw up the United Nations' annual "human development index" in 1990, along with a Pakistani colleague, Mahbub ul Haq. It measures life expectancy, the education levels of boys and girls, and income per person, ranking countries by the outcomes. Sen wanted a tool that would get economists and policymakers to pay more attention to the well-being of real people, not just to cold, abstract numbers.

This focus on human well-being feels intuitively right—that the point of economics, or almost any pursuit, is how well it helps people to live better or happier lives. Sen's approach is bolstered by an argument drawn from the real world, suggesting that successful economies first create strong human capital as the basis for getting materially richer later. In the twentieth century, for example, China did a far better job than India in three areas: educating its people; improving public health, nutrition, and hygiene; and making sure fewer women die in childbirth. The World Bank, in 2010, offered a measure of just one failure, calculating that lack of sanitation costs India $54 billion a year, from illness, early deaths, lost productivity, and more. This is a problem that China has more or less left behind.

India is not uniform. Sen spelled out how the south of the country has flourished, thanks especially to stronger human capital. In Kerala, incomes are roughly equal to those in some well-off northern or western states, but the proportion of children in the south who suffer early deaths—the infant mortality rate—is only one-third of that in Gujarat, for example. By the 2010s, if you were born in Kerala you could expect to survive into your late seventies—almost as long as in European countries. That is about a decade more than somebody born in Gujarat. Investment in public health and in schools explains some of this. Also, girls receive more support in the south. In Kerala, long before independence, local royalty had promoted education for girls; churches and mosques did the same, as did politicians, after independence, in the Communist and Congress parties, which took turns running the state. Remittance money from workers in the Gulf also helped, and much of that was spent on private schooling. Hospitals and hygiene are relatively high-quality, too.

The broad case Sen and others make for creating human capital early is convincing, though one might argue about the best ways to create it—for example, over how big a role the state should have in running schools and hospitals, or the degree to which foreign groups, such as the mammoth Gates Foundation, can supplement health efforts in poor states. But the fact remains that India urgently needs to improve the well-being of its people, as its lowly ranking on the human development index suggests. By 2015, even as some Indians described themselves as an emerging great power, it ranked just 130th out of 188 countries on that index. On education, crucially, India lags. In 2016 a big Indian chamber of commerce, Assocham, published a report warning that India's education system was failing its people: the country spent less than 4 percent of its national wealth on education, whereas Britain spent nearly 6 percent and Denmark nearly 9 percent. Even with some recent improvements, Assocham predicted, India will need another century, or more, to get its education standards to match those in rich countries.

Such concerns with human capital make sense. But not everybody is happy with Sen's approach. The Bengali academic has an academic nemesis: Jagdish Bhagwati. A long-standing rival, a similarly bright, witty, and self-confident intellectual drawn from the other coast of India, in Gujarat, Bhagwati is a figure who hails from an alternate part of the political spectrum. A prominent economist who has also long worked and lived in America, he is just as brilliant and as argumentative as Sen. A few months younger than Sen, he was widely said to be furious that his rival, not he, was the first Indian to get an economics Nobel. He once admitted in an interview with the *Financial Times* that he gets "worked up a bit" each year over the fact that the Nobel committee failed to award him "the bloody thing." (His anger over losing the prize is so well known that even *The Simpsons* referred to it in an episode of the show.) Bhagwati is no shrinking violet. Perhaps in jest, he once told a journalist colleague of mine that he not only deserved the Nobel for economics but should really get one for literature, too.

Feuding between Sen and Bhagwati became public and notorious, played out internationally, and offered a handy perspective on arguments about India's economy. The two octogenarians exchanged excoriating letters, published in *The Economist* (in response to reviews I had written of their respective books, both excellent) and then elsewhere. Bhagwati accused the Bengali of failing to grasp that economies first have to grow quickly, as the priority must be to create resources for redistributing later. India's greatest weakness, he argued, is not its weak human capital but its failure to set policies for rapid GDP growth. He wrote that Sen "belatedly learned to give lip service to growth, which he has long excoriated as a fetish," as "he continues to assert that redistribution has led to rapid growth in Asia, a proposition that has no basis in reality and puts the cart before the horse. Growth has made redistribution feasible, not the other way round."[1] Bhagwati, writing elsewhere, attacked Sen for failing to back liberal reforms in India, and also got personal. He once suggested that Sen's "lip service" paid to growth was insincere, "much like an anti-Semite would claim that Jews are among his best friends."[2]

Sen shot back, writing that "I have resisted responding to Mr. Bhagwati's persistent, and unilateral, attacks in the past, but this outrageous distortion needs correction," that he long championed rapid growth as essential for cutting poverty, and that public efforts to tackle "illiteracy, ill health, undernutrition and other deprivations" do not count as mere redistribution of incomes. He cited examples of Japan, China, Korea, Singapore, and other countries to back up his argument that human capital must improve early.[3]

Bitter exchanges between two economists might seem arcane. But their argument mattered, especially before the election of 2014 when public debate arose over the success, or not, of Gujarat as an economic model for the rest of India to adopt. Bhagwati was an eager supporter of his fellow Gujarati, Narendra Modi (though not of Modi's Hindu nationalism), and lauded his economic record in running Gujarat. Bhagwati loudly cheered progress in Gujarat's industrial growth and road-building, and he predicted that dramatic improvements in social indicators would soon follow its rising incomes. He accepted that Kerala had higher levels of literacy and life expectancy, and did better on other social indicators, but argued that Gujarat would catch up fast as it got richer. Higher incomes could come first, he said, pointing to faster economic growth across India that obviously benefited many: the World Bank counted 133 million Indians lifted from the worst poverty between 1994 and 2012, an amazing achievement that coincided with rising growth rates.

The trouble with Gujarat as a model, however, was that too many of the weakest in society got left behind. "Modi thinks he can deal with human capability after India gets rich," snapped Sen one evening as we chatted, "but even Milton Friedman said India is neglecting its human capital." Sen, a close ally of Manmohan Singh, the Congress prime minister from 2004 to 2014, called Modi "obtuse," as "he is not a learner." Modi, including in interviews with me, had claimed he was replicating Singapore's success in Gujarat and had long praised Lee Kuan Yew, the city-state's old authoritarian leader. But Sen, who had known the Singaporean, dismissed Modi's understanding of what made Singapore rich, pointing out big efforts made to get its residents healthy and highly educated. "There are two things that Modi should have learned from Lee Kuan Yew: the value of human capital, the value of a multi-ethnic society where all groups are treated equally. Lee Kuan Yew was a really intelligent politician. He thought about education. I don't think Modi in a thousand years would get close to Lee Kuan Yew or Margaret Thatcher," said Sen.

Across India, average incomes are rising, but deep pools of the worst deprivation—for example, among tribal people and the lowest caste—will not drain without public help. That means the state needs to do better—for example, by spending more on basic, public health. Yet few Indian leaders seem to grasp Sen's arguments. The World Bank suggested that overall spending on health in India was equivalent to just $75, per person, for a year, in 2014. Public spending was just one-third of that, a pitifully low amount. By comparison, China spent $420 per person, overall, and Brazil $947. In Gujarat, in particular, health or education did not appear to be priorities. As chief minister, in an interview with me, Modi had denied doing too little for health, education, and human welfare, talking of getting more girls into school and stopping them dropping out. He pointed to lots of new universities in Gujarat, to colleges that taught forensic science and children's psychology, and to a special center for training recruits for the army, navy, and police. "We are first in India, we have started a university for the teachers. The whole world requires the best teachers, and India is a youth power, so we want to train the teachers and we can export even teachers," he said. He spoke of innovation to lift survival rates of new-born babies, with the state paying private doctors to help mothers. He said that previously fewer than half of the women in his state, Gujarat, gave birth in clinics, but "today it is 98 percent, so it is safe delivery."

That all sounded appealing, but upon closer analysis the results from his model disappointed. An international health official, dismayed by Gujarat's lack of social progress, described to me how she had once made an unannounced visit to a clinic for tribal women, on the edge of Gujarat's capital, Gandhinagar. In a mostly empty building she found a mother who had given birth two days earlier, her child lying on a cot nearby, unwashed, dangerously cold, and not yet breastfeeding. Asking a nurse for warm water to wash the child, she was told the taps were dry. Taking bottled water to do it, she asked for soap and was told the clinic had none. This medical center with its poorly trained staff was not in a remote desert or forest. It was around the corner from a massive concrete convention hall where billionaires gathered to brag about showering hundreds of billions of dollars on Gujarat, which they said "shone like a land of gold."

In fact, contrary to Bhagwati's expectations, there is evidence indicating Gujarat's continued poor record on health and human well-being. In 2015 an official passed along to me a remarkable set of unpublished data, gathered in the previous two years by the United Nations and the Indian government. Based on a massive survey across every state, it assessed basic progress on health. It counted how many people had been vaccinated against measles, polio, whooping cough, and diphtheria. It checked rates of hunger and nutrition among babies, young children, and pregnant mothers. It assessed the height and weight of children, comparing people by income and other background measures such as caste and wealth. It recorded the weight of teenage girls, efforts to deworm children and to get women to give birth in clinics, and much more.

The results were a trove of information, updating decade-old official figures. They were leaked to me because government officials were refusing to release the results, even though these data showed general gains across India. It was obvious why the information was being kept secret: it embarrassed Gujarat. Many states had delivered steady gains on human capital, but the best performers had been those that (perhaps

persuaded by Sen's arguments) targeted public help for the most vulnerable—for example, tribal people. In Gujarat, improvements lagged
badly. It failed in the simplest actions, such as giving universal basic
vaccinations. About two-thirds of all Indians received these shots, but
in Gujarat only about half got them.

Most damning was the failure to make sure that people were properly nourished. Hunger fell only gradually in Gujarat, at a rate no faster
than across the rest of India, despite the state's fast-rising incomes.
Across India, nearly 30 percent of children were still reckoned to be
underweight, a level ten times worse than in China, and also much
worse than in Africa, where 21 percent of children were underweight.
Gujarat lagged behind India as a whole, with 33 percent of its children
underweight. It also did badly on other measures of malnutrition, such
as stunting and wasting. Kerala and other southern states, as before,
performed well. The best comparison for Gujarat was with its neighbor
on the western coast, Maharashtra, where incomes were roughly the
same but health indicators had improved much more quickly. Better
outcomes were the result of political leadership: Gujarat had failed to
develop public health schemes, whereas next-door politicians and *babus,* the civil servants, targeted help at the neediest populations, especially tribal people.

Talk of hunger, especially afflicting tribal people and the low caste,
stirred little interest among India's rising urban population. Yet roughly
one-third of Indian babies remained stunted or underweight in 2015,
a long-term burden. The brains of malnourished children often fail to
develop as fully as those of well-nourished kids. One-third of India's
future population could fall badly short of their potential. Gujarat did
well in some areas, notably in building infrastructure and getting investors to act. But it stumbled in human capital, the sort that Sen saw was
essential. If Gujarat were to be seen as a model for India, such a model
would be a badly lopsided one.

Some parts of India deliver far better lives for their people than others. One rule of thumb is that states along the coast (and especially in

the south and west) have long been better off than most landlocked ones. Those farthest from the sea are often the least prosperous or well-run of all. Those territories with a history of being open, trading with the outside world, still seem to flourish most happily. Roman coins unearthed in southern India and on its western coast showed there had been trade over the Indian Ocean for millennia. In Ancient days, gold and silver flowed eastward from Europe across the ocean to pay for silk, cotton, and animal skins as well as for tigers, elephants, peacocks, and other exotic animals. In Roman Pompeii, in an ordinary home, archaeologists found an ivory figurine brought from India, a small indication of something Pliny the Elder complained about: the fact that trade with India, China, and the Arab peninsula drained at least 100 million sesterces from Rome each year. (It is impossible to give a modern dollar conversion for that sum, but to get a rough comparison, 1 million sesterces was considered a large personal fortune, the minimum required to become a Senator.) At the time of Roman Emperor Augustus, two millennia ago, at least 120 ships crossed yearly from ports in Egypt to India and Sri Lanka, carried by monsoon winds. A papyrus dating from the second century AD detailed hugely valuable cargo on board a ship traveling from southern India to Egypt, listing boxes of oils, spices, and around one hundred pairs of elephant tusks, presumably destined for Roman buyers. Subsequent centuries brought other traders, from Europe and from China, to the same ports on India's coast.

In modern India the most southern states, Kerala and Tamil Nadu, boast relatively high incomes, decent social indicators, and political stability. A zone of southern prosperity that began to spread northward in the twentieth century has continued to do so in the twenty-first century. Andhra Pradesh, which was formerly plagued by Maoist insurgents, plus a newly formed state, Telangana, and a third one, Karnataka, is starting to match the far south in terms of rising incomes, at least in larger cities like Hyderabad and Bangalore. Family sizes have shrunk in the south, education levels and life expectancy have risen, and social indicators show that many southern Indians are living comfortably mid-income lives, not too far behind some people in Southeast Asia. Without migrants from north India, the population of the south would no longer grow. The western seaboard has also become wealthier, even if it does not parallel the industrial might of China's eastern coast. Taking a path along the coast, one finds decent roads and schools, rising cities, new airports, hotels, malls, and other businesses running up from Kerala, through Karnataka, to Goa—a former Portuguese colony where average incomes are just about India's highest—into Maharashtra through a manufacturing area in Pune, to the financial capital, Mumbai, and finally up to Gujarat. In such places India is blossoming.

Farthest west is Gujarat, which was carved from Bombay State and boasts a long history of trade. On its long, wiggly coast—Gujarat has about a fifth of India's coastline—dhows and wooden fishing boats are yet built to ply the Arabian Sea, as they did for centuries (reportedly smugglers to Pakistan like to use the boats). Old habits of entrepreneurialism help to explain why Gujarati sons and daughters have done so well, often as small businesspeople, diamond-dealers, hoteliers, and shopkeepers. Extended family networks, the Patels especially, support each other and finance expansion abroad. Gujaratis flourish in Africa, Europe, America, and beyond—a prime example of a footloose trading community.

A second broad point about the parts of India that have done well concerns the role of the state. India's perennial problem, despite being a democracy, has been the failure of its state to deliver basic services of all sorts. Gujarat became a revealing example as a part of India where civil servants have proved efficient at some tasks, mostly in terms of helping investors set up manufacturing businesses, even if they fall short on human capital. Its spin doctors and supporters would liken Gujarat to Guangdong, the great manufacturing region of China. In fact, other bits of India also have decent economic records at getting factories running, and some tall stories about Gujarat have had to be discounted. Official bragging about its efforts for the environment seem misplaced in a state that has depended hugely on oil refining and the production of chemicals and fertilizer. And a much-heralded "ministry of climate change," opened in 2009, achieved little of note.

But some things certainly worked. Functionaries who ran Gujarat were more efficient than most, important in a country where administrative dysfunction and graft holds the economy back. India appears to have plenty of government: by the 2010s it employed over 20 million people who (in addition to staffing administrations, schools, hospitals, and the like) oversaw the railways and the national airline, managed large parts of agriculture and big steel companies, were responsible for much of a troubled banking system where crony businesses took out big loans, and a great deal more.

An author friend, Gurcharan Das, argued that India's biggest weakness is state capacity that cannot match its growing duties. A park in Delhi where he liked to walk is dotted with six-hundred-year-old tombs, built by Lodhi invaders from Afghanistan, a reminder of how Delhi had seen waves of rulers over the centuries. None had been able to establish anything to equal China's more efficient, often more repressive, administrations. Gurcharan further noted that China, beginning more than two thousand years ago, built its Great Wall, defining and defending its border and also strengthening central authority, as its state put untold numbers of people to work and gathered funds. India, by contrast, made do with oceans and the Himalayas to mark and defend its frontiers, and its central state remained relatively weak. Mughals who ran north India often had patchy control of their empire. British colonists, who took over from trader-adventurers in the East India Company, controlled territory with remarkably few people. Much was run indirectly by princes and kings. Gurcharan pointed out that, in 1938, the central government in Delhi was staffed by just eighty-one civil servants. Even at the time of this writing, in 2016, many Indian frontiers remain undefined, unmarked, unguarded. The state is thin.

Another observer likened India's state to the body of a middle-aged man—with fat in all the wrong places. Too many *babus,* the civil servants, tried to do things better left to markets. Officials ran steel, coal, airline, hotel, and watch companies but had skewed incentives—for example, doing what pleased politicians rather than customers. They fixed artificial prices for rice, wheat, fertilizer, some forms of energy, and more. Meanwhile, too few *babus* achieved crucial things like running efficient customs, registering businesses quickly, getting towns policed after dark, or stopping factories from polluting rivers and air. Crucially, too few did anything to improve education. The thin state is also meddlesome: thus, Indian business can grow only "at night," said Gurcharan, when no officials or politicians try to extract rent or block one firm's progress to benefit a favored rival. The great boom in cellphones is an example of success when nobody looked: officials were prevented from interfering, slow to grasp how valuable the industry would become and how much rent they could extract (though crooked politicians and officials did eventually take massive payoffs). Gurcharan reckoned that India's state had been crumbling for decades. "It is a flailing state," he said. "No single institution has disappointed Indians more than the bureaucracy."

Yet there were times when the state really worked well. My favorite example comes from Surat, at one time a town well-known for the wrong reasons. It is on the coast of Gujarat. Early in the 1990s it suffered overcrowding, chaotic planning, and floods. Mud and decaying animal carcasses in the streets, heaps of uncollected rubbish, rotten food, open sewers, swarms of rats—all combined to produce the filthiest city in India. An outbreak of pneumonic plague was reported, causing international alarm. But Surat responded thanks to its chief *babu,* the municipal commissioner. Go today and you see (and smell) a city transformed. Tour the municipal underbelly and you find a place notably better run than much of India. The sewerage plant has neat gardens, reservoirs, imported German machinery, computer control rooms, aerators, tanks, and waterfalls of progressively less stinky water. A bio-gas plant generates electricity. A city rubbish dump has covered lorries that drop trash in compactors imported from Britain. Even at the height of summer, there are no bad smells, flies, or dust piles; nor is garbage spilled about. "Surat used to be so dusty and unorganised, I've seen the city change in front of my eyes," said Himanshu, a local journalist. Even allowing for local pride, the absence of grumbling there is exceptional.

Surat's population exploded more than six-fold from the early 1980s, exceeding 6 million by 2016. Its diamond industry, run especially by Jains, is said to polish eight in ten of all the world's diamonds. The industry's operations are slick: factories are sterile, air-tight, and dust-free; trays of precious stones sparkle under bright lamps. Young men and women sit in rows at long white tables and peer through powerful lenses to study the rocks that they shape. Once a week, a train trundles down the coast to Mumbai, with men on board whose coat pockets are sewn closed around polished diamonds, to be traded around the world. Other industries, such as synthetic textiles, draw hordes of mi-grant workers. Shopping malls, palm trees, and coconut-sellers line its well-swept streets.

What went right in Surat was local government. The sitting admin-istrator of the city explained during a visit: Manoj Kumar Das was young, professional, and marvelled at the progress unfolding around him. He called Surat the "fourth-fastest growing city in the world" and predicted it will have 9.3 million residents by 2031. He boasted of re-liably fresh, piped water, a steady supply of electricity, proper sewerage, a power surplus, and growing industries. These were big achievements given deficiencies elsewhere. Unlike in some parts of Gujarat, he said that "great harmony" existed between religions, too.

Surat improved partly because a crack-down on corruption sent a message that the state functioned. *Babus* had to be transparent, to complete tasks wherever possible online, where decisions such as those regarding public tenders could be monitored easily. Civil servants were not rewarded for raising bribes for political bosses, the *netas*. The ad-ministrator exaggerated a bit. Himanshu, the journalist, said corrup-tion did still happen, but, crucially, it was kept within bounds that everyone understood. Surtis, people from the city, distinguished among three forms of graft, Himanshu explained: "One is *nazurana,* a gift of appreciation; a second is *sukurana,* a thank you for a specific transaction; a third form is *jaburana,* or extortion. In Surat the first two sorts of payments can be tolerated, but never the third." Elsewhere, more debilitating forms of corruption-as-extortion remained more common.

Surat's story showed mainly that civil servants could be motivated to get the state to work—and its approach could be replicated. The city planted 200,000 trees every rainy season, as protection against more floods. It fumigated for mosquitoes, which cut rates of malaria and dengue. Most Indian cities left heaps of rubbish in roadside piles, but a private company was contracted in Surat to incinerate trash and generate electricity—something other cities could do, too. Slums were cleared and tens of thousands of new homes built. The administrator claimed that 96 percent of residents paid municipal taxes, many early. "There is a positive environment across India compared to twenty or thirty years ago. More resources are at our command, better consultants, there is a desire to improve, there is better education, people expect more," he said. Shame had spurred the city to act, after some countries refused visas to Indian travelers because of fears of the plague. Local ambition had soared. "We want to be like China. We will be bigger, we have a great opportunity," he said.

The turnaround in Surat mostly happened long before Narendra Modi took office in Gujarat. But Modi talked a lot about *vikas,* or development. On trips to China as chief minister he would have heard its leaders recite a slogan that "development is the only hard truth," and he adopted similar mantras. He talked of his state as a home to good infrastructure, honest civil servants, lots of investment, and fast-rising incomes, where far more people than average had electricity at home. He once bragged to me, exaggerating somewhat, that every village in Gujarat got uninterrupted power, implying he could make that happen nationally. In fact, Gujarat had specific advantages, being well placed to import oil and gas from the Gulf. It had a grid of gas pipelines. But the state government had broken an indebted electricity board into parts and split power supplies for farmers (who got it cheap, eight hours daily) from other consumers (they paid a market price, but got it non-stop). He boasted of hiring five hundred dedicated electricity police to "stop theft in power supply." Elsewhere vote-hungry politicians ignored such theft, heavily subsidized power for all, or granted farmers unlimited free use of electricity. Such populism led to waste, lack of investment, and bad service. In this area, Gujarat was a bright exception.

Modi, too, claimed that his rule was honest. With no wife at his side, he said he had no relatives to abuse his position. Others lauded his refusal, early on, to let political cronies run state firms. It would have been better if more firms were permanently removed from any political control, but, despite saying that "government has no business to do business," he did not seek a smaller role for the state. Pressed to say whether he wanted any state-run firms sold into private hands, he demurred. He appeared most comfortable with a limited form of state capitalism: tough political leadership to get state firms managed less badly. Once I suggested to Modi that his anxiety to keep a personal grip implied he was an authoritarian, "a dictator." He called the idea "absolutely baseless," claiming that he got his state to function by inspiring "team players."

Modi measured economic success mainly by how many industrial investors, especially manufacturers, set up in Gujarat. For example, Tata, one of India's biggest companies, had planned in 2006 to produce a tiny, cheap car—the Nano—to wow the rising middle class. Tata began in West Bengal, where the government provided one thousand acres of fertile farmland, and Tata built most of its factory. But two years later, after protests by dispossessed Bengali farmers and populist politicians, Tata fled to Gujarat instead; it was one of many car firms that did well there, even though the Nano itself flopped. (Demand for the car did not take off, in part because some early models burst into flames, but also because few consumers aspired to buy a vehicle best known for its cheapness.) Business leaders lauded the progress being made in Modi's state. At a summit for investors in Gandhinagar, Gujarat's capital, Ratan Tata, who long ran Tata Group (the firm was worth around $125 billion in 2016), recalled that Modi won him over beginning with a text message that simply said "welcome." Critics hinted at behind-the-scenes deals for investors, saying they got excessively cheap land, power, and other good terms. But Ratan Tata, revered for increasing the value of his firm enormously, was a supporter. He thanked Modi for helping big businesses to thrive, saying that "he [Modi] is embarking on advancement of rural people, their health, and wealth," and telling Modi himself that "your leadership has been exemplary."

Tycoons heaped on praise, making grand pledges (never entirely fulfilled) to bring billions to Modi's state. An investors' meeting in 2003 announced collective promises to spend $14 billion in Gujarat; by 2011, their pledges topped $450 billion, roughly a quarter of India's entire GDP. That was as likely to come as snowfall in the Rann of Kutch. But the inflated numbers won headlines. And Gujarat regularly did get either the most or the second-most investment of any state. Anand Mahindra, chairman of Mahindra Group, said that Gujarat had an exceptionally business-friendly climate: "it's different here, you can see it, breathe it." Anil Ambani, another billionaire, simpered that Modi was "one of the greatest change agents for India in the last decade."

Investors liked smooth roads, reliable power, a bureaucracy that worked—a functioning state that took and implemented decisions relevant to them. The state's economy almost tripled in size under Modi (who ruled from 2001 to 2014), growing by about 10 percent a year. Gujarat matched China's performance and outpaced India as a whole. Despite having only 5 percent of the national population, it had roughly one in ten of all formal jobs and 16 percent of industry and it pumped out a quarter of all exports. In addition, around a quarter of all sea cargo passed through Gujarat's ports.

Cronyism did not stop entirely. Political opponents said that big firms, such as Adani—another conglomerate whose bosses were close to the ruling politician—grew rich. Investors knew they had to meet

Modi and get his personal support to clear the way for any project. Dependence on access to the big man undermined the idea that institutions were strong and independent. Tax holidays, allegedly cheap prices for land, low-cost power, and other incentives lured big firms from other bits of India. Those who ran smaller companies, especially Muslim Gujaratis, did not get the chief minister's ear and grumbled that the benefits of growth were not equally shared.

Gujarat's above-average infrastructure helped a lot. Ahmedabad, the main city, was better planned than many, and its suburbs were home to a new middle class. Residents lived in swish-looking housing developments often with bizarre names, presumably rejected titles for ringtones such as "Riviera Blues," "Pegasus Earth," "Pacifica Reflections," and "Fantasy World." The state, largely desert, got water thanks to a new, 300-mile-long canal, the Narmada, which cheered farmers even though green activists called it destructive. Gargantuan projects that involved millions of tons of poured concrete worried environmentalists who alleged that the main purpose was to stroke Modi's ego.

A grand scheme rose in scrubland north of Ahmedabad, an area known for heat and earthquakes. An artificial lake and 110 glass towers were to be built there by the early 2020s and already, by 2015, two seventeen-story towers shimmered above the dust. An estimate that the promised city would deliver $50 billion worth of financial services to India appeared to be a notion plucked from the thin desert air. Known as GIFT (Gujarat International Finance Tec) City, it was to be an example for one hundred "smart cities" that Modi promised he would bring to the country. One tower stood empty, but the other had offices filled with morose young men, employees of state-owned banks, presumably sent there to please the government. "GIFT came about because Modi wanted a flashy vision, it is ridiculous," said a town-planner, pointing out that GIFT City was built in part by a Chinese firm using a Chinese model—an Ozymandias-style folly in the sands.

But not all big projects were misguided. India needed better-organized cities, and a project in the heart of Ahmedabad was more appealing. Enormous riverside walkways had been built on reclaimed land, along with new parks and a market for traders who were previously jammed into a slum. If you walked with tens of thousands of people along its carved stone paths as families cheered and laughed, it was obvious how the right public spaces improved lives. Far too few cities provide anything similar. The redevelopment came at some cost: twelve thousand former slum-dwellers, in a prime location, were rehoused miles away on the edge of the city. Those displaced might get new homes, but far from jobs or proper public services. The Ahmedabad scheme was also artificial: the "river" was a man-made puddle, on which jet skis and speedboats took tourists for rides. An activist complained that "the center of this redevelopment is really a big, stagnant pond that flows nowhere" and pointed to a layer of thick green weed on the unmoving soup. But the economic activity and the excited faces of the tourists were real enough.

Does Gujarat offer evidence that India would take a new course, letting its economy deliver higher rates of growth, encouraging the state to become more responsive, and allowing better infrastructure to get built along with improved human capital? In the dispute between Sen and Bhagwati, it was clear to me that the humane argument—that India's most grievous problems are its failures to see people properly nourished, cared for, and educated—is the more powerful one. In this regard, Gujarat is far from a model for others to follow. Yet in other respects, such as getting civil servants working, building better roads and power systems, and attracting companies that create jobs, some of the answers offered by Gujarat have been essential for the rest of India to follow.

3

AFTER THE SONIA-AND-SINGH SHOW

ALMOST ANYTHING YOU SAY ABOUT INDIA COULD BE TRUE—
and the opposite, too. Progress under Manmohan Singh, the
prime minister from 2004 to 2014, for example, badly disappointed many observers. Yet the economy had also performed better,
on the face of it, than in any comparative period in the past. Singh's
government, led by the center-left Indian National Congress, was supported (and sometimes constrained or compromised) by a gaggle of
smaller parties, including Communists for the first five-year term. The
real center of political power in any case was Singh's boss as head of
Congress, Sonia Gandhi, a woman with a remarkable political story.

Born just after World War II in Italy's northeast, Edvige Antonia
Albina Maino (she later switched to "Sonia") was the daughter of a
mason who had supported Italian fascists under Mussolini and served
in the Italian army. In the 1960s Sonia enrolled at a language school
in Cambridge, in Britain, and there she met a young Indian, Rajiv
Gandhi, who attended the famous university. Sonia reportedly earned

her income as a waitress at a Greek restaurant when the two met. After marriage and moving to India, the two expected no political career: Rajiv trained as an airline pilot and flew for Air India. In the 1970s his ambitious and unscrupulous younger brother, Sanjay, had instead been groomed to join and eventually succeed their mother, Indira Gandhi, in politics. Gossipy accounts depict Rajiv and Sonia as determined socialites, passing their evenings at Delhi dinner parties, uninterested in politics to the point of guilelessness.

But after Sanjay and Indira both died—the first after crashing a stunt plane, the other murdered by her Sikh bodyguards—Rajiv became India's youngest prime minister yet, at the age of forty. Sonia Gandhi adopted Indian citizenship and then, after Rajiv in turn was assassinated by a Tamil suicide bomber, it fell to her to assert dynastic control over Congress. That took some years, but by the late 1990s she had led Congress and had crushed a rebellion by rival party leaders who said her Italian heritage disqualified her. Having been elected as an MP, and winning devotion from voters in Uttar Pradesh, she went on to head the national opposition in parliament. She grew in confidence. By the time of a general election in 2004, she was a strikingly effective campaigner, drawing on a personal story of family sacrifice (the loss of her husband, the murder of her mother-in-law) and adopting some of the mannerisms and guile she had witnessed in Indira Gandhi. She made a point of dressing like Indira Gandhi and talking of the former leader's "innate sense of fashion." Such details mattered: in the early 1980s, Sonia had outdone the widow of Sanjay Gandhi for the affections of their mother-in-law, Indira, by picking out saris for the elder woman, winning endearment and raising her status.

Other democracies have their dynasts. Americans are now used to seeing Clintons, Kennedys, and Bushes vying to be president. But dynastic stories are most remarkable in South Asia. In 2004 Sonia Gandhi delivered a surprise electoral victory for Congress, then shrewdly renounced any claim to be prime minister and appointed Singh to the post. The nominee couldn't have suited her better: Singh, who reliably wore a pale blue turban and a pleasant but somewhat docile expression, would serve for a decade as her front man. He was bright, kind, and timid, more functionary than politician, often mute in public. Unable to win a seat in the lower house of parliament, he posed little or no political threat to her, however great the office he held. Nor was he troubled with charisma. His old college in Amritsar, in Punjab, offered no sign that this alumnus was celebrated, or much remembered. But he had a reputation for integrity and a record as a sound economic manager. Singh's presence suited Gandhi, letting her hold political power but without the tedious responsibility of assuming office.

It had been Singh, directed by a previous Congress prime minister, Narasimha Rao, who guided India through its first liberalizing economic reforms in the early 1990s. By 2004 it was clear how those and subsequent changes, though initially painful, ushered in an economic boom, especially in the services economy. The Gandhi-dominated faction of Congress under Sonia nonetheless had denied Rao credit, seeing him as disloyal and objecting to evidence that the party achieved most in the few years when the Gandhis were sidelined, immediately after Rajiv Gandhi's death. When Rao died, in 2004, an embittered Sonia Gandhi and her supporters prevented his getting a full funeral in Delhi, as a former prime minister is usually due. Rao's family was told to make do in Hyderabad instead. In a display of abject pettiness the Gandhis even prevented his funeral procession from entering the Congress headquarters in Delhi.

The Bharatiya Janata Party (BJP), the largest on the center-right, had also carried out liberal reforms in the late 1990s and early 2000s. In national office the BJP bragged about "India shining," rapid growth, and drawing in foreign investment. But Sonia Gandhi and Congress displayed greater electoral skill, convincing voters that the center-left party had the interests of the *aam aadmi,* the common man, most at heart. Congress promised that economic growth would be matched with more help for the needy, that farmers' loans would be written off, and that a great splurge of spending would flow to the poor as subsidies, welfare, grants, and pensions.

Congress's leaders believed that their talk of a "rights-based approach" for voters won them two national elections, in 2004 and in 2009. A "right to work," for a modest wage, was introduced for one hundred days for villagers who built dams, roads, and other publicly useful things. A right to subsidized food was unveiled, to cover some two-thirds of the population, expanding earlier cheap rations aimed at the neediest. The right to a free, midday meal for all schoolchildren had proved successful in Tamil Nadu, so the lunch was rolled out nationally. Other rights included state-backed health insurance (for some) and universal education: all children were promised places in state schools and minimum standards, at least in theory. Farmers also got rights to cheap supplies of fertilizer, gas, and other rationed goods. Many of these rights, naturally, turned out to be less than ideal in practice, and they relied on officials to administer them. The right-to-work scheme, for example, was often mismanaged, involved officials taking cuts of wages as bribes, or saw the shoddy building of public works washed away in the next monsoon. Right-to-education rules were often little more than an excuse for extortion by inspectors.

The ten years under Singh up to 2014 were mixed, but they undoubtedly gave rise to real improvements for many. The new rights—promoted by an advisory group of social activists and left-leaning thinkers close to Sonia Gandhi—were supposed to improve human capital, of the sort Amartya Sen emphasized. At the same time, Singh tried to deliver economic growth through limited liberal reforms—for example, by allowing foreigners to invest in supermarkets, so as to improve supply chains and markets for food. Singh also tried to remove subsidies on petrol and, more slowly, on diesel—subsidies that distorted markets and rewarded the rich. He also wanted to create a single market, with standard tax rates, across India. Yet liberal reforms were painfully slow in coming. Singh lacked the political clout, or even the appetite for politics, crucial to getting parliament to pass reforms. That goal required active backing from Sonia Gandhi, who remained head of Congress for a record eighteen continuous years (and counting, as of 2016) and who was boss of the ruling coalition of parties. In many matters she directed Singh, appointed his ministers, set policy, negotiated with allies, and haggled with opponents to get bills through parliament.

Singh had limited say over some policies and appointments. But one of his most important achievements, in September 2013, was the selection of a much-respected figure, Raghuram Rajan, to run India's central bank. Rajan won over international investors, speaking bluntly about widespread crony-capitalism in India and the need to fix up the country's troubled banks. His influence was benign; his presence somewhat made up for an earlier, awful, decision to make Pranab Mukherjee—an ally of Sonia Gandhi—finance minister. A veteran, Machiavellian figure who cared little about economics, Mukherjee conspired to scare off investment, and bullied timid Singh. Mukherjee was booted upstairs in 2012 to be India's ceremonial president, a post in which he could do less damage.

Singh's presence did cheer international observers, plus urban voters. But Sonia Gandhi had to reconcile different camps. Congress was divided, with a left-leaning group opposed to liberal reforms and a minority that saw their benefit. (Inside the opposition BJP, nationalist politicians also fiercely opposed reforms that would let foreigners win access to markets or threaten the interests of small traders.) Congress's coalition allies, such as the Communists and Trinamool, from West Bengal—the state that included Kolkata (formerly Calcutta)—also opposed any "neoliberal" change, such as easing labor laws so that companies could more readily hire and fire workers. Worse, several big businesses—the cronies that Rajan and others opposed—had strong influence on some in Congress and government. Many business leaders sought official favors, contracts on preferential terms, and minimization of competition. The strongest firms even got direct influence over who should run the energy and telecoms ministries. A scandal known as the "Radia tapes," in 2010, revealed recordings made by intelligence services of business leaders, or their fixers, trying to shape ministerial appointments and decisions. In effect, big firms donated to politicians and bought political influence. Some coalition partners, such as a party from Tamil Nadu, were brazenly corrupt. Though Singh was personally honest, he utterly failed to get a grip on such graft.

The prime minister was more active in foreign affairs, which helped the economy. He promoted better relations with America, delivering a civil-nuclear deal just before the election in 2009. It was designed to open up imports of uranium and make the running of nuclear power plants easier. That deal, pushed through parliament, broke Congress's alliance with Communists. (Some opposition MPs apparently were bribed to support the legislation.) It was the highlight of Singh's career as leader and an opportunity missed to begin pursuing other reforms or initiatives. Singh also yearned to improve ties with Pakistan, showing remarkable restraint after Pakistani-backed terrorists attacked Mumbai in 2008.

But as global economic conditions got harder, as the financial crisis from 2008 onward dragged on, Singh lost his way. He agreed not only to borrow and spend to stimulate the economy and pay for the new welfare but also to write off big loans to farmers (often through crooked agricultural banks, whose bosses no doubt cornered much benefit). Gandhi saw these outlays as politically essential, though years of high public spending crowded out private investment and stoked up infla-tion. Singh's economics team presented grand schemes—dressed up, Soviet-style, as "five-year plans" under a "Planning Commission"—for long-term investment, promising over $1 trillion to improve roads, railways, ports, airports, and other infrastructure by 2020. The plan-ners said private capital would fund much of that, along with toll roads and other "public-private partnerships." But these involved ever more dubious ties between politically connected contractors, officials, and badly managed state-run banks. Back-handers and dodgy spend-ing were widespread and stored up painful problems for later. Roads improved only slowly. The main highway from Delhi to Mumbai, for

example, had for years on end the same half-built flyovers and partially finished road-widening schemes, however much official money
was dumped on them. Ministers who oversaw such projects became
strikingly rich.

None of that seemed to matter for a time. The economy boomed despite worsening tangles of bureaucracy, corruption scandals, and slow
decision-making in government. New property rose: forests of concrete
towers that sprouted on the edges of cities. Any car journey from Delhi
required an hour or two of trundling through the shadows of this concrete sprawl. More homes were needed in huge urban areas, and politicians and tycoons found investing in residential blocks (often sending
cash via hard-to-trace funds routed through Mauritius) a handy way
to launder stolen and untaxed money. Soaring prices for minerals, and
other finite resources such as the land or telecom spectrum, created the
impression that the economy was racing. Demand from China pushed
up prices of natural resources, such as iron and other minerals. The
splurge of public spending kept many incomes rising, and state-run
banks, under political pressure, kept on lending to favored companies.
Global capital also gushed to emerging markets, as central banks in
America, Europe, and elsewhere in effect printed cash. Indian stock
markets, property, and other sectors boomed.

Unfortunately, much was destined to come to a juddering halt. By
2012 the economy showed real strains. Despite high growth, almost no
new formal jobs had been created. India had roughly 30 million or so
formal jobs in 2015, no more than five years before. Large chunks of
the economy, such as agriculture and manufacturing, had hardly grown.
Power cuts were a national bane, the result of bad management at the
state-run coal company and failures of distribution firms. Big firms like
Tata invested little new at home, preferring to expand overseas—for
example, by buying Jaguar Land Rover in Britain. That was a smart deal
(buying British steel mills was not), but the sight of Indian firms rush-
ing abroad suggested they lacked confidence at home. Many firms were
also increasingly loaded with debt—much of it in foreign currency, or

raised from those dodgy state-owned banks. Local banks, as a result, looked vulnerable to a run.

Many problems got more intense in the last couple of years under Singh. High inflation, especially of food, worsened when droughts and daft rules on trading some food-stocks choked supplies. Rocketing global oil prices punished India, a big energy importer. The government ran up debt, as the country imported far more than it exported; the rupee looked poised to crash. Whopping corruption scandals—estimates of bribes paid to politicians and officials during Singh's last five years in office ranged from $4 billion to $12 billion—caused public fury and indecision in government. The failure of many "public-private" schemes spread dismay and bad debts. The country's first high-speed train, from central Delhi to its airport, was trumpeted initially, with Reliance Infrastructure, as a co-owner, helping to build it. But it opened late, then closed for several months amid problems with cracks in iron beams beneath the tracks, and then trains plodded at half speed with often empty carriages. Public anger at Singh's passive, silent style also spread. The opposition repeatedly boycotted parliament, making it impossible to pass any laws. Some normally sober analysts even muttered about the threat of a revolution.

Singh was a terrible communicator, partly hamstrung by a fear of contradicting Sonia Gandhi or being seen as personally ambitious. He found it difficult to make a case for liberal economic reforms, to explain how foreign and private capital helped the economy grow or to argue that looser labor laws would encourage firms to employ more. Reforms were usually painful for some at first, and always threatened some vested interests. If you cut a subsidy on diesel, the growing car lobby got upset. If you opened up for foreigners to run supermarkets, small traders might be hurt. A better politician would have tried to narrate a story of progress since the early 1990s and explain what gains could come next. Singh's efforts fell flat. Few listened to his mumbled speeches. In cabinet meetings he was often silent for entire meetings, deferential to those with more political clout. He almost never gave press interviews or even met journalists for conversation, lest he rile Sonia Gandhi or the likes of Mukherjee.

Singh should have sent all sorts of messages, such as saying government would stop running hotels, airports, banks, insurance firms, and companies that made watches, fertilizer, and steel, among other things. He should have spelled out how food could be grown more efficiently at much greater scale, and brought to consumers' plates at vastly lower cost. Reforms of farming—specifically, letting investors develop commercial agriculture on large plots and freeing markets to be competitive—would boost food supplies. A braver leader would have tried to shift more wasteful subsidies that distorted markets, and pushed investment in irrigation, cold stores, and warehouses. Internal limits on trade should have been scrapped. And Singh should obviously have cracked down on crony ties between business and politics, confronting his most destructive ministers—especially Mukherjee, who demanded "retrospective tax" from foreign firms. Under him, India was listed by the World Bank as one of the worst countries, anywhere, to do business with.

The big question was not why Singh failed to do these things but why he hardly seemed to try. His harshest critics said Singh had no strong beliefs. Early in his career, in the 1970s, he had meekly gone along with daft economic decisions to isolate India and have the state grow ever more intrusive, under Indira Gandhi. Then in the 1990s, he went along with welcome liberalizing reforms, because that was what Rao demanded. He appeared to be a straw that bent as the wind changed. Milder and more plausible criticism suggested Singh deeply understood and believed in liberal economic changes, but he lacked political guile, and rarely dared to push Sonia Gandhi. She in turn had to balance the interests of factions inside Congress and beyond, including those with dubiously close ties to businesses or others that opposed reforms.

Sonia Gandhi rarely spoke about what would make the economy grow faster, preferring (like most politicians) to focus on spending the proceeds. Her son, Rahul Gandhi, whose influence on Congress rose starting in Singh's second term, rarely expressed thoughts on policy. Amiable and apparently well-meaning, he was also ill at ease amid the aggressive thrusts of politics. No one in his party discussed how some politically connected firms slurped up credit from state-run banks, or how others were held back by terrible bureaucrats. Few seemed to understand the cost of dubious interactions between business bosses and politicians. Populist efforts—for example, a new land law—threatened to make it even harder for investors to function in India without political godfathers to smooth their way.

In 2014 voters dumped Congress, largely in frustration over a slowing economy, high inflation, corruption, and weak leadership. Modi baldly promised *acche din,* meaning good times, but he would also struggle to change the mood on the ground in the years that followed, even if official (though questionable) GDP figures looked rosier. With little grace, he rubbished Singh personally for what had occurred in the previous decade. In opposition he had jeered that the elderly prime minister, a trained economist, could not stop onion prices from soaring. In office, even abroad, Modi dismissed Singh as a failure and spoke of his own earlier embarrassment over India. In conversations with me he said: "Consider India's identity in the last years. You would say the key features of the old government were policy paralysis, corruption, weak governance. But if you take my government, we have made major initiatives in the economic sectors, auctioned coal mines, telecom spectrum." He bragged of touring the world to invite investors to see a new, reinvigorated India. He claimed that blackouts would end and promised to kick-start nuclear civil power and channel hundreds of billions of dollars to solar, hydro-, and wind-power plants. By 2022 renewables, he said, would supply 175,000 megawatts (MW) of electricity, five times more than in 2015.

Rising confidence in the new government and better decision-making brought some gains. Luck helped too, such as a windfall when global oil prices collapsed from $115 a barrel in June 2014 to $40–$50 two years later, lowering a huge import bill. The lower oil price also cut inflation and steadied the rupee and deficits. Meanwhile, Rajan at the central bank calmed nerves, helped to shore up the financial system, discouraged domestic drivers of inflation, and put pressure on banks to get the worst crony-businesses to repay debts. There was no love lost between Rajan and the new government, and the central banker was unusually vocal about many problems, doubting the merits of a new plan to boost manufacturing and skeptical over new official statistics on growth. His comments on social concerns, such as the need for harmony between Hindus and Muslims, infuriated Hindu nationalists. Yet he reassured those who worried about a lack of economic expertise in the new administration.

The trouble was that many early improvements under Modi looked fragile. A series of bad droughts, for example, would threaten to lift food inflation once more. In the early summer of 2016, in rural Maharashtra, villagers had poured into relief camps, battered by the worst local drought in a century. Oil prices would eventually rise again. Eventually Rajan, in the summer of 2016, was hounded out of office by members of the Hindu nationalist right. That sparked fears of an outflow of foreign funds from India.

A more thoughtful politician than Modi would have acknowledged that not everything under his predecessor had been a disaster. The previous decade, for all Singh's timidity, had brought the highest sustained rates of growth ever in India. The previous leader did not deserve all the credit: benign global conditions helped, as did benefits flowing from earlier stability and reforms. Nonetheless, under Singh many tens of millions of people escaped absolute poverty. Starting in 2000, the size of the economy quadrupled, becoming worth more than $2 trillion by 2016. Keeping up previous growth rates would deliver an economy $3 trillion strong by about 2020.

The new government put an end to the worst corruption of the later Singh years. Dodgy tax officials and ministers' fondness for extortion-like taxes were largely stopped. Lobbyists and middlemen for bigger companies were mostly chased away—it was remarkable how much quieter the lobbies of ministries in Delhi became after the change of government. Most dramatic, in an evening speech in November 2016, Modi announced that large-denomination 500- and 1,000-rupee banknotes would no longer be legal tender (other than when exchanged in banks). The idea was to force those who held great quantities of such cash as "black money," unmonitored by tax authorities or for corrupt uses, to deposit their funds into banks instead.

Modi's "demonetization" program proved to be a big political and economic gamble—perhaps the biggest of his administration. His action appeared genuinely popular with the public as people welcomed a dramatic effort to address corruption. But it had widespread, painful effects. He had ordered the removal of nearly 90 percent (by value) of banknotes from the Indian economy, equivalent to taking $227 billion out of circulation. The economy is hugely dependent on cash to function—98 percent of consumer transactions are done with it—in part because little infrastructure exists, at least in villages, to do anything else. The implementation was botched. New 2,000-rupee notes were issued, but far too few had been printed, and they proved too small to be dispensed from Automatic Teller Machines. For weeks on end Indians formed immense queues at banks, trying to deposit old banknotes or obtain new ones. Banks were ill-prepared to accept, without warning, 8.5 trillion rupees of deposits that flowed to them in the first three weeks after the announcement. The early signs were of a short-term shock to the economy, as small businesses and manufacturers, dependent on cash, suspended work, and as payments for casual labor (the form of employment for most Indians) dried up.

Modi's action was dramatic and in some cases the corrupt were inconvenienced. One acquaintance told me in December 2016 of a relation, a wealthy businessman who dealt in "black money" and built hotels in Goa, who reportedly had been stuck with enormous quantities of cash, in bundles of rupees worth hundreds of thousands of dollars, at his large home south of Delhi. (My acquaintance urged his relation to burn the banknotes.) A month after Modi launched the initiative, the governor of India's central bank, Urjit Patel, offered his first full defence of the measure by claiming, not entirely convincingly, that "detailed deliberations" had been made before the cash was withdrawn and suggesting benefits would, eventually, outweigh the costs of the action. But the bank had to admit, at least in the short term, the economy was suffering. Sadly, too, the central bank itself looked diminished as an institution. The dramatic withdrawal of most legal tender, done for political reasons, was widely understood as a decision taken by Modi and not the bank. That raised doubts about the institution's independence as more than a rubber stamp for decisions of a powerful prime minister.

The cash withdrawal did show a strong desire by Modi to crack down on crime and surprise political rivals who, presumably, had stockpiled banknotes ahead of an important regional election. But the action was an example of the state happily inconveniencing huge numbers of ordinary people who were forced to waste millions of hours, collectively, standing in line at banks. In the weeks following Modi's announcement, a baffling array of additional rules were introduced by bureaucrats, such as exemptions from limits on currency withdrawals from banks for those who stated they were organising a wedding. Where India needed liberalisation and a removal of the deadening hand of bureaucrats, to help unleash economic growth, Modi instead delivered the most dramatic economic intervention of a strongman in office. The great cash withdrawal was followed by suggestions that tax officials would begin to raid homes and look for families that had suspiciously large stocks of gold. That was further evidence of an increasingly intrusive state.

Kaushik Basu, a former chief economic adviser to the Indian government and chief economist at the World Bank, wrote in the *New York Times* that withdrawing the banknotes was a "major mistake" and warned that "one inept government intervention against shadow activities can do a lot of harm to the vast majority" of Indians. Far better, he suggested, if India tried to cut corruption by reforming how political parties were funded. Lawrence Summers, a former US Treasury Secretary who had long campaigned for bans on large denominated notes—the $100 bill in America and the 500 euro note in Europe—wrote in the *Financial Times* that the Indian move was "the most sweeping change in currency policy that has occurred anywhere in the world in decades." But he also doubted India would see lasting benefits from the disruption, because the most wealthy and corrupt would have anyway stored most of their assets as property, jewelry, in foreign currency or in banks abroad. Amartya Sen, a Nobel laureate, called the demonetization scheme "despotic."

Few experts spoke in favor of the move. Vivek Dehejia, a commentator on economics in *Mint* newspaper, did laud Modi's boldness. He predicted there would be fundamental benefits in the long-term because withdrawing the notes could spur "digitization" and "modernization" of India's economy. He foresaw a big increase in people using bank accounts, following disruption in the use of cash. In an echo of his earlier clashes with Sen, Jagdish Bhagwati defended Modi's decision to demonetize, dismissing Sen's suggestion that the move was despotic. Two months after the first announcement, he called critics of the action "cockeyed" and said they were "shooting from the hip". He argued that economic hardships, though significant, were only "transitional". A think tank, the Centre for Monitoring Indian Economy, had estimated that transitional costs over the first 50 days were some 1.28 trillion rupees. Others noted how investment by companies in India slumped in the months following demonetization. Nonetheless, in an article for the *Times of India*, written with two fellow academics, Pravin Krishna and Suresh Sundaresan, Bhagwati called the move a "courageous and substantive economic reform" that would bring big benefits. He said Indians would begin to conduct more transactions without cash, relying on online payments, bank transfers, credit and debit cards. This would help to reduce the size of the "black economy" and more people would pay tax. Bhagwati did complain that "frequent changes in rules" detailing how people could hand in old cash, or obtain new notes, caused needless confusion. Overall, his support for Modi's radical change was in tune with the mood of the public. Despite the disruption, it appeared most ordinary Indians believed demonetization showed Modi was sincere in fighting corruption.

Other changes were modest in comparison. The old Planning Commission was abolished. But optimists who had predicted a rush of dramatic, pro-growth reforms, quickly tackling areas where Singh failed, were disappointed. Modi talked of being pro-business, when India really needed a leader who was pro-markets. Unlike Singh, he could communicate brilliantly and had political authority, but he was slow in delivering liberal reforms. He recited slogans, saying he wanted "less government and more governance" and "minimum government," promising to "unobstacle" problems with government. He said "men, machines, and money must work together." But he failed to explain such phrases.

When asked during a private conversation a few months into office if he would send a pro-market signal by selling part of Air India, the troubled national airline, Modi demurred, saying he would not battle unions early on because he planned to be in office for at least two terms. "Basically he doesn't want to sell," said a businessman friend in Ahmedabad. Even modest schemes prepared by Singh—for example, to sell more state-run airports to private buyers—were scrapped. The new finance minister promised to raise revenue by selling state-owned assets, but he did not deliver much.

Modi cast himself as a modernizer who wanted an economy that looked and felt more like one in East Asia: he seemed to believe in state-capitalism, not the more liberal Western sort. Two years after he came to office, he said nobody had explained to him what "big bang" reforms referred to, but argued that changes he brought about had already made India "the most open economy in the world" for foreign investors. That, sadly, was a fantasy. A ranking by the International Chamber of Commerce, in 2015, listed India as the sixty-third most open of seventy-five countries it measured—behind Russia, China, Vietnam, and Saudi Arabia, for example. But at least India was moving in the right direction, gradually becoming more open to investors and traders than before.

One broad question was how much any Indian government would trust markets, rather than bureaucrats, to bring improvements to the country. Consider those state-run firms. India was never totally dominated by them—they made up less than 10 percent of the economy by 2015. (In China the figure is 40 percent or higher.) But the wider impact of these firms could be large. Dodgy state-run banks, for example, existed beside better-run private ones; but as the state-run ones held the bulk of industry assets and high levels of questionable debt, they posed a threat to the whole banking system. Similarly, though private firms could get involved in energy distribution, India's power sector relied heavily on production by state-controlled Coal India, which sent the fuel to power plants. Coal India was huge and disastrously run. The government, with enough political will and decent managers, hoped to knock such state-run firms into shape, as Modi had done on a small scale in Gujarat. But if Modi would not sell firms, freeing them from political meddling, doubts would remain regarding how professionally they would really be run. Hesitation on selling firms raised doubts for the long term. It was the same with the railways: the new government repeatedly bet on the state doing a better job than before, and declined to open up quickly to private actors stepping in. Pressed to explain what "minimum government" meant, Modi spoke of efficient administration and cutting red tape—a welcome but limited vision.

Few politicians in India really cheered liberal reforms, and the average voter certainly did not trust the idea of markets doing better than governments—for example, at putting capital to work. Voters didn't choose Modi hoping for a Thatcherite privatizer but, instead, wanted a strongman to somehow deliver rapid growth and lots of jobs, and didn't mind at all if that meant jobs in state-run companies. The new government wanted the economy growing, but also remembered how the BJP lost its "India Shining" election in 2004 despite rapid growth. Worried that Congress and others might accuse him of crony-capitalism, Modi also, at first, kept many of India's richest business leaders at arm's length. That was a smart calculation. India had perhaps one hundred billionaires by 2016, but only a few, such as Dilip Shanghvi of Sun Pharmaceuticals, could tell stories of creating wealth by building impressive firms from scratch (his began with a $1,000 loan in 1983 and was worth some $14 billion by 2016). Instead, too many billionaires had done well through political connections, had become rich passively from rent on land, or had inherited a lot of their wealth. Mukesh Ambani of Reliance Industries, for example, had a personal fortune worth some $21 billion but received a big leg-up by inheriting valuable assets from his well-connected father.

The new government understood that economic growth had to be seen as helping a broader swathe of people. But two years after Modi came into office, his arm's-length treatment of billionaires appeared to be changing. For example, Modi's office, in September 2016, allowed his image to appear in an advertisement for new cellphones being sold by Ambani's Reliance Industries, and Modi himself granted a rare television interview to Ambani's television channel (where the interviewer asked only soft questions). These incidents raised the suspicion that cozy old ties between politicians and tycoons might be restored.

Modi seemed to believe much would change in India if only perceptions of the country were different—missing the point that facts also had to change on the ground. He talked up the prospects for India's economy, with him at the top, as an emerging engine of global growth. In one conversation with me, in 2015, he said that "at the beginning of the twenty-first century, there was great expectation from India. It was said that BRICS [Brazil, Russia, India, China, and South Africa] would change the world. Suddenly, in the past few years, it was felt that the 'I' in the BRICS had become a burden." He said he had rushed around the world in his first year in office to "understand what the international expectations from India were. And I think we have reclaimed the position of 'I' in the BRICS, in terms of being an engine of economic growth." He said there was a "big set of global expectations from India, and it is India's responsibility to address those."

The first years of his administration brought limited gains, despite its enormous political mandate. The government might have focused on fixing the frail banking system (in order to get investment flowing fast again) or tried to shake up old laws on labor or do much more to improve public education and health. It might have brought in outsiders to bolster a limited economic team (Congress, in office, had inducted Nandan Nilekani, of Infosys, to run some projects). Outsiders might have known how to sidestep *babus* who often stifled change. The new government might have used early budgets to send signals to encourage high domestic investment, invested more in schools and universities to improve skills, and cut some wasteful subsidies. Ministers might have made early, possibly unpopular, decisions knowing how rewards from reforms often lag. If wise, they would also have shown grace to the opposition, which still controlled parliament's upper house, to agree on a core set of reforms—both parties said they favored many of these reforms, such as spreading the pitifully small tax net and trying to create a single market across India—and to share credit for getting difficult laws through.

Modi as a political outsider in Delhi, unused to parliament or to making any political compromise, was also deeply embittered against Congress after years of confrontation in Gujarat. He talked about entirely destroying the other party. And his style of governing was remarkably centralized. He stuffed much of his administration with political lightweights, running much from an unusually powerful prime minister's office, as if he were still chief minister of a single state. He also got distracted by foreign trips and winning state elections. His finance minister, Arun Jaitley, in poor health, had little interest in economic matters, leaving it to the prime minister's office to write large parts of the national budgets. The early result, demonetization aside, was mostly a continuation of the cautious policymaking of the prior decade. Two years after the new government took office—and despite grand headlines—many corporate leaders in India were downbeat, confidence remained low, and domestic investment did not flow (though the foreign sort did). For example, investment in industrial production, the bedrock of much expected growth, looked anemic. By May 2016, the value of exports from India had diminished for eighteen consecutive months. Yet despite all this, official statistics claimed the economy was thriving more than any other big one on the planet.

Some old plans were expanded. The new government extended Singh's old efforts to scrap subsidies on diesel (those on petrol were already gone). It promised, eventually, to replace subsidies-in-kind on cooking gas and kerosene with cash welfare. It oversaw the opening of over 200 million new bank accounts, to allow cash welfare to replace rations eventually. (A great many of these, however, were hardly functional, as they contained only 1 rupee or less.) And it pushed on with a biometric identity scheme—Aadhaar—that was useful for cleaning up welfare, which the World Bank reckoned would save the government $1 billion a year. Parliament agreed to let foreigners invest more in some sorts of shops, the insurance and defense industries, and the railways, though there were sometimes complicated restrictions and foreigners were at times barred from outright control. Big blocks of coal and telecom spectrum were sold to private buyers, an open process that helped to fill government coffers and avoid corruption. A chunk of public spending was also devolved from central government to states. A welcome new bankruptcy law was planned to make it easier to do business. And though the government dared not tackle India's difficult labor laws nationally, it told willing states to try. It also pushed states to compete to cut red tape and improve the business climate. A few capable ministers did work to improve railways, roads, and the power sector. Public spending was also cut, which helped to lower inflation.

Most of this was welcome, and suggested that the pace of economic change might gradually pick up. It would need to, if faster growth were to be sustained for a long time, in order to match the decades of high growth that China had achieved. Modi did eventually deliver on a particularly important promise to pass a big new tax law, called the Goods and Services Tax (GST), designed to create a single market for India. The GST at last became law in mid-2016, and it was to be implemented during the next year. Investors saw that as a test of his ability to reform, and if implemented well—without too many different tax bands—it could boost growth in India somewhat: the idea was to make it simpler for factories, and others, to sell to all of India as one market.

Talking sensibly about India's economy was tricky, however, partly because of doubts about new official statistics, introduced in 2015, that appeared to be divorced from experiences of businesses and consumers in the real world. Official statistics showed India's economy racing at well over 7 percent a year, a much giddier pace than a slowing China. (The same method suggested it had rattled on almost as fast in the final years of Singh's government, which nobody believed.) On the ground, however, India felt more like an economy in the relative doldrums, growing at perhaps 4 or 5 percent. Construction sites were silent, many malls were quiet, armies of casual laborers remained out of work, perhaps because the flow of dodgy money had slowed. Higher foreign investment could not make up for the fact that domestic investors, especially companies that had become stuck in broken infrastructure deals, were cutting back on spending. Government spending also dragged, though it usually rose prior to national elections.

Modi, naturally, was upbeat. He chatted one evening at Race Course Road, the prime minister's official bungalow in Delhi, as peacocks bawled like noisy teenagers on lawns outside. He ticked off the reasons for his confidence. "All rating agencies say India's is the fastest-growing country in the world. I think 7.5 percent growth: this is the highest growth," he said. "Look at any aspect of economic growth, we have taken so many steps, all vigorously implemented," he claimed. Investment by foreigners was up by 35 percent in his first seventeen months, compared with Singh's final seventeen months. More tourists were coming into the country, and manufacturers were thrilled that red tape was getting snipped. "We have focused enormously on bringing strength to our economic progress," Modi said.

But wariness lingered. Businesses grumbled that India remained a painfully difficult place to work. Improvements came slowly and rewards were often limited. The head of a big German firm, Kion, which sold forklifts trucks—a handy indicator of how many warehouses were in use—dismissed India as still "an extremely small market." China had 250,000 forklifts compared with India's 12,000, Kion's CEO said, in 2015. The boss of another foreign firm rolled his eyes in dejection when asked about investing, telling a grim story of corrupt local judges, apparently in the pay of local tycoons, who postponed a court case long enough to destroy a business opportunity. A boss within a huge American industrial company already investing in India said the country had interesting prospects but was nothing yet compared to China. The manager of one of the biggest investment bodies in the world, who oversaw some $800 billion of assets globally, said he wanted to invest more in India but could not find suitable, big, trustworthy, and attractive targets. Political risk in India remained too high.

But perceptions of India would improve. Assessed over decades, India had notched up real gains. The 1990s brought the first, big, liberal reforms and excitement that the economic restrictions of previous years would be lifted. By the 2000s, the BJP and then Congress were presiding over mixed progress, thanks to mostly benign global conditions. Amid rocketing expectations, as many anticipated that they would get rich quickly and that inequality would grow, India struggled to launch a second big round of reforms. Those years at least coincided with rapid growth, even if far too few formal jobs were created. The 2010s, however, would see even tougher economic challenges: global conditions are indeed difficult for a country hoping to generate lots of new exports, and India will have to move on to deeper economic reforms to take advantage of its great bulk. Those challenges risk dwarfing the achievements that came before.

BRING BACK THE GOLDEN BIRD

THE YEAR 2022, OR THEREABOUTS, WILL SEE A MOMENTOUS statistical turning point for the world. For every year of known history before, China has been the most populous country on the planet. From that year on, say demographers, India will be the world's largest. Nearly 1.3 billion strong as of this writing in 2016, India's population is likely to keep on growing throughout much of this century, and will peak at about 1.7 billion. Talk of India as number one in a more general sense will also pick up. Those who call demography destiny have points to make. If a country's population is huge and growing, each year adding 16 million or so, all sorts of other things become possible. Additional warm bodies are potential future workers and consumers. Some might turn out to be brilliant inventors or philosophers, brave soldiers or inspiring artists, clever entrepreneurs, successful athletes. Plus, having lots of young people will be increasingly valuable. Given aging populations in much of Asia, Europe, and beyond, more people will be dependent on shrinking labor forces in most countries.

Along with some African countries, India will be an exception, keeping a youthful advantage for decades to come.

This great potential bounty is only theoretical, because it depends on getting those extra people to be productive and useful. Already in the 2010s an estimated 1 million extra workers, every month, had to be absorbed into India's economy. Yet India failed not only to create formal jobs at anything remotely close to that rate but also to create conditions that would allow entrepreneurs to thrive. Youngsters certainly yearned to escape the dust, broken roads, and brainless farm work associated with village life. The overwhelming demand for salaried jobs was extraordinary. Take an example from 2015 in Chhattisgarh, a poor and landlocked central Indian state. Its government advertised for applicants to be peons, the lowliest office staff who are bossed about by others, sent to open doors, bring tea, or carry files. Peons are badly paid and hardly enjoy glittering career prospects. But they do get job security, a pension, and perks. For just 368 available posts, a stunning 2.3 million people applied, including postgraduates and engineers.

That story was just one sign of a wobbly, partially reformed economy that had to travel an enormous distance to catch up with middle-income countries elsewhere in Asia. India was better off than some of its neighbors: the people of Pakistan, for example, would have loved to experience similar economic progress. India's middle class was growing, but it remained small. By 2016 only 25 million or so people had credit cards, and roughly 30 million had formal jobs. Average incomes were far below those in China, and earnings and wealth were shared unequally. Extreme poverty had declined, but the lifestyles of only a tiny minority would have counted as middle class elsewhere. A ten-year boom in sales of "fast-moving consumer goods," such as tiny sachets of shampoo or packets of biscuits, reflected the fact that low incomes had been rising a bit in villages. But gains were modest.

Rich corners of India were still small. Billionaires and millionaires thrived in pockets. Capgemini, a consultancy, estimated that 200,000 Indians had investible assets worth more than $1 million in 2015, up from 127,000 Indians in 2009. The consultancy suggested that India's wealthy held assets worth nearly $1 trillion. But their wealth did not trickle far. By one estimate Delhi, the huge capital, had fewer restaurants than Lisbon, Portugal, a city one-twentieth its size. An Indian academic once mentioned to me that Shanghai alone had more hotel rooms than all of India. In 2016, Apple said that it would open its first iPhone store in India a full eight years after setting up in China. IKEA, the Swedish flat-pack furniture seller, said it would finally open a store in India in 2017, many years after first announcing it would come there. Such firms had long been deterred by oppressive regulations and surprisingly small markets. The Swedes, who had hired anthropologists to try to understand Indian shoppers, talked of having twenty-five huge shops by 2025. But a consumer boom was starting late in India, and growing relatively slowly, compared with many other countries in Asia.

If you ask the brightest minds in government, universities, or think-tanks how to get the economy into fine fettle and how to spread the benefits of growth much more widely, they usually recommend the same medicine: get more workers into factories. After all, much of East Asia's growth late in the previous century can be attributed to its having been the world's workshop. Manufacturing counted for about a quarter of the value of the average economy across much of Asia. In India, by contrast, it added up to just 17 percent. That had a human cost: India missed out on many millions—probably tens of millions—of formal jobs. If it could only get its manufacturing sector to resemble that of other Asian countries, many people would be much better off.

Of course, India's policymakers did not intend to wreck large parts of its manufacturing sector, though in retrospect one might question that. During the late twentieth century, the country cut itself off from trade, did a poor job of building infrastructure, and failed to get people educated, to improve public health, to encourage entrepreneurs, or to generate jobs for the population beyond working on small farms. India did try to protect its industry from foreign competition, ordering that some goods—such as boxes of matches, small hinges, and pencils—could not be imported and had to be made locally by small producers. The unfortunate result, however, was rotten production and mostly awful standards. Try to strike an Indian match and the flimsy stick would almost always snap in your fingers. Hinges and even pencils tended to be wobbly. India failed even to trade with its closest neighbors, so South Asia remained the world's worst integrated region.

Once India began to open up to more trade, in the 1990s, many manufacturers were ill-prepared. Makers of pharmaceuticals did extremely well, thanks to India's bold decision to ignore patents on many medicines, so its generics industry flourished. But other manufacturers were clobbered by far more competitive foreigners. Imports, especially plastics, flooded into India from China. Local manufacturing was so inadequate that producers found it paid to export plastic granules to China, make them into buckets there, and bring them back to India. By 2016 only some 50 million Indians—11 percent of workers—had factory jobs, and most of these were informal, in tiny firms with few staff. Amazingly, most Indian factories did not even operate with electricity.

The economy instead owed its rise to services, as India tried to be the world's "back-office" by providing business processors, phone operators, and software engineers. Service firms thrived with new technology, outsourcing, call centers, information technology (IT), and programing, boosted by lots of engineering graduates who spoke English and learned to write code. Southern India, where education levels were high, did best—especially in cities like Bangalore and Hyderabad (which also drew clever graduates from good universities in cities like Kolkata). What especially helped is that many people of Indian descent—about 3 million by 2016—lived in America, creating ties between the countries. Gradually, higher-skilled service jobs—that is, for designers, accountants, and lawyers, among others—were also outsourced to India. An American friend in Delhi recounted how he managed more than one thousand Indian lawyers who reviewed documents for legal teams in America in 2015. Business was exploding, he said, as American firms learned to trust even sensitive and technical work to skilled Indians, at a fraction of the cost of paying legal assistants at home.

Some did well betting on growth in such services. In Hyderabad, an attractive city with a less oppressive climate than most in India, Chandrababu Naidu, chief minister of the southern state of Andhra Pradesh, recalled how he became a darling of global business. A slender man with a trim white beard and a natty dress sense, Naidu was most responsible for getting outsourcing and business processing firms to thrive in Hyderabad from the mid-1990s on. He had bet on creating a "knowledge economy," he said, encouraging hundreds of new colleges to open in his state. In 1995 it had just 32 engineering colleges, which turned out 8,000 graduates a year. A decade on, it had 230, producing 75,000 graduates. "We in Andhra have a track record. We started colleges, then we built hi-tech city, Cyber city, campuses for businesses. Microsoft and others came to Hyderabad," he explained.

Naidu talked of "a very inspiring time for India" and recalled that "we started economic reforms in 1991; before that there was single-party domination for decades, the growth rate was very nominal, people used to heckle and talk of the Hindu growth rate." He praised liberal reforms by the previous BJP-led government under Atal Behari Vajpayee, prior to 2004. The deregulation of telecoms allowed the mobile industry to take off early in this century. The power industry improved. The sale of some state-run power companies brought gains. Naidu said that reforms stalled under Singh, and that there was only "tremendous hype about India and India added to the hype."

By 2015 Naidu again saw a "clear cut mandate" for rapid change: "All the world is forecasting the bright future for India, there is no uncertainty. People expect that this decade, this century, belongs to India. China's economy is slowing down, Europe is in stagnation, Japan has a problem. America is a stabilized, advanced economy. In India there is untapped potential. In the future, India and China will be the two countries that count." Naidu was an articulate optimist, saying that "India is a sleeping giant, with a lot of untapped potential. It has a population size, demographic advantage. The average age by 2022 will be twenty-nine years. We have abundant natural resources, a big market, rule of law; the judiciary is very strong; our people do well all over the world. Then there is our use of English. In ten years there will be more English-speaking people here than in America. We will be the number-one country for English speakers. Everyone has the aspiration to do more."

Naidu was a rare politician who proposed that India's place in the world would be strongest if it competed among high-skilled industries, which required, especially, a massive investment in higher education. Rather than follow Naidu's path of services and knowledge, however, India's national government was more anxious to try an East Asian–style path to lower-skilled production, getting more people into factories.

One way to begin that process was to provide much more power: bringing more lightbulbs, machinery, and computers into the most basic workshops would lift production fast. New sources of power, thankfully, were already blossoming. Construction of massive solar plants occurred in southern India especially, and big hydropower plants built by Indian firms in the Himalayas, including Nepal, allowed electricity generation on a huge scale. Visiting one of these plants in Nepal meant hiking for hours along the upper reaches of the Marsyangdi River, in a beautiful valley near the border with China. Crickets screeched at night and the river roared. It was a magical place: wooden homes had yellow maize cobs hanging from balconies in the sunshine; small red-and-green birds flitted by; beehives clung to mountainsides. At times the track was literally bored high into a cliff, leaving a sheer drop hundreds of feet to a glacial river below. Engineers from an Indian firm, GMR, explained how they would blast a 7-mile-long tunnel, 18 feet wide, into the mountain, sending the river through a steel-lined pipe to spin underground turbines. This operation would one day generate 600 megawatts of electricity, just one of several hydro schemes nearby. Nepal could in theory produce 40 gigawatts (GW) of electricity from its rivers (up from less than 1 GW in 2015)—enough to light all of north India and beyond. Across the Himalayas there was potential for about 200 GW of such hydropower.

A liberal reform early in the 2000s had freed India's power sector, letting firms trade electricity first domestically and then with neighboring countries. That sort of change brought big, long-term effects, encouraging investments in production and the grid. Governments had to find similar reformist efforts to give private actors incentives to do more. Modi called for factories to produce textiles and cellphones and to assemble cars. He lined up tycoons to promise to do more manufacturing, launching a big PR campaign called "Make in India," which was part of his oft-repeated promise of "good times." He admitted that he was "not a big economist" but set grand targets for manufacturing jobs to double to 100 million by 2022. He had a deft turn of phrase, saying pre-industrial India was known as a Golden Bird, and should now be known as a golden opportunity, because "here is a government that is dedicated to development . . . it is an article of faith." He also promised that an implausibly large number of Indians, half a billion, would somehow get vocational training by 2022. "It pains my heart," he said, that investors preferred to leave India rather than set up factories at home. "You may not feel it is a big vision," he said, promising to make India an easier place to do business.

Some companies, such as those assembling cars, did bet on India becoming an industrial hub—at least for small, basic models, including for export. By 2016 the country had produced 3.4 million vehicles a year. General Motors started exporting from India to Central and South America. Daimler Chrysler invested to export cars from Chennai. Hyundai, Toyota, Honda, Ford, and others had similar plants. Around a quarter of Chinese households owned cars by 2016, compared with only 5 percent of Indian ones. That suggested growth ahead. The manager of the French carmaker Renault called India a big hub for carmaking and praised its long industrial history, though he grumbled about its rotten infrastructure. Renault's factory in Tamil Nadu was just 25 miles from the port, he said, yet it typically took many hours to get vehicles to their ships.

India needed better roads, and to be rid of awful rules that prevented businesses from growing. The new government won lots of praise in 2015 for scrapping 125 outdated laws, as Modi called for an end to "archaic rules" and promised to eradicate a "maze" of 3,000 "useless laws," deleting one for every day that passed. There were plenty to target. India saw its last telegram sent in 2013, but it had long kept a law forbidding private possession of telegraph wires of a specific thickness. A "treasure trove" act, from 1878, ordered anything more valuable than 10 rupees (a few US cents today) found in the ground to be handed to the government for the benefit of "Her Majesty," a reference to Queen Victoria. A law from 1923—the "Indian boilers act"—required that inspectors regularly check the safety of boilers in factories, but in actuality let those officials gather bribes from companies. States had many laws and rules that should have been killed off decades before. Babies born to foreigners in Delhi immediately accumulated fines for being present without visas. In Andhra Pradesh, a thirty-nine-page document listed eighty-nine different electricity rates for consumers: people farming rabbits or mushrooms were charged differently from other farmers, or from those who put up advertising billboards.

Some specialist manufacturers flourished. Over dinner in Delhi, Vivek Gambhir, who worked for a conglomerate, Godrej, related a quirky example to me, saying his company had a profitable sideline in exporting human hair. Dark, lustrous locks were snipped during religious ceremonies and, woven into wigs and hair-extensions for women in Africa, were supplied into a market worth $400 million in 2015. By one estimate a single temple in Tirumala, in Andhra Pradesh, earned nearly 2 billion rupees (some $40 million) by selling more than five hundred metric tons of hair that had been snipped from devotees' heads. Other niche manufacturers succeeded as well. One was in Puducherry, a tiny coastal territory in the south, an ex–French colony with well-tended streets, brightly painted houses and police in red *kepis*. There Dilip Kapur, a man with an open face and wide eyes, had founded Hidesign, a maker of fancy leather bags and belts sold around the world. He was bullish about India rising. "You are going to see a very sophisticated consumer class, with more confidence, the first generation without an inferiority complex," he predicted. "There are no doubts. They know something great can come from here." Hidesign did well. Staff were loyal, on average remaining for more than fifteen years. Kapur showed off studios and workshops where seven hundred women, mostly in sky-blue saris, each wielding an Italian steel knife, sliced and stitched. But he worried that it would grow harder to find skilled workers, as younger recruits preferred jobs in banks or offices.

Getting reliable employees was paradoxically a problem, even if many millions were hunting for jobs. An Indian tycoon who produced chino trousers on a massive scale from factories in Hong Kong, China, and Bangladesh explained that he would never set up in his native India. He called the "work culture" unhelpful, describing how Indian workers would quit tedious jobs in factories to seek more interesting or easier work, or just to have a break, unwilling to be drones. Many workers, understandably, grew fed up with mind-numbing toil: "Eight to ten hours of intense work on a sewing machine is not much fun, and we need very high-efficiency models," he said. His fellow Indians, he suggested, were not inclined to endure prolonged drudgery: "I compare notes with competitors who work in India and I find Indian factories very inefficient. When I recruit managers from Indian firms, they confirm that we are right."

In Puducherry, Kapur did well by producing high-quality goods on a small scale. He sold to wealthier consumers, emphasizing craftsmanship over cost, so he did not have to squeeze out every rupee possible. He said it took thirteen hours to cut and stitch a single Hidesign bag, whereas workers in China churned out a synthetic one, mostly glued, in less than an hour. But Kapur did not dream of scaling up. "We have two to three thousand people, but does anyone want five thousand? Who wants to employ five thousand people? In India it's extremely difficult. It's like a noose around your neck and not just because of the government, the laws. If I closed this factory they would all come and stand outside my house and make me miserable," he said.

India's government, however, really wanted large-scale manufacturing. That happened in relatively few places. One was a big factory in Rajasthan called Kajaria Ceramics, the country's biggest tile-maker. Dr. Rajveer Chaudhary, its boss, said proudly that his plant produced 54 million square meters of them a year, enough to tile Manhattan, should the need arise. India had previously imported shiploads of tiles from Italy, Spain, and China, but became an exporter instead. Over small cups of green tea, Chaudhary said that "every year we add capacity, in Andhra Pradesh, also in West Bengal. We have a plan to open a plant in the United States, in Tennessee." His company aimed for $1 billion in annual turnover by 2022. "We can do it because we expand everywhere," he said.

Kajaria Ceramics did well. It put up wind-turbines and a solar park to sell energy into the grid, and it had neat lawns, tidy warehouses, and great stacks of tiles loaded into colorful lorries. Yet the firm had relatively few workers. Driverless carts shifted tiles from kilns to conveyor belts, and digital printers automatically added designs. Much machinery was controlled remotely. Dr. Chaudhary called his huge factory "mostly automatic." It ran nonstop, all year, with nine hundred employees spread over three shifts (plus some casual labor). That total was likely to fall, despite expansion. Managers had bought machines from China to pack tiles, eliminating wages and saving a princely 4 rupees per box. Dr. Chaudhary said the problem with human workers was not just arcane and contradictory labor laws (though even officials in India admitted that these laws were "worst in the world"). You could avoid those, he said, by hiring temporary staff. But like the Indian trouser maker, or Dilip Kapur in Puducherry, he also worried about culture. "We employ a mix of local people and distant ones, but the locals are mostly illiterate and don't want to work hard," he said. A machine from China would not disappear for a week, drinking in its village after getting its monthly wage.

Those awful labor laws did help to keep Indian firms small: seven in ten manufacturing jobs were in companies with fewer than fifty workers. Few firms would risk getting much bigger. Employing over one hundred workers meant the application of a law, dating from 1947, obliging them to get permission from government before laying anyone off, let alone closing an unprofitable business. Formal jobs come with mind-numbing levels of bureaucracy, such as baffling definitions of what counts as wages or what category of worker an employee belongs to. All seemed designed to create lucrative chances for corrupt labor inspectors to extract bribes. Complicated duties and taxes were detested by many workers and employers alike. Nearly half of wages, even for the low-paid, were supposed to be deducted by employers and paid into official schemes and funds to pay for various state-sanctioned benefits. A shrewd commentator on Indian labor laws, Manish Sabharwal, pointed out that a draconian law on apprentices, from 1961, was routinely (and necessarily) flouted. In theory, he said, some 15 million apprentices, or 5,000 company bosses, should have been jailed long ago for breaking its provisions.

Finding skilled laborers could be especially difficult, and growing manufacturers competed for these. Apollo Tyres was a hopeful case, with four big plants that served a surging domestic market and exported a handy 1 million tires a year. Tamil Nadu in the south became India's "knitwear capital" as textile factories expanded there. America's GE made low-cost electrocardiographs in India. Tetrapak churned out packaging from a hi-tech forty-five-acre factory in Maharashtra. "India is joining the global supply chain," an excited official in government said. But much of this was capital-heavy manufacturing. It seemed unlikely that such new factories would really create tens of millions of jobs.

Some big foreign manufacturers said they would bet on India, if only to get access to its growing consumer market. For example, Foxconn, which made smartphones, said in 2015 that it would spend $5 billion on an Indian factory. The man in charge of attracting investors like

Foxconn was an energetic figure called Amitabh Kant, who had a gift for slick marketing. He spoke of nearly 100 mini-reforms under way, mostly to cut mind-numbing paperwork, saying that "within three or four years, we will reach up to the top thirty" in a World Bank index measuring the "ease of doing business." India did improve a bit by 2016 from a low level of 142nd, reaching 130th by 2016. That modest gain hopefully presaged much more dramatic improvements. "We have become far more market friendly," Kant said. "For many years India talked the language of socialism, but that is changing."

Kant also wanted a tourism boom. In 2015 India was getting just 8 million foreign visitors a year, compared to France's 84 million, despite an amazing array of forts, palaces, beaches, tea estates, temples, tombs, ancient cities, and other treats. A goal was set to attract 11 million foreign tourists by 2018, and many people could be tempted by luxury train travel across the deserts of Rajasthan, dare-devil skiing in Kashmir, white-water rafting elsewhere, and lion safaris in Gujarat—as well as the usual visits to see tigers and the other treats mentioned above. Despite a big effort to promote tourism, many astounding sites simply remained unknown to many foreigners. Favorites of mine were two extraordinary spots, the Ajanta and the Ellora caves in Maharashtra, western India. The UNESCO world heritage sites were popular with Indians, but might have attracted many more foreign visitors were it not for the pot-holed and congested roads and lack of hotels at such sites. Those who did go were rewarded with several dozen majestic structures, including Hindu, Buddhist, and Jain temples, exquisitely carved deep inside cliffs and hillsides. Each had taken generations to construct. Inscriptions and other evidence suggest that work on the elaborate sites dates as far back as to the second century, BCE.

India, perhaps because it developed more slowly and chaotically than China, left much of its great heritage relatively undisturbed. It is exciting to witness what lives on from its ancient cultures. It is awe-inspiring to see Hindu devotees assemble, in their largest numbers every twelve years, to celebrate the Kumbh Mela, near Allahabad in

Uttar Pradesh. At the festival in 2013, over the course of two months, some 120 million pilgrims attended, many taking freezing dips in the River Ganges. Reportedly 30 million gathered on a single day, with experts in organization marveling at the efficiency in providing temporary housing, transport, food, and water, as well as ensuring safety at the occasion. Inevitably observers would ask how it was possible for the Kumbh Mela to get its infrastructure so well organized, when India more generally struggles to do so. The best answer: Indians are brilliant at organizing at the last minute, as with elaborate and prolonged weddings. Huge events, like the Kumbh Mela, appear to be an extension of that approach.

Other delights exist, from spice markets in Old Delhi to houseboat tours in the backwaters of Kerala. Stumbling on attractions created by eccentric individuals is the best of the lot. In Chandigarh, a Punjabi town designed by Le Corbusier, one can lose absorbing hours in a once-secret, illegally built rock garden created by a former official of the public-works department, Nek Chand Saini. Over the course of decades Chand used rubble from demolished houses, shards of crockery, bottle tops, broken tiles, glass beads, mounds of rags, and old coal-tar drums to create a sprawling and beautiful series of palaces and gardens. His creations eventually covered twenty-five acres and included waterfalls, ponds, statues both huge and tiny, hidden tunnels, and shady pathways through forests. (Chand's statues have also been exhibited in galleries in New York and Liverpool.) Millions of visitors have seen his gardens, a tribute to his individuality and good humor.

But for tourism to really thrive in India, many basic problems must yet be solved. Safety for women is a big concern: it hardly helped the country's image when a minister, in 2016, advised female tourists that they should not wear skirts. Unless rickety infrastructure improves, foreign tourists will also remain hesitant. India has also done a poor job of selling its attractions. A telling example is the ruined city of Hampi, a spectacular fifteenth-century collection of great buildings in a beautiful southern spot. Stretched across a valley scattered with mighty volcanic boulders are splendid temples and mosques, stone stables for elephants, an intricately decorated bathing house for a princess, plus a giant granite chariot. Hampi's walls are adorned with statues depicting explicit and entertaining scenes from the Kama Sutra. The ruins are as glorious as those at Angkor Wat, and worth exploring for days. It is hugely rewarding when you get there. But whereas the Cambodian attraction draws 2.3 million foreign visitors a year, the Indian one gets a paltry 47,000. It is simply too hard a slog to reach Hampi, assuming you've even heard of it. For all of India's aspirations to be Superfast, travel in the country can be slow and difficult.

Making the most of manufacturing or of tourism, therefore, will be a slow march. An added problem is that the rest of the world is changing and will not simply wait for India to catch up. Rising wages in China did encourage firms to seek new sites for their factories, with Bangladesh and Vietnam winning investment. But global supply chains are also becoming far more complicated. Lower energy and labor costs in America, the phenomenon of "near-shoring" (finding manufacturing sites close to the biggest markets in Europe and America), and new sorts of production such as 3D printing all threaten to change the twentieth-century model used by East Asia—including, notably, China. India has failed to join regional trade deals, designed to lock countries into logistics chains and to set minimum standards and regulations. One risk for India is that, by the time it is ready to set up lots of factories to export goods, many industries will have changed.

India's infrastructure did improve a bit. The new government had a goal of building 19 miles of properly surfaced roads every day by 2017—a rate three times faster than the Singh government had aimed to achieve. The country was unlikely to meet this goal, but new roads did appear. Over 600,000 villages were also supposed to have broadband Internet by 2017, but this scheme fell far behind schedule. As for future goals, the River Ganges is to be clean by 2019; measles and tuberculosis are to be eradicated from the country by 2020; one hundred "smart" cities are to be built by 2020; by 2022 there are supposed to be long-distance, high-speed trains whizzing on a "diamond quad-rilateral" of tracks linking big cities, plus twenty-four-hour-a-day electricity for every household; thirty river-linking schemes are to be put in place by 2024; and a huge defense production as well as the creation of a $650-billion-strong textiles industry are planned for 2025. We may question whether such goals are realistic, but they do signal grand ambitions.

What is missing, however, is a much-needed push to develop more high-quality schools and colleges of the sort that flourished to such great effect under Naidu in Andhra Pradesh. One can't be sure exactly what jobs tens of thousands of graduates will end up doing, but at least highly educated and entrepreneurial graduates will be well placed to adapt to uncertainty. The trouble with Modi's visions of building factories is the risk of opting for low-margin industries where human workers will come to compete with machines, robots, and artificial intelligence as industrial processes become increasingly automated. Little in this scenario would benefit jobless Indians, especially as designers and those who own the highest forms of technology usually end up grabbing the most value from industrial production. In short, India needs to be more future-oriented. For example, it can do a lot more with new technology. Luckily, it has made a good start at that.

TECH DREAMS AND SILVER BULLETS

H E HAD A BUSHY WHITE BEARD, RIMLESS GLASSES, AND A PASSION for classical Indian dance. In his day job, Koppillil Radhakrishnan focused on modern maneuvers: getting the first Indian spacecraft into the orbit of Mars. As boss of the Indian Space Research Organisation (ISRO), India's counterpart to NASA, he knew that reaching the red planet would bring a big national fillip. Manmohan Singh had vowed that India would be the first Asian power there after news broke of a failed Chinese-Russian effort. On the eve of the launch, in 2013, Radhakrishnan said an unmanned craft would take nine months for its trip. He explained how ships in the South Pacific would track the craft's ignition, launch, and separation of its parts, before the orbiter deployed into space. The craft had the look of something you might have hammered together in a garden shed: seemingly a box taped over with golden foil, plus a few solar panels. "The trans-Martian injection" would begin after the craft rose, in five steps, 124,000 miles above Earth. He was serious, methodical, quiet-spoken—not quite getting across just how thrilling it must be to send stuff whooshing off Mars.

Most of the launch vehicle and orbiter were made in India, and the goal was to show that India could navigate a spacecraft so far away. Radhakrishnan sniffed at talk of national propaganda, promoting India as a tech-savvy place and attempting to get a marketing boost for other bits of his space program, such as its successful satellite-launching service. The orbiter, which others nicknamed *Mangalyaan,* had a serious job, he said: to take photographs, measure the Martian atmosphere for methane (a potential sign of life), and expand scientific knowledge. What about winning the race with China? "Absolutely not," he said, primly. "We are in a race with ourselves to excel in this area." It was the sort of comment one was accustomed to hearing among more tech-savvy, and mathematically minded, Indians who saw opportunities to solve social and political problems using new technology.

Historians trace India's fascination with astronomy back more than 2,500 years. The Vedas, ancient Sanskrit texts, include references to movement of the planets, the sun, and other stars as aids for setting dates of religious festivals. Later texts, known as Vedangas, deal with astronomy. By the sixth century AD, a more accurate understanding of planetary movements was being recorded in Indian texts. In Mughal times, emperors showed intense interest in what swirls above. Humayun, who ruled in north India in the sixteenth century, and whose impressive tomb is in Delhi, was fond of his observatory. One story of his death, in 1556, suggests that he fell from a steep staircase as he rushed to prayers after star-gazing. In the eighteenth century, a Hindu ruler—the Maharaja of Jaipur, Jai Singh—built five observatories, including the Jantar Mantar, an elaborate red-brick construction in Delhi that looks a little like a rollercoaster structure. Jawaharlal Nehru, India's first prime minister, was a buzzing enthusiast for science and space, launching a department of atomic energy in 1950, three years after independence, that helped to pay for space research.

Actual space activity in India began in 1975, said Radhakrishnan, when the Soviet Union launched an Indian-built satellite. Some forty years on, his organization got an annual budget of 60 billion rupees (about $1 billion) and kept busy nearly ten thousand scientists and engineers—a "good pool of young talent," as he described them. They worked frugally: for the Mars mission they spent a reported $74 million, less than the cost of making the Hollywood movie *Gravity.* "If you compare our activity with NASA, it's not that big," said Radhakrishnan, totting up only 107 missions since the 1970s, as of 2013.

India's frugal program shares something of the spirit of new space entrepreneurs such as Elon Musk, who anticipates low-cost human flight to Mars, even settlements there, within a few decades. India, too, has been signalling its growing clout on Earth by being more active in space—also at low cost. The rich world has lessons to draw from various frugal techniques dreamt up, notably, in India. In medicine, for example, "production line" surgery, where similar heart operations (or others) are done on dozens of patients, one immediately after another, has allowed the cost of operations to fall to just one-thirtieth of identical ones performed in America. Standards are maintained because the high volume of surgeries allows doctors to perfect techniques. Among others, teams from Britain's National Health Service have visited India to study its medical program.

Radhakrishnan's real dream, like Musk's, was for manned space flight, but that would be expensive. "Instead we are always focused on space applications, to benefit the common man," he said, referring to satellite launches, better communication, and more precise weather forecasts. The Mars visit went without a hitch—a resounding success in terms of reaching the planet, though the craft did not sniff out any methane. *Mangalyaan* reached its orbit in September 2014, sending back pictures that excited the Indian public, adding to a triumphant, patriotic mood. Scientists created a Twitter feed, supposedly the orbiter's, showing the Indian spacecraft in chatty conversation with American ones. Modi gave a celebratory speech at mission control headquarters in Bangalore, saying "we have dared to reach out into the unknown and have achieved the near impossible." Speaking in English, he tried to reassure those who worried that his *sarkar,* or government, mostly conducted in Hindi, would be alien for many southerners who do not speak the language. "Indians are proud people despite our many limitations—the success of our space program is a shining symbol of what we are capable of as a nation," he said. Later he asked: "Should a poor nation like India develop a space program? This question is raised time and again. How to make maximum use of technology and ensure it reaches the poorest of the poor—this is our main challenge."

It was a good question. Techno-optimists argued that technology would allow short cuts to faster development and better government. Some innovations already helped, such as satellites for predicting weather (essential for farmers and insurers) and preparing for disasters. A big cyclone arrived on India's east coast, in Odisha, around the time *Mangalyaan* launched. It was a devastating storm, but it killed only a few people because accurate forecasts had allowed early evacuations of low-lying areas. Fourteen years earlier, a cyclone of similar strength, in the same spot, drowned over ten thousand people. That was a telling measure of progress. The space story was instructive for strategic reasons, too: India had worked with America's NASA, particularly in the area of navigation—one of many indications that the two big democracies were working ever more closely.

The Mars success coincided with a general outpouring of enthusiasm for new technology. In business, the idea of frugal innovation had grown trendy, centered on some clever but low-cost developments such as efforts to produce cheap family cars like the Tata Nano (modern India's answer to the Model T in America, the Volkswagen in Germany, or the Mini in Britain). India saw the rollout of low-cost medical devices, such as cheap machines for checking blood pressure. General Electric bet that the no-frills medical gear it developed in India would find markets elsewhere, such as in Africa, but also in richer places. By 2016, more than a quarter of the company's new health-care products were being developed in India. Godrej promoted a tiny "Chotukool" fridge for low-income Indians. A rival firm produced "MittiCool," a clay container that keeps contents cool through the evaporation of water. A group in Jaipur touted its cheap prosthetic leg. Renault-Nissan, an alliance of two carmakers, set up a center for frugal engineering in India. It remains unclear, however, whether such frugal innovations will turn into large-scale commercial successes.

Some of the talk about technological successes has been a bit whacky. Ruling politicians at times alluded to a mystical understanding of scientific history, presumably to cheer the more fanatical wing of the Bharatiya Janata Party and its nationalist hangers-on. Soon after the Mars success Modi spoke in Mumbai, describing plastic surgery and "genetic science" as ancient Indian practices, described in texts such as the Mahabharata, an epic tale from over two thousand years ago: "We can feel proud of what our country achieved in medical science at one point of time," he said. Apparently serious, he talked about the elephant God, Ganesh, saying, "We worship Lord Ganesh. There must have been some plastic surgeon at that time who got an elephant's head on the body of a human being and began the practice of plastic surgery." Indian surgeons do have a long history of conducting plastic surgery, such as nose jobs, dating back nearly three thousand years. But at times, such bragging about ancestors' achievements has been exaggerated. Modi, for example, reportedly wrote the preface to a book, published in Gujarat, that said ancient Indians had invented motor cars, planes, television, and the basics of stem-cell research.[1] It drew on passages from the Mahabharata referring to horseless chariots and aircraft—*vimanas*—with smooth bodies and flashing lights that could land softly on the ground. Supposedly, ancient Indians of a Vedic civilization could fly.

All sorts of politicians have drawn on history in peculiar ways. A minister for water, Uma Bharti, once ordered a geological search for a mystical river, the Saraswati, described in ancient Vedic texts as flowing from the Himalayas to the west coast. She apparently hoped to find a massive new supply of fresh water. And a junior minister in Singh's government told archaeologists to excavate a site in Uttar Pradesh to look for a thousand metric tons of buried gold, after a local guru with a straggly, straw-colored beard dreamt of treasure buried there. Neither the subterranean river nor the gold was unearthed.

On balance, Indian rulers have been more excited about new technology than about mysticism. Gujarati friends of the prime minister recalled how, as a younger man, he routinely returned from trips to America agog over a new computer or other gizmo he had picked up. When Modi visited Japan as chief minister he saw bullet trains, which he later ordered to run in India, too. As chief minister, in conversation, he played up how useful tech could be for government. Putting policies online and inviting ordinary folk to comment, he said, allowed democracy to become stronger. Tech helped in other ways as well, such as monitoring others: "If you have technological advancement, then there is very less scope for corruption. We are using technology a lot, we are an e-government state, because of e-governance I'm a beneficiary. You see all my vehicles have a GPS system, so we can know whether [bureaucrats are] traveling or not, working or not; we can find out."

The rumor in Gujarat, widely believed, was that Modi's office avidly used technology to snoop on officials, rival politicians, and others. For example, phones were widely said to be tapped, with reports sent directly to the chief minister. Whether or not Modi engaged in phone tapping, the rumor, if believed, deterred gossip and graft, and the implication was that Modi kept a tight grip on others. A day spent with Gujarati officials allowed me to witness their understanding of e-government and the usefulness of putting land records online, making it easy for even small farmers to prove what they owned. That, in turn, helped them to raise loans to invest in irrigation, say, or warehouses. The government added online systems for filing complaints about misbehaving officials, and for contractors to bid for official tenders. Reducing personal interactions with civil servants made it harder for them to demand bribes.

As prime minister, Modi has been equally gung ho about tech. "He is driven, he has tasted blood by using technology in so many ways in government," said an official close to him. Modi said he began each morning, before yoga, reaching out for an iPad. At cabinet meetings, ministers were made to work from tablets loaded with documents. In election campaigns Modi again ordered GPS trackers to be fitted to cars of BJP workers and candidates, so he could check on their travels. Beginning in 2012, he created a buzz by projecting what appeared to be 3D holograms of himself (in fact, the images were simpler optical tricks) to address several election rallies simultaneously. At one point, he apparently spoke to fifty-three rallies at once. In the general election he addressed roughly one thousand rallies this way, most commonly with recorded speeches taken on tours of villages using special cinema trucks. He wowed rural voters, as one fellow politician explained: "It creates a sense of awe" because "the illiterate in India's villages are used to films but this is better—their faces are so surprised." There was no evidence that the special shows swung many voters. But the use of new tech added to the sense that the new prime minister was a modernizer, open to innovation and to the potential of new tools.

No politician, anywhere, has been a more avid user of social media. By 2017 he had over 26 million Twitter followers who received a steady flow of selfies and statements on current events, as Modi did away with a press spokesman. He made the fondness for technology among many Indians abroad part of his promotion of a new era for India. In 2014 he jokingly told a crowd of eighteen thousand people in Madison Square Garden, New York, that "our people used to play with snakes—now they play with a mouse."

"Whenever societies walk with the times, they progress faster. Acceptance of modern science and technology is an essential part of working with developments of the time," he said during a chat with me the following year. For a country that aspires to develop at a Superfast pace, or at least to catch up with other parts of Asia, some tech could clearly bring shortcuts. But it has proved much harder to deliver on the ground than to make promises. Modi's plan for 600,000 villages to have high-speed Internet by 2017 was in trouble from the start because it relied on slow-moving civil servants. "Digital India is a very big programme of ours," he said. "One goal is to have Internet access to all. A second is for optical fiber to reach every village." But the project was underfunded and poorly run: Modi would end up blaming state governments when the scheme fell short.

In fact, new technology spread when businesses had incentives to roll it out, rather than when officials did so. An evening I spent with a group of entrepreneurs in their twenties and thirties, at a friend's home in Bangalore, indicated how rapidly the private sector could move. The youngsters were low-key, in casual clothes, and might have been mistaken for students, though most were self-made billionaires. In common among their successes was the booming use of smartphones. An unassuming man, Sachin Bansal, chatted about the future of shopping. In 2007 he had co-founded Flipkart, an online marketplace (a local version of Amazon, where Bansal once worked, or of Alibaba), with $8,000 borrowed from his parents. "The name is meaningless, I just liked the sound of it," he explained. By 2016 the firm was said to be worth $5.5 billion. Industry experts talked of annual online merchandise trade soon being worth $30 billion.

"The best thing about India is we don't have to replace anything," Bansal said, noting that most people had never had a landline but by 2020 some 500 million people would have smartphones. Shopping online could make sense in a country where supermarkets had never flourished. Consumers were notoriously price conscious and accustomed to tradesmen bringing goods to their doors. Most urban folk relied on corner shops, kirana stores, or traders who brought vegetables, fruit, and other produce on carts. As of 2015, only 1 percent of shopping in India happened online, but that share would rise dramatically. Bansal predicted that Flipkart would create jobs for 2 million people. Even if his company fell short, digital firms and small online entrepreneurs were more likely to create lots of new jobs than the factories Modi was betting on. Smartphones were crucial, said Bansal. "Consumers are shifting to them, but more interesting for us, and more significant, is that every trader and delivery person uses them, so we can trace deliveries through smartphones. The shift away from laptops and tablets to smartphones, it's huge. People live their lives on smartphones: it is how they look for jobs, holidays, love, and news. And we get the data on what they are doing," he said.

Another entrepreneur, Bhavish Aggarwal, was just as optimistic. He had founded Ola, a smartphone-based taxi-hailing service, in 2011. Four years on, he claimed that his start-up had 150,000 drivers, mostly first-time entrepreneurs, and that Ola was far bigger than Uber in India. It was valued at $5 billion as of 2015. "We are riding on mobile penetration, on-demand consumption—people expect things in five to ten minutes," he explained. Indians were quick to adopt new technology and habits rather than simply following the old practices of the Western world, such as owning cars. "We see sales of 100 million smartphones a year in India, but only 2.5 million cars a year," he said, predicting that in the future Indians would hail cabs rather than drive and park their own cars. He pointed out that his mother's ex-driver, in Punjab, became a taxi driver for Ola, buying his car with a loan from the firm. "Now he is his own boss. He may go on to own two or four cars. People are becoming businessmen. They expect more," said Aggarwal. For the energetic and creative, tech opened up chances to be entrepreneurial where none existed before.

Thanks to new technology, businesses may be able to skip some of the problems associated with broken infrastructure. Naveen Tewari and Abhay Singhal, two founders of InMobi, an online firm that has supplied billions of advertisements to users globally, described how start-ups boomed in Bangalore. The city had plenty of engineers and creative types good at programming, and India as a whole had centers of excellence in Indian Institutes of Technology (IITs). Tewari told me that students at IITs were launching a new generation of tech businesses, many smartphone-based, at a dizzying pace. He had invested in nineteen of these, and some were growing quickly. Bangalore also got a boost from its ties to the Indian diaspora in California's Bay Area. "You don't have six or seven years to build a billion-dollar business now; you have to move quicker. We don't have time to make mistakes," he said. Many Indian firms are registered in Singapore, because of tax and bureaucracy in India, but they are a testament to the idea that India is home to creative, imaginative tech innovators.

Tech could improve government, too. One visit to Mumbai showed me the best example, a scheme launched by Singh's government and then expanded under Modi. Aadhaar, the national biometric scheme, was set up to give every Indian a secure, unique digital identity—for use in interactions with officials, companies, or one another. The government hired private firms to register over a billion people in a few years. In Mumbai a big IT firm, Wipro, sent teams to record the identities of tens of thousands of people daily from 2010 onward. They fanned out with laptops, webcams, and iris scanners, gathering biometric data from volunteering residents—a process that would have made George Orwell tremble.

The team members on the road faced many challenges. They crept north from Mumbai under a remarkably heavy monsoon downpour, as water rushed off tin rooftops and hammered on the car roof. Cows waded on flooded roads as the team leader described "ground challenges" in the region. Inland, in the hilly bit of Maharashtra state, his staff had to deal not only with terrible roads but also with Maoist revolutionaries who planted landmines and ambushed the police. Analysts talked of a "Red Corridor" that stretched from northeast India to the center, through the isolated inland bit of this state. In forested areas, revolutionaries are known to attack busloads of policemen and to block roads. One morning in 2012, a bomb exploded under a bus filled with paramilitary police, killing fifteen. Understandably, others were wary of following in their tracks.

For the Wipro team on the coast, difficulties were more mundane: poor public transport and recurrent theft. Sixty-eight laptops had been stolen from this team; thieves usually ignored more expensive scanners and other equipment. Religious festivals were also a pain because team members wanted to attend them rather than working and residents did not turn out to be enrolled. "The second half of the year is full of celebrations," grumbled one Wipro man. "Now there is Eid for the Muslims, then comes eleven days of Ganapati when Hindus celebrate the god of prosperity." After those came Navratri (a party for nine nights) and finally Diwali (the festival of light).

A ceiling fan swirled warm air and mosquitoes inside a small fire station in Uttan Gaon village. Villagers queued up as operators scanned irises using a machine that looked like an oversized pair of binoculars. Nester Gharshi, a villager in neat blue trousers and a crisply ironed shirt, was able to get his fingerprints recorded only after vigorous rubbing on the scanner: many laborers' fingers were so worn it was difficult to identify the thirty different points required. He told me that he hoped a new, digital form of identity verification would stop police from hassling him while he drove his rickshaw. "This is a good idea, a good process," he said. His details, and those of hundreds of millions of other people, were sent to a repository for digital identities in Bangalore, and each was allocated a unique number. Because it is virtually impossible for one person to get more than one such number, millions of old duplicate "ghost" recipients of government services could be eliminated.

Bangalore was also home to Nandan Nilekani, the man who oversaw the massive iris-scanning scheme. He had helped to found Infosys, an IT and business consulting giant that he ran for five years until 2007. Infosys became India's second-largest IT company, worth some $40 billion as of 2016. But in 2011, when we met in his office in Delhi, he was in government to direct the Aadhaar scheme, bursting with pride at having signed up his first 14 million people. "The goal is to give everyone in India an ID, and for there to be no fakes or duplications; with this we can improve public services, and, crucially, provide everyone with a reliable online ID, to use on a mobile network or on the Internet," he said. He pointed excitedly to graphs of enroll-ments, an online dashboard that showed how many people had signed up and where. All jagged lines pointed sharply upward.

Over the years Nilekani expanded Aadhaar, arguing that technology was the key to making government efficient. Manmohan Singh gave him the rank of a cabinet minister and, crucially, the freedom to exper-iment. India spent about $50 billion yearly on welfare. In an economy of over $2 trillion that was not much, but the share of total spending was rising, from 1.6 percent of GDP in 2004 to 2.5 percent in 2014. In a few years India's welfare bill would reach hundreds of billions of dol-lars. The McKinsey Global Institute and others estimated that as little as half of that money reached the intended recipients.[2] That might have been a generous estimate. Rations in kind were most prone to being stolen, damaged, or lost. Rajiv Gandhi, India's prime minister in the 1980s, said that for every rupee spent on helping India's poor, only seventeen paisa (i.e., 17 percent) reached the needy. A 2009 study of public distribution of food in several states suggested that he was about right.[3]

Good monitoring helped to cut theft and waste, but another op-tion was just to give cash directly to the poor—as direct transfers to personal bank accounts, or as vouchers, at least where markets existed to use the funds. Some paternalistic observers worried that villagers, especially men, would waste such cash on booze. But money could instead be directed to women, who might be better trusted to care for whole families. A new system could use technology to cut out "middle-men"—shops that sold rations of subsidized food and other goods to the poor, or lorry drivers and others who shifted low-priced rations in kind. It was such intermediaries who were most likely to steal or lose the welfare-in-kind.

The new technology helped to begin this shift to cash welfare. The poor needed bank accounts and a reliable way to be identified. Modi oversaw the opening of 255 million new accounts in state banks by 2016, though many, at first, were empty accounts. The idea was to match these new accounts, and older existing ones, to the biometric system Aadhaar, which in turn would help identify who got benefits. Neeraj Mittal, an official in Delhi, described the pieces that were being put together to transform some of the massive welfare spending. He began with cooking gas, claimed by about 150 million households. The removal of "ghosts," partly thanks to Aadhaar, cut waste. By 2015 India was handling 3 million daily transactions for gas, as cash benefits, making this the world's biggest cash-transfer program.

Aadhaar had other uses. Ram Sewak Sharma, who oversaw hi-tech programs for the national government, said that it encouraged civil servants to work more efficiently. Iris scanners at government offices, connected to the Aadhaar database, helped to monitor who turned up and when. A pilot scheme in Jharkhand, an eastern state, plotted, in real-time, state employees' attendance at their offices or other places of work on a website that anyone could check. A similar scheme monitored more than 120,000 civil servants of the national government in Delhi. Suddenly golf courses fell much quieter during the working day, though civil servants were said to be teeing off at 4:30 a.m. instead, to complete rounds before getting to the office. Truancy had long been a plague across India's government. In 2014, in the state of Madhya Pradesh, a teacher was sacked after a twenty-four-year career, having been absent for twenty-three of them. A year later, an engineer employed by the central government finally lost his job because he hadn't shown up for work since 1990. In theory, the monitoring scheme could cover millions more people employed by the state—in schools, hospitals, and offices—where absenteeism has long been a scourge. More benefits could follow, to the dismay of civil libertarians. Taxpayers' records could be linked to bank accounts, using Aadhaar, making it harder for the rich to dodge tax payments. Those buying an expensive property might have to supply their unique identity number, a problem for money launderers.

Technology was supposed to improve administration, and states were encouraged to compete. Better-run ones rolled out government services using similar technology. Karnataka state found a way to get forty departments to share a smartphone app, Mobile One, to provide public services such as property records, birth certificates, and car registrations. Nilekani wanted technology to be used far more widely—for example, to tackle India's rotten standards of education. He developed a platform (for use on smartphones, computers, tablets) called Ek Step, to improve literacy, numeracy, and language skills. Of course, tech cannot cure every problem, and it is no substitute for fixing the most basic deficiencies. Students need electricity supplies and light in order to learn to read and write. They also need clean water and good nutrition and hygiene to be healthy and able to concentrate in the classroom. The impact of free midday meals for schoolchildren has been significant and is obviously low-tech—it helps to explain why school attendance has risen steadily in the twenty-first century. For many children, simple needs are the most urgent ones, even if technology brings benefits too.

This broad lesson is relevant everywhere. The likes of Ola and Uber, Flipkart and Amazon, and other agile digital companies will succeed, but all require the basics, too, in order to function: roads that are not too crowded or pot-holed, Internet infrastructure that's up to speed. Talk of "smart cities" has become fashionable under Modi, conjuring images of hi-tech urban areas with clever traffic-management systems, advanced electricity grids, and high-speed Internet connections. These ambitions are fine, but cities most need to fix basic problems first: they need to get good public transport, proper sewerage, decent housing and schools, and they need to tackle smog, the deaths of pedestrians in the streets, and other mundane but serious difficulties. Technology will fix some problems, but not all. Better municipal government, fewer corrupt city politicians, higher rates of tax collection—these are all essential. Most prosaically, India has to educate and deploy armies of town-planners, so that land can be better used and infrastructure can be built in a more timely way.

Better education will improve in the old-fashioned way: by getting well-trained teachers to instruct and inspire students. Girls will have to feel safe and welcome if they are to remain in education late into their teens and beyond. It is hard to imagine that an app could make that possible. More tech is certainly welcome, as it can make government, business, and other actors far more efficient. But on its own, it is no silver bullet for myriad problems.

Yet by the late 2010s it was possible to be cautiously more hopeful for India's economic prospects than was the case in past years. At that time India was unlikely to match the decades of sustained high growth that turned China into an economic rival to the United States. But India was pushing out, albeit gradually, more reforms such as the new Goods and Services Tax to make itself, at last, into one big market. The result is likely to be higher rates of economic growth, lower rates of poverty, and the eventual emergence of India as the third-largest economy on the planet. Would that count as Superfast in the broadest sense? More Indians would see improved lives, with health and education levels (human capital) rising. And more could expect to find productive jobs in services like tourism, in factories, and in the tech field. Under Modi it appears likely that infrastructure, such as railways and roads, will also improve. Yet without effective leadership from government, there is a risk that such benefits will be skewed toward a small minority. To ensure that they are more widely spread, politics has to function better. That is the topic of the next section of the book.

PART 2

PRIMETIME—POLITICS

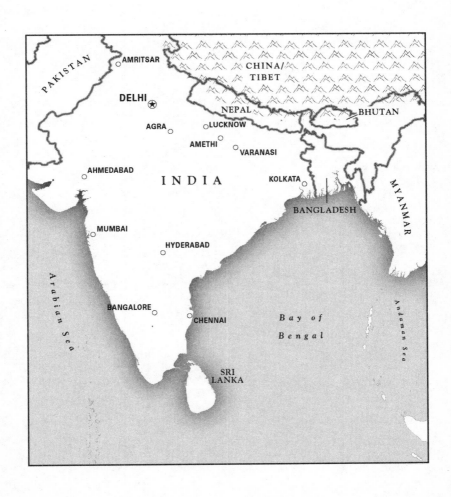

WEAKER FAMILIES, STRONGER DEMOCRACY?

I T IS A CURSE, OR A DEAD WEIGHT. DEMOCRACY IS A BURDEN: ALL those expensive elections, the corruption that comes with crooked political parties and crony-capitalist allies. Pesky laws and courts protect individual property rights, making it harder to build railways and roads, or to open up mines, dam rivers, and log forests. Remove democracy from India, make it more like China with a strong and more capable state, then rapid economic development could surely follow. All that energy wasted by politicians in parliament and at campaign rallies could be harnessed to delivering rising living standards. Who needs the chaos of politicians obsessed with winning elections, rather than governing well?

Such an authoritarian argument is never seriously aired in India, though in Pakistan it has been used repeatedly to justify military rule for many of the years since independence. But at times, frustrations with failures of Indian democracy do grow intense. Democracy is often described as a sort of tax, responsible for slower economic growth than could otherwise be possible. Evidence of imperfection in Indian democracy is not hard to find. Take the biggest fact of all about Indian politics: that three generations of just one family supplied prime ministers who dominated politics for the first four decades after independence—first Jawaharlal Nehru, then his daughter Indira Gandhi, and then her son Rajiv Gandhi. A fourth figure from the same family, Sonia Gandhi, de facto led government for another decade, until 2014. That hardly points to a democracy working at its prime.

The argument in the chapters that follow, the "Primetime" section, is an optimistic one. Its premise is that Indian democracy is potentially a huge advantage, rather than a curse or a tax. Even an imperfect democracy delivered a lot of the country's greatest successes so far, including the relative peace, tolerance, and stability that have distinguished India from all of its neighbors. Freedoms of expression, movement, belief, and political organization in India are enormously valuable. But democracy is not simple: some forms of it function better than others; democracy changes as society and the economy grow. Democracy is far more successful, for example, when voters are informed and demanding, and when strong institutions (such as the Election Commission) work independently. The coming years will hopefully see democracy functioning better—for instance, if politicians realize they get rewarded for responding to voters' broad economic demands, and if voters (who have become more urban, educated, informed, and active) attain a better understanding of what their country could achieve. The political Primetime of India could even be associated with declining corruption, more competitive elections and assertive voters, and politicians who start to address long-term challenges, such as the need to improve the prospects of women or to respond to environmental threats. It should all begin, ideally, with dynasts' power declining.

During my years of living in India, it was possible to see dynasties almost anywhere in the country. The example closest to me was my delightful Delhi landlord, an aging Sikh businessman with a wispy beard and a perfectly tied turban. He was kept active and happy well into his eleventh decade thanks to nightly, generous shots of scotch and the loving support of several generations of his family. I would occasionally help with the whiskey drinking and listen as the family described his role as a magistrate in Shimla, a mountain resort town, and how he had prospered by running small businesses and owning property in postwar Delhi. Long after his hundredth birthday he made daily trips to supervise a shop he owned in the city's white, colonnaded shopping center, Connaught Place.

This Sikh patriarch produced three sons. His eldest had two of his own, and they, in their time, sired more. Four bustling generations lived together in one home, attended on by several servants. In the evenings they ate together, drank, and gossiped about business and private lives, or about the art they liked to make and exhibit. They told of corrupt demands by Delhi inspectors, or of feuding in the extended family. At times they went to Delhi's grandest club, the century-old Gymkhana, where the city elites sit at tables of starched linen or lob tennis balls back and forth in neat courts. Now and then their house filled with flowers and wedding guests, the smell of spice and the roar of a tandoor oven, and its tables were weighed with plates of Punjabi delicacies. Birthday parties were followed by explosive Diwali parties, then nights of gambling at cards, winter drinks around bonfires, Sikh festivities, Christmas caroling, water-fights, and clouds of powdered paint for Holi and—eventually—sessions of prayer, recitals, and music to mark the end of the old man's long life.

His dynasty prospered, typical of many in Delhi. It also turned fractious, which was typical, too. Two brothers accused a third of cheating on the old man's will. For months, then years, the case sank into India's flawed legal system. Hearings and depositions were postponed, and rival lawyers invented mischievous ways to prolong the process, in a modest version of Dickens's Jarndyce and Jarndyce. It crawled on, one of millions of cases involving families, businesses, and others who scrap in slow motion over assets—houses, jewelry, farmland, firms—all ill-served by a sputtering, often overwhelmed and sometimes corrupt, legal system.

The case was a reminder of how the family is central to India's economy, from its most profitable firm down. As of 2016 Reliance Industries, a conglomerate involved in energy, supermarkets, broadcasting, and more, was being led by Mukesh Ambani, routinely ranked as one of the richest people on Earth. He was undoubtedly among the most influential people in India. He moved with armed guards, breakfasted with cabinet ministers, craved public acceptance, and showed questionable public taste: he built a monstrous, twenty-seven-floor home in Mumbai for nearly $1 billion, earning widespread scorn, not least because the land had previously been owned by an orphanage and was allegedly bought below the market price. As both an ugly building and a symbol of crass insensitivity to concerns about inequality, "Antilla" could hardly be matched for bad taste. Its maintenance required a staff of six hundred, so at least it created a few jobs.

Ambani once called his firm a "role model for all Indians who dare to dream," but of course it is easier to realize your dreams if you had first inherited big advantages. Reliance was huge. By 2014 it accounted for 15 percent of all Indian exports and 4 percent of the value of the stock market. Like many tycoons in India, Ambani had done well largely thanks to an inheritance from his father, Dhirubhai Ambani, a yarn trader who founded the firm and prospered enormously in the 1980s, partly thanks to mysterious, anonymous investments routed from overseas. Mukesh Ambani himself also did well, having won a battle for control of the firm's most valuable assets against his brother, Anil.

Big companies in India—like its little ones—are often family affairs: over half of India's large business groups were controlled by families as of 2015. Anand Mahindra, boss of Mahindra Group, was a self-aware tycoon who led a big family firm. Three generations of the Mahindra family had run his Mahindra Group, but when asked about family businesses he grew uncomfortable and said such firms were usually stuffed with relatives "99 percent of whom should not be there." Sanjiv Goenka, the head of another business family, the Goenkas in West Bengal, said he saw opportunity in this family-oriented arrangement: members of smaller and newer business families needed training, which could be provided by relatives working at the same company. The Goenkas' firm, RPG, with sprawling interests in property, tires, IT, private colleges, and more, had been around since 1820, when it traded with the East India Company in Calcutta. Over a Bengali lunch in his boardroom, he told me of his plans to sell services to new dynasts in other families. "We will target family-owned businesses, that's a gap. The rich send kids abroad to learn, but some don't want their kids to go away. We will target families who have revenues of $10 million to $20 million," he said, identifying those "who keep their kids in Delhi, or elsewhere in India, and want to get an education and professionalize their family business." The richest pickings would be in rural areas, such as those in Jharkhand and Chhattisgarh, where families prospered from mining and political connections but had little understanding of how to invest or develop further.

Firms in India are often built around families, because relatives are more likely to trust one another. And for businesses to flourish, especially during the license Raj before liberalization, they often needed access to politicians and officials. If your firm needed land, licenses, an electricity or phone connection, the right to import goods, or access to foreign currency, achieving this goal almost always depended on your having political clout. So it was natural for business families to fund politicians, or to develop political wings themselves; ruling political families also found sidelines for developing businesses. Across South Asia powerful families became almost the default unit in much of politics, and such families were often deeply involved in business, too. In Pakistan the Bhuttos—Zulfikar, Benazir, Asif Ali Zardari—came and went at the head of government, prospering along the way, notably through corruption. Benazir Bhutto's husband, Asif Zardari, was widely known as "Mr. Ten Percent," a reference to the benefits his family was rumored to have earned. In Bangladesh, Sheikh Hasina, the prime minister, dominated the country her father had founded, amid talk that her daughter would rule next.

In India many political parties are, in effect, public expressions of a single family's power. As of 2009, around 9 percent of sitting legislators in America's Congress, and the same level in Britain's parliament, were dynasts (defined as rulers who have a relative who has also served there). On the same measure, dynasts account for a much higher share, 29 percent, of India's lower house of parliament, the Lok Sabha. Even after bachelor Modi stormed into office in 2014, lambasting dynasty politics, the share fell only slightly to 21 percent. His finance minister, Arun Jaitley, declared "an end to dynasty politics," but in reality it remained a big factor in both regional and national politics.

Dynasts are expected to rise again, not least because many voters seem to like them. A survey of sixty-five thousand households in twenty-four states conducted by the Center for the Advanced Study of India before and after the 2014 election found that 46 percent of the public preferred a candidate, all else being equal, who hailed from an established political clan. Many believed that a dynast brought experience, that being a politician "is their occupation"; in addition, it was the poorest and least educated voters who were most likely to favor candidates from politician-families. Perhaps most important, political parties—including the BJP and regional parties—were more likely to nominate (and re-nominate) candidates who were dynasts rather than candidates who lacked existing ties to political families. Sympathy for dynasties did not trump everything—Modi did well as an outsider who was not from the established crowd of political families. In the same election, two-fifths of candidates of Congress in the state of Rajasthan had strong dynastic ties and none got elected. But political cycles turn, and some of those candidates were likely to return and win later.

Yet the long-term sympathy for dynasts might yet decline for other reasons. India is under the sway of dynastic politics partly because deference for powerful families reflects a conservative society, especially in villages. India has never had a revolution, and it seems that Indian society is more used to gradual changes, and seeing power passed within families, rather than to sudden ruptures. Invaders, at least not recent ones, were not crushed or thrown out: India instead assimilated outsiders, or saw one lot of foreigners displace the last. The Mughals, intruders from the north and west, lost control of India only gradually as local princes took some territory and then British traders and colonists grabbed power, culminating in the nineteenth century. The British, in turn, were not forced out by revolutionary violence—despite a bloody uprising for the sake of independence in 1857—but they quit after prolonged negotiation and after being weakened by two global wars. Because of its relatively stable parliamentary democracy, India escaped the worst bloodshed and horror inflicted by ideologues in Russia, China, and many parts of Asia, Africa, and Latin America last century. A result of such stability, at least in rural India, was that traditional ways of organizing society—through families, village councils, and timeworn gatherings of elders or religious leaders—appeared to remain little changed from centuries before.

India had a relatively weak state (and a liberal constitution) clamped on top of a society with strong traditional and conservative structures. The institution of the family, in turn, appeared unusually powerful. Caste divisions, traditional village councils led by male elders, extended families dominated by patriarchs, religious communities—all those bodies helped to ingrain habits of deference to the powerful. Despite some modest land reform and the scrapping of financial aid to royals, in the years after independence Indian politicians were slow to shed their feudal and royal past, the vestiges of Mughals, Maharajas, and colonial Britons. Much of wider India, until the British left in 1947, had been run by princes, kings, or queens: 562 princely states accounted for one-third of the land. A few liberal royals encouraged education and social progress for their subjects, but many did not. Big landowners or the high caste long retained great power.

Some ex-royals, with crumbling palaces, aged retainers, and walls crammed with portraits of their ancestors, were politically active deep into the twenty-first century. An up-and-coming leader in Congress,

Jyotiraditya Scindia, was the third generation of his family elected to national parliament. Pudgy faced and foreign educated, he was descended from maharajas who ran the central Indian state of Gwalior from the eighteenth century on. Their splendid, four-hundred-room Jai Vilas Palace in Gwalior had the world's heaviest chandeliers and an elaborate, raised, indoor swimming pool. Asked if he agreed that voters were fed up with dynasts, in 2015, he prickled, straightened his starched white kurta, and said, "Dynasty is not relevant, and is it a crime that I happen to be born with this name?" He argued that "politics in India is about entrepreneurs," more than about families or old privilege, but he undermined the effect of his argument by then ordering a bare-footed, middle-aged servant to adjust the air-conditioning and bring us tea in fine china cups. Scindia in fact had a decent record as a politician. Although young, he had spent over a dozen years in parliament, where he spoke early and often, making an effort for his constituents. He also spoke frequently on news shows to defend his party—an act that required stamina and strong vocal cords, given the shouting typically involved. The most pampered dynastic leader in his party, Rahul Gandhi, refused such trials.

Other young dynasts were active. One was Omar Abdullah, who became chief minister of Kashmir at the young age of thirty-eight, in 2009. With a boyish face (and a British mother) he was also the third generation of Abdullahs to run the mountain state. It was a tough job amid uprisings against Indian rule, and some older political commentators dismissed him as weak. His police mishandled bloody summer protests in Kashmir: in 2010 alone they killed at least 110 young men in and around Srinagar, the summer capital. Abdullah was also pilloried for inaction when floods washed through Srinagar in 2014, just before he lost elections. At least he was open, ready to admit to mistakes. In the autumn sunshine in the garden of his residence he discussed the nature of dynasty politics, accepting that it was unhealthy if a few families dominated public life. "I have at least lost an election," he added, "and there is no better learning experience than losing an election." He mentioned Rajiv Gandhi, prime minister from 1984 to 1989, saying that he "would have come back as a much better leader after losing his election had he got a chance to prove it." (Rajiv Gandhi was murdered in 1991.) Abdullah was tighter-lipped about his friend Rahul Gandhi, son of Rajiv and Sonia Gandhi, who struggled to perform despite his family's control of Congress.

No dynasty has shaped modern India more than the Nehru-Gandhis, who for thirty-seven of the first sixty-nine years of independence supplied the prime minister. Whole shelves in bookshops, and in the homes of any reader on Indian politics, heave with tomes on the lives, letters, loves, and political activities of the family. The foremost figures include the prewar Congress leader, Motilal Nehru; then his son Jawaharlal Nehru, India's first and most dominant prime minister (he was also a prolific and insightful writer); and, subsequently, Indira Gandhi, who brought India closest to dictatorship. Nehru undoubtedly benefited from the wealth, education, and political status his father helped to bestow. But it was Indira (who had married a supporter of Congress, Feroze Gandhi, no relation of the Mahatma) who really put the family stamp on modern politics. From timid beginnings—backroom operators in Congress accepted her as prime minister in 1966 believing she could be easily controlled—Indira emerged as a fierce champion of the family's interests. By the 1970s, one of her closest confidantes and most powerful advisers was her son, Sanjay Gandhi, a man who oversaw brutal acts, such as the forced sterilization of members of the urban poor, and who used draconian powers to crush opponents, flatten parts of Old Delhi, and empower himself. He also profited personally—for example, in winning favors to set up a car company. With his backing, Indira centralized power, overturned governments in states opposed to her, and ruled there by decree. She also encouraged a cult of personality, as supporters chanted that "India is Indira, Indira is India."

The Indian military intervention that helped Bangladesh (then East Pakistan) to secede from Pakistan in 1971 led to praise of Indira as a tough, even ruthless leader. Some called her the Goddess Durga, a reference to an invincible warrior goddess. But she could be ruthless at home, too. She felt a threat to her grip on political power, in 1975, and then suspended Indian democracy for nearly two years, declaring a state of emergency. Personalizing power to an extraordinary degree, she twice recreated the Indian National Congress, first in 1969 after being expelled from it, then in 1978 when she adopted a new party name, Congress (I), in which "I" stood for Indira. The fact that she triumphed each time showed that voters had more loyalty to her and to her family name than to the institution of the party.

She claimed to be a champion of the poorest—for example, in 1971, when she campaigned saying she would "eradicate poverty." In fact, her policies punished the poor in the long run. She promoted a bigger role for the state, encouraged political meddling in much of the economy, nationalized banks and other companies, proved increasingly protec-tionist, and intensified bureaucratic control on business—ultimately hobbling economic growth and setting inflation soaring. Despite grand gestures such as an official declaration of state-socialism in 1976, she was not really a committed ideologue; rather, she chose leftist economic policies for reasons of political expediency. By the 1980s she was ready to change course, at least in part. But her actions, and the isolation of India, had hobbled the economy even as much of East Asia began opening up for more trade. The result was the continuation of poverty in India for hundreds of millions of people.

After Indira, who was murdered in 1984, the Gandhi family re-mained ascendant over Congress. Her younger son, Sanjay Gandhi, had been the more active in the politics of the next generation. But he killed himself one morning in 1980, while trying to perform a stunt in a new plane over Delhi. That left Rajiv Gandhi, who took over immediately following his mother's death and then, after his own election, ruled as prime minister for five years until 1989. He left office under a cloud in part because of his role in a big corruption scandal involving a Swed-ish maker of artillery pieces, Bofors. Then he too was murdered, by

Tamil separatists from Sri Lanka. As discussed earlier, his widow, Sonia Gandhi, eventually got control over the party in the late 1990s and would dominate the Congress-led government of 2004 to 2014, led by Manmohan Singh.

Two minor Gandhi figures, Sanjay Gandhi's widow Maneka Gandhi, and her son, Varun Gandhi, were also political actors, but they found their berth in the Bharatiya Janata Party. They were occasionally offered ministerial positions when the BJP held national office. Maneka had fallen out bitterly with Sonia Gandhi in the early 1980s and knew that neither she nor Varun had any prospect of a career in Congress. It suited the BJP to have its own Gandhi dynasts to deploy—to appeal to voters in rural Uttar Pradesh, where the family had strong appeal. Varun Gandhi proved more dynamic than his cousin, Rahul, but also readier to appeal to ugly tendencies. In the 2009 election campaign he cast himself as a virulent Hindu nationalist, and a tape emerged of him allegedly talking to voters about cutting off the hands of Muslims or slashing their throats. He denied making the comments. Later, he presented a new persona, writing earnest newspaper columns on current affairs as well as books of occasionally mournful poetry. He said he turned to verse "when I am feeling most tender, most raw" as part of a "journey inwards."[1] (Many politicians, perhaps inspired by Mughal leaders, showed their softer sides with poetry. Even Modi, who usually liked to present himself as muscular, turned out books of verse. "At times various, I seem like a honeybee," he once wrote; another time, he explained his poetry to be "streams of thoughts, like a spring of fresh water.")[2]

By 2017, the figure who will do the most to decide the future of the Nehru-Gandhi dynasty, and perhaps decide whether the Indian National Congress can survive as a significant political force, is Rahul Gandhi. Arun Jaitley, the finance minister, liked to sneer at his opponent, calling him "an empty suit." "He is just family charisma, not coupled with wit or competence," Jaitley once said to me. Rahul Gandhi, first elected as an MP in 2004, proved to be timid, unable to think strategically, and ill at ease in the aggressive sparring of Indian politics. He had refused an offer to become a minister in Manmohan Singh's government. A relative of his claimed that Rahul had scorned the idea of taking responsibility, supposedly saying he would not bother to be minister when he could take the job of prime minister. Nor did he get experience running a state government, which might have been good training. Instead, the scion lamented that politics was a "poison" and carried the air of a well-meaning non-governmental organization worker, one who lamented the failures of politics but who was forever shy of taking charge. His own family, though they remained relatively popular, had done the most to create the political system he criticized—for example, when he grumbled that politics was "decided by a handful of people behind closed doors" and that elites rob people of their voice. "Why do a handful of people control the entire political space?" he once said, decrying politics as "designed to promote mediocrity" and claiming that "mediocrity dominates discussion."[3] His proposed solution, to introduce internal democracy in Congress, flopped badly. Beyond that, he did not articulate any strong views on policies or reforms to lift Indian politics from its mediocrity.

Rahul Gandhi, rather bravely, did speak about the curse of family in politics and once described himself as a symptom of a problem that needed fixing. But it was unclear what solution he offered. Congress always stood ready to do the family's bidding, like a well-upholstered Ambassador car waiting at the front door, as a colleague of mine put it. The family name was attached to some 450 different public schemes and institutions nationwide. An official estimate in 2013 found that just three members of the Nehru-Gandhi dynasty had their names on 74 roads and buildings, 64 public schemes, 39 hospitals and clinics, 28 sports tournaments, 19 stadiums, 5 airports and seaports, 98 schools and colleges, 51 awards, 15 fellowships, and 15 natural reserves, among other schemes funded by public money. That was the sort of self-aggrandizing and self-promotion one might expect from a ruling family in a monarchy, not a party that supposedly promoted meritocracy.

Another young dynast was Sachin Pilot, an amiable figure who got a big leg up because his father, Rajesh Pilot, had been a minister and a long-serving politician (after a stint as a squadron leader in the Indian Air Force). From a family in Uttar Pradesh, the elder Pilot once worked as a milkman in Delhi, delivering to politicians' grand houses where, years later, he and then his son would live. The younger Pilot always looked cautious—his default expression was of a man startled by something and who hoped not to show it—but he did capable work as a junior minister. Pressed about Rahul Gandhi's failure to step up, he loyally said in an interview with me that Gandhi is not "hankering" for high office. "It is not about occupying positions of power. It is about building the party, democratizing it. You can't criticize him for wanting power."[4] In fact, it was Gandhi's lack of leadership, his long absences from parliament while abroad on holiday, his failure to give speeches or interviews, and his lack of effective work for constituents that were troubling. Pilot defended his friend: "Rahul has proved he's not power hungry. It is a good feeling to have, here's a guy who is not going to compromise. Rahul is not holding others back. Who do you think can galvanize, motivate like he can? He can do so anywhere, in Kerala, the North East, Tamil Nadu, Jammu. There is a buzz around him. He is not associated with a region, a caste, an ethnicity."

In small, private meetings, Rahul Gandhi could be fluent and engaging, though fellow MPs complained that he was often dismissive, curt, vague, and uninterested. In public he showed little political aptitude. The more Modi the showman-outsider rose, the worse the Rahul-of-the-establishment struggled. And when the shine first began to come off Modi, it was regional politicians, not Rahul Gandhi or Congress, who benefited.

Even in his own parliamentary constituency, Amethi, in western Uttar Pradesh, voters grumbled about Gandhi during visits I made to take his measure. It was harvest time and women in fields were lifting sheaths of wheat over their heads before whacking them onto cloth on the ground, threshing seeds. Their technique owed nothing to twenty-first-century farming. Two elephants passed, tusks cut off, on a stroll from a nearby *mahout*-training center. The road was patched and pot-holed; many houses were tumbledown. A roundabout was topped by a white statue of Rajiv Gandhi, reminding everyone that the family dominated. But nothing hinted that this dusty place was part of an emerging superpower. The Gandhi family told locals to be proud of living in a "VIP constituency," yet the absentee politicians did little beyond setting up the occasional institute—for example, to train youngsters in designing shoes. By night Amethi fell dark, during a prolonged power cut, and only one building kept its lights shining: an official guesthouse where Rahul Gandhi and his sister, Priyanka, stayed that night.

The scion might have tried to turn his constituency into a thriving model of what he would do if given national power. He did not. Nor was he popular among his own workers, party colleagues, and supporters. Some constituents dismissed him as ineffective or lazy. "Rahul Gandhi walks alone; there are not many people he is taking with," complained a supporter, who considered Sonia Gandhi to be "a goddess." Another man trying to get him reelected complained that the candidate had a weak image and lacked spontaneity, preferring to read from prepared speeches. The scion's father used to sit in the town petrol station and chat to all-comers, but "RG," as the worker called Rahul, was aloof. When people complained to him, "he waves his hand and goes away." His sister, Priyanka, knew "all the local party workers by name, face and remembers them publicly later on; RG does not seem to have the same skill," said the party man. Even when he campaigned, grumbled another worker, he stayed mostly in his air-conditioned car and shunned pesky locals. "People complain that RG prefers to play games on his smartphone, rather than meet voters," said a volunteer.

Rahul Gandhi was a flop in 2014 and beyond: Congress was walloped in the general election campaign that he helped to lead and then, subsequently, in the state elections of the next two years. Some Congress figures hoped that Priyanka Gandhi could be an alternative leader.

She looked more driven, and her resemblance to her grandmother, Indira, got some analysts' hearts fluttering. But their assumption that only someone in the family could hold together the party was dispiriting. She, too, played up the dynastic factor. On one occasion, in her brother's constituency, in Lalganj village, I watched as Priyanka lectured a crowd of farmers not to trust anyone else: "Other people who come here are unattached to you, they do not love you, they come for their image," she said, whereas "we consider you as family." Her speech called to mind a feudal chief chiding her peasants—people who were largely destitute, ill-educated, and backward, even as other parts of the country prospered. Pressed about the speech afterward, she said she had "just been speaking my mind and talking about the Congress and its policies." Asked why she did not raise subjects like corruption that voters cared most about, she said blithely that no one brought up such topics.

On the campaign trail, Rahul Gandhi give similarly uninspiring talks. His said that he and his constituents shared a "relationship of love" and dreamed of "making Amethi shine." In blistering heat, voters had trudged along bad roads and waited hours for him to show up— late. Those in the crowds complained of a lack of electricity to spin fans, run irrigation pumps, or charge cellphones. They wanted jobs, the higher incomes that they knew others were beginning to enjoy. Talk of love and family from a distant man who promptly drove off in a luxury SUV, then whirled away in a helicopter, left behind mostly resentment. If someone pointed this out to Congress or the Gandhis, they blamed others—the state government of Uttar Pradesh, the disruption by other parties, anyone but themselves for the backwardness in the family seat in Amethi.

Rahul Gandhi could have been cannier in his public efforts to win popularity. Take the example of Semra village in his constituency, where, one evening, children were clanking a hand-pump in the gloom. The only light came from a solar-powered street lamp, a few candles, and the moon. A widow in a red-and-gold sari, Shiv Kumari, said that she had five children and worked in others' fields for 50 rupees, roughly a dollar, each day. Unusually, Rahul Gandhi had once stayed in her crumbling home. "He came at midnight," she recalled. "I don't know why he came, but he stayed until 3 a.m. and left. He chatted, he was a nice man, and he promised my house would be repaired and a loan from the moneylender paid," adding that "I fed him a pure-veg dish, just vegetables, cooked by a self-help group of women." But she complained that nothing had since been done for her, pointing at her broken walls.

Gandhi's visit was a gesture to appeal to Dalits, once called "untouchables" or those considered below caste. Eating food, taking water, and being in proximity to Dalits were long considered taboo by other castes. For some it was unacceptable even to let a Dalit's shadow fall on them. By showing that such barriers meant nothing to him, Gandhi hoped to please Dalit voters, who constituted one-fifth of the population of Uttar Pradesh—over 40 million people. It was a fine gesture, but he apparently failed to follow up, to build a system to improve lives in Semra, nor did he explain a mechanism for cutting poverty and raising incomes. His party promoted welfare for the rural poor, but even Gandhi, in a private conversation in 2015, said that rights-based politics no longer chimed with voters.

The poor of Amethi rolled their eyes at the Gandhis. So did the rich. A local princess, a former badminton player for India, Ameeta Singh, had married into the Maharaja's family, owners of a yellow and red palace. She called Rahul Gandhi "a fun guy, great to be with, full of energy," but said that times were hard for his dynasty. Whereas Sonia Gandhi put in fourteen hours of work daily to win support for Congress, and was strong in taking decisions, Rahul dallied. Singh, in an interview with me, called politics "much tougher for him. No longer can you just say 'come, we are the Gandhi family, that is all we need.' There was a time when Congress would win because it was the Nehru-Gandhi family, but voting today is different, now we have transactional politics and voters have no family loyalty like before."

Faced with Modi, who made brash appeals to Hindu nationalism and, with a swagger, promised rapid economic growth for all, the Nehru-Gandhis looked tired and out of touch by the mid-2010s. Nor did they have a response to the growing clout of regional political parties, many of which drew on the appeal of local populist figures such as Mamata Banerjee (in West Bengal), Jayaram Jayalalitha (in Tamil Nadu), Kumari Mayawati (in Uttar Pradesh), or Nitish Kumar (in Bihar). Congress's failure to ally with such regional outfits, or to preserve its own regional support, meant that it shriveled from the roots up. The old family offered a liberal and moderate outlook on society that an urban class of left-leaning voters might one day find appealing again. Rajiv Gandhi had been a modernizer, a dashing former airline pilot who promised new technology to benefit all. Sonia Gandhi had transformed herself from demure Italian housewife to canny, hard politician—the widow of one martyr and the daughter-in-law of another. But Rahul Gandhi looked adrift and pampered, barely aware of the growing power of social media, unable to reach out to young Indians online, lacking either forcefulness or warmth.

Fortunes could turn again. I recall a palm-reader, cross-legged on a white mat beside a Delhi metro station, who read a photo of Rahul Gandhi's open hand and predicted to me that "he will reach the topmost post." Polls late in 2016 showed that Rahul Gandhi retained much public sympathy. But political experts were skeptical. A newspaper editor, sympathetic to Congress, once described him as "not very bright, with a sense of entitlement, almost royalty," adding that Rahul Gandhi "doesn't know which world he wants to be in: he hangs out mostly with dynasts of politics or business despite posing as a champion of the poor." Ramachandra Guha, an astute historian of modern India, suggested in 2015 that Rahul Gandhi, "a child of privilege," could not connect with voters in the face of Modi, son of a tea seller. Each time Congress was thumped in elections, Gandhi disappeared for long stretches, adding to a sense that he lacked commitment or stamina. Guha summed up the scion as a "dud."

In an interview with me, a senior party figure, a former minister, complained that "Rahul Gandhi intrinsically doesn't want it. If you do not have the intrinsic will to power, no one can supplant it in you." Congress has to escape its dependence on one family and find policies, a purpose, that will appeal to more modern voters. A senior ex-minister, in another interview, said of his party: "It can't evolve yet beyond the Gandhi family. Since the 1991 economic shift, Congress has not been able to reconnect its ideological moorings. In an ideological vacuum, Congress has to substitute personality for the ideological. Its philosophical underpinnings are unknown. It becomes a vehicle for getting people elected to office." The problem, then, was structural decline. As the party failed to win regional strongholds, nobody would join Congress in the hope of patronage.

Another senior figure, Palaniappan Chidambaram, who had been finance minister, told me in an interview some months before the 2014 election that he could imagine Congress beyond the dynasty, and perhaps thought of leading it himself. He pointed out that for much of the 1990s "we had a period without a Gandhi as a prime minister, or a Congress president [and] the Congress did hold together." Chidambaram's son contested the 2014 election. Under Narasimha Rao, the prime minister who oversaw the first big economic reforms in the 1990s, Congress had delivered dramatic gains. The challenge, as voters grow more demanding, is to shift from reliance on dynasties to something more modern and focused on policies. What India needs, therefore, is a party on the center-left able to appeal to urban voters especially and to respond to anger about current issues (such as corruption, demonetization, and inequality), but also to promote smart policies to lift economic growth as well as push for basic welfare.

7

SEASONS OF SCAMS

IN THE ALLEYWAYS PEOPLE HELD THEIR PHONES ALOFT, GLOWING like fireflies in the dark, as they filmed a short man who walked among them. "We are with you, be strong," came a refrain. As the crowd mobbed him, he tried to press forward, his assistants pushing hard to make space. Occasionally he would stop, give a short speech, usually about resisting police violence, then walk on. It was a steaming summer night in 2013, and Arvind Kejriwal, an anti-graft campaigner, was walking the streets of east Delhi, a low-income neighborhood. He was a driven man, impatient to launch a political career, and he knew the subject that would carry him on among the city's voters: their fury over corruption. He dreamed of leading a movement, swept along by anger over graft. "The personality of the leader is extremely important, because politics is in complete turmoil and people are fed up," he explained.

In the last years of Manmohan Singh's government, examples of awful graft in India popped up faster than champagne corks at a dodgy

politician's dinner party. Not all could be blamed on Singh's administration. In Uttar Pradesh officials stole billions of rupees—some $1.5
billion—from a single public health scheme for poor villagers. After
that scandal broke, murders followed. The most senior health officials
in the state were mysteriously killed. But some of the worst examples of
graft were in national politics. A rigged sale of telecom spectrum cost
the treasury, by one official estimate, nearly $40 billion in lost revenues.
It was widely said that some senior members of Singh's cabinet were
closely influenced by India's biggest business houses. A former cabinet
minister said he believed some of his most senior ex-colleagues, whom
he named, did the bidding of particular big businesses. Singh sat impassive in cabinet meetings, he said, culpable through inaction.

Corruption was not at all new, but anger over graft reached extreme
levels in the 2010s. The rise of India's high-profile billionaires, soaring
prices of many goods, and obvious signs of extreme inequality added to
public fury over the theft of public funds by those with political power.
If there was one issue that threatened the legitimacy of the political
system, it was this. If India were to develop a healthier political system,
then finding some way of cleaning up corruption was essential.

Dynastic rule and corruption could seem intricately bound together.
One man became a particular target for public scorn in the early 2010s:
media claims swirled over the alleged provision of soft bank loans and
questionable property deals in Haryana, near Delhi, connected to Rob-
ert Vadra. He had no official role, but he lingered at the edge of dynastic politics, part-owned a luxury hotel in Delhi, and cultivated a
moustache and a dress sense that owed much to the memory of Freddie
Mercury. He was politically powerful—notoriously, he was permitted
to skip being frisked at airport security lanes—because he was the husband of Priyanka Gandhi and thus the son-in-law of Sonia Gandhi.
When allegations arose against him, he posted a sneering message on
Facebook calling anti-graft activists "mango people in a banana republic." It was a bizarre way to assert his innocence. When a TV journalist
confronted him in a hotel and asked about the allegations, he panicked,

grew furious, tried to slap away his microphone, and blustered "Are you serious? Are you serious? Are you nuts? What is wrong with you?" before storming off.

Vadra's talk of fruit and nuts, and the many scandals that swirled around Congress, its ministers, and its dynasty, made it easy for opponents to say that corruption was closely bound to tired old dynastic politics. If India checked the power of old political families and got stronger political leadership, said the BJP, then it could tackle corruption. There was something to the argument, as many dynasties were indeed associated with crooked behavior. But proponents of that view ignored abundant evidence that politicians without large families were also often corrupt. The first serving chief minister of a state ever convicted and jailed for corruption, for example, was Jayaram Jayalalitha, in 2014. Jayalalitha, an immensely popular movie star in the 1960s and 1970s, was convicted of having assets unjustified by her declared income. Some details were breathtaking. In her home in Tamil Nadu police had found 10,500 saris, 91 designer watches, 750 pairs of shoes, 1,760 pounds of silver, over 61 pounds of gold, 44 air-conditioning units, and 660 million rupees (about $10 million) in cash. She denied any wrongdoing and a court later overturned her conviction. She died in December 2016.

In Uttar Pradesh another serving chief minister, Kumari Mayawati, had earlier been investigated for her inexplicably abundant personal wealth. Her political story was striking and she was also no dynast: from a modest family and with an early career as a teacher, she triumphed by leading a party predominantly for Dalits. Along the way she somehow acquired such a large income that, one year, she paid the equivalent of over $6 million in tax. A legal case against her was eventually dropped and she denied wrongdoing. But perceptions lingered: American diplomats, in a diplomatic cable that was made public by WikiLeaks, once suggested that Mayawati had sent her private jet more than 1,000 miles to Mumbai to collect a single pair of sandals, an act that Imelda Marcos would have appreciated for its gall.

She denied it. Both Jayalalitha and Mayawati were unmarried and without a large family or dynasty.

Corruption looked endemic to the Indian political system and beyond, not only among the dynasts. Many politicians felt they had to scramble for illicit cash to fund elections and because they saw that others—especially in business and sport—were getting crazily wealthy. Indian cricket, though exciting to watch, was riddled with bribes and match-fixing. Commentary on the flashiest and wealthiest format of the game, known as the Indian Premier League, was often less about the sport itself than about cases of rigged games, individual cricketers caught accepting bribes to perform in certain ways, and—occasionally—prosecution and bans for the most exposed of the sportsmen.

Teams were owned by Bollywood stars and by some of the most high-profile industrialists in India. Vijay Mallya, a brewing and airline tycoon, owned a prominent team from Karnataka, though he left the country in 2016 as government agencies tried to chase him for $1.3 billion in unpaid loans from Indian banks. Two entire cricket teams were suspended from the league for two years, in 2015, after police taped phone calls suggesting they had taken part in match-fixing. Three well-known bowlers were arrested in 2013, as evidence mounted that they took bribes from bookmakers to play unusually badly. All were later cleared. So closely was this form of Indian cricket associated with scandal that Pepsi, in 2015, stopped sponsoring the league, though a Chinese sponsor, perhaps less troubled by the talk of graft, stepped in.

Business in general could be terribly crooked, with some firms keeping two sets of books, dodging taxes, and cheating customers, investors, or partners. An interior designer who worked in the homes of Indian tycoons once told me about how his clients had breezily discussed ripping off minority investors in their firms: the tycoons bragged about holding large reserves in cash for paying bribes or to plunder personally, he said. The designer added that he had witnessed "insane corruption" among businessmen, yet most public talk of graft was focused on politicians: "Those who say 'just get the government out of the way and let business do things, then you'll cut corruption,' they are naive, they don't realize how many businessmen break rules for private gain." A foreign investor, lamenting how difficult it is to find trustworthy companies in India, said that "minority shareholders exist to be cheated." The boss of a prominent Indian company described having hugely overpaid for an asset overseas, from another arm of his firm, to create a slush fund.

Some firms lied about emissions from their factory chimneys, the quantity of pesticides in food, and the source of mineral water in their bottles; others ripped off their workers, and many cheated on their taxes. Corruption within firms was common. A private detective told me about the prevalence of rule-breaking and said that his own snooping business did well because fraud was so widespread within firms. "People are not so honest," he said. "Larger companies need people to crack fraud, both internal and external. They can't use their own team to investigate, so they need us. Even long-serving employees cheat."

People cared especially about petty public graft: a traffic policeman who demanded 100 rupees for an imaginary or real transgression, an official who refused to issue a driving license without a bribe, teachers who sold high marks in exams. In some state administrations and police departments, officials were rumored to have bought their posts with big payments to superiors. They then demanded bribes to make good their initial investments. A colorful case in 2015 suggested just how big these problems were: Police in Kolkata raided the small home of a municipal engineer whose job had been to issue construction permits. They found great bundles of rupees hidden in cupboards, inside sofas, under mattresses, spilling from pillows, in an enclosure under his bed, beneath a marble floor, in the cistern of a toilet, above a false ceiling, and stuffed in a bathroom. It took a full day, using four electronic note-counting machines, to tot up rupees worth $31 million. On the engineer's monthly salary, equivalent to $700, it would have taken him nearly four thousand years to save up that sum legitimately.

Police removed it in silver boxes on a cycle-rickshaw, as neighbors gawped and giggled.

Companies typically paid "speed money" to get permits from officials in good time. Businesses knew they should host lunches for officials and their friends and fund projects run by relatives of politicians (an activity that could then be called "corporate social responsibility") as ways of donating to those with power. In general, Indians often seemed relaxed about a limited degree of rule-breaking. Drivers in Delhi and other cities often took shortcuts by propelling their cars along sidewalks, merrily drove the wrong way on one-way roads with their extended family balanced on a motorbike, or skipped through red lights. Drunk driving and other reckless roadway behavior resulted in sixteen deaths every hour in India. Avoiding income tax was a common habit: barely 3 to 4 percent of the population paid it in 2015. Encroachment on public land—shifting a garden wall three feet outward, adding an extension that jutted into a road—was common, too. Cheating in exams occurred on an industrial scale. So many qualifications were bought, including papers for airline pilots, doctors, engineers, and inspectors, it was a surprise that planes or buildings did not fall to the earth more often.

At times it seemed that bending rules was a sport, and was socially acceptable. Even mountaineers were caught cheating: in 2016 a husband-and-wife team of police constables from Pune, a town in Maharashtra, was banned from visiting the Himalayas in Nepal for ten years. A government investigation found they had faked photographic evidence in claiming that they climbed Mount Everest that year. It was hard to imagine corruption decreasing until it became more widely frowned upon, and not just illegal. One creative effort to spread a debate on the problem involved a website in Bangalore, "I paid a bribe," which encouraged bribe-payers to make public how much they had to pay to buy a driver's license or some other official document.

Politicians grumbled that they were simultaneously condemned for corruption and asked by members of the public to break rules. Kapil

Sibal, a cabinet minister and lawyer whose real passion was writing poetry, made that point as anti-corruption protests raged in the streets in Delhi: "The same people, my constituents, come into this office and ask me to get their children admitted to a school when they do not qualify, or for a job or promotion for someone in their family, or to get the police to back off when they have built something illegal. Day in, day out, I get requests from voters to do something corrupt," he said. Another politician, pointing to boxes full of cash stacked in his office, once said languidly: "There is an election coming." Some voters expected a polling day payout from politicians, even as they condemned corruption.

Well over $1 billion was probably spent on the 2014 general election—approaching the cost of an American presidential one. But unlike America, India lacked a fully transparent system for big corporate donations to parties, and also lacked state funding, so much of this cash was raised and distributed without scrutiny. Those in office knew how to deploy money to wield power. India's spies (like those in all countries) used cash to shape events abroad and in troubled places at home. In Dhaka, in Bangladesh, a figure close to leaders of the ruling party, the Awami League, described witnessing a visiting Indian official hand over large bags of cash for use in an election there. In a memoir, an ex-chief of the Research and Analysis Wing (RAW), India's answer to the CIA, justified paying off politicians and others in Indian-run Kashmir. "Corrupting a person by giving money is not only a lot more ethical than killing him, but a lot smarter in the long run. And no one has yet come up with a better way of dealing with Kashmir. Money in Kashmir goes back a long, long way," he wrote, in 2015.[1] The same happened in India's northeast, and in regions where Maoist rebels were active. Activists in remote areas said that the constitution of India did not apply—that instead there was "constitution of PC," meaning percentages or bribery.

If India's political system was to become more effective, respond better to public anger, and make the country more business friendly, it had to crack down on corruption. But attempts to do so were only occasionally effective. The legal system worked sporadically: now and then a prominent figure got caught and prosecutions followed. The dodgy sale of telecom spectrum eventually led to the rare arrest of a former cabinet minister, Andimuthu Raja, from Tamil Nadu. Another scandal involved allocation of coal deposits to politically favored companies; this embarrassed Manmohan Singh, because he had been in charge of the coal ministry. Other allegations centered on an environment minister who put off approving investors' projects to extract under-the-table payments. Scandals over road-building were so widespread that the relevant minister in Singh's cabinet was routinely referred to as "ATM" or "Cashpoint," followed by his family name. The problem was that Singh, though not corrupt personally, made no effective effort to punish others who evidently were. Sonia Gandhi, too, was more concerned about keeping together the ruling coalition, in the years before 2014, so she did not appear to object when her allies or members of her party were found to be flagrantly corrupt.

Corruption had wide costs, deterring investors—both local and foreign—who found India too difficult a place to operate. Yet some politicians seemed not to care. In 2011, when Pranab Mukherjee was finance minister, the Bengali veteran of forty years in national politics suggested to me that corruption was not "a problem for Foreign Direct Investment. I don't find any correlation between corruption and FDI." That went against other evidence. A poll of 1,700 business leaders in sixteen countries, mostly in Asia, ranked India as more corrupt than China or Vietnam, for example. Another survey, of 100 bosses in India, found that one-third had deferred long-term investment, or distrusted institutions like the stock market, because of widespread graft. Often the first question visiting business figures asked foreign correspondents, such as me, over coffee in Delhi, had to do with the awfulness of corruption in India. Corrosion hurt in unexpected ways, too. For example, honest politicians and civil servants, worried that they might later be accused of wrongdoing, put off making any decisions at all—in some cases, bringing government work almost to a stop.

As India's economy slowed sharply in the mid-2010s, inflation also rose and public grumpiness grew. Much anger was focused on corruption. Pollsters found that over 90 percent of respondents believed graft was getting worse, and support for Singh and Congress plummeted. "Black money"—raised illicitly or with no tax paid—reportedly poured out of India to be stashed in foreign accounts. Some was routed back, via Mauritius (which became, suspiciously, the biggest source of "foreign" investment), to be laundered in big construction projects. At least that paid for many informal building jobs. Other dodgy money stayed abroad. An American think-tank once estimated, while Singh was prime minister, that Indians held more than $450 billion overseas. That was perhaps an exaggeration, but no doubt Indians did hold large assets abroad. The opposition made a popular (but hard to deliver) promise to bring home "black money" within months of coming to office.

Could Indian democracy really tackle graft? Growing protests indicated that many people were furious about it. The Arab Spring—street demonstrations, especially against corruption and bad government—had shown how huge protests spread beyond north Africa and the Middle East. In Pakistan, Imran Khan—a populist politician, playboy, and former cricketer—drew enormous crowds of urban, middle-class people to rallies against graft. A rabble-rousing cleric, Muhammad Tahir-ul-Qadri, also excited crowds in Pakistan. Both attacked massive corruption (though neither mentioned Pakistan's biggest problem, the over-powerful army).

As noted, India saw big protests, too. Demonstrations erupted daily at the gate to the prime minister's residence. Pew Research Center polls found that 70 percent of respondents were unhappy with India's direction under Singh and 89 percent were angry over food costs, as grumbles over inflation and corruption merged. Crowds came out in Delhi, around India Gate and in the street of protests, Jantar Mantar. In 2011 one spark came from Anna Hazare, an elderly campaigner with a passing resemblance to Mohandas Gandhi. A seventy-four-year-old man, Hazare said that he could banish corruption easily if only given a powerful, unelected, independent body to veto any decision taken by politicians. Foolishly, police arrested him, provoking 1,300 supporters to get detained too, causing a frenzy of media attention. Prison officials tried to release Hazare, but he refused to leave, saying he was launching a second campaign for "independence" for India. Hazare's proposed anti-corruption body sounded unaccountable and authoritarian, but he touched on a hugely sensitive issue and the crowds grew.

On a monsoon day at a parade ground, the Ramlila Maidan in Delhi, tens of thousands of Hazare followers gathered. Many, like their leader, were on a hunger strike and passionate for change. A middle-aged man said that Hazare was his "guru," his eyes glistening. "My legs have cramp because I have been fasting for more than a week," he explained. "But we train our bodies, we can go without food for thirty days and to lose flesh is to gain energy." Hazare, who lay beneath a poster of the Mahatma on a nearby stage, had lost over thirteen pounds of bodyweight after many days of fasting, and was worrying his doctors. Before him a forest of photographers and television cameras broadcast nonstop, as the media helped to spread demonstrations nationally. The atmosphere was festive, verging on rebellious. Hazare supporters said democracy was "bunged up" by corruption and needed a "jolt." Young men sported white hats known as Gandhi caps, with "I am Anna" lettering, and Anna Hazare rosettes, headbands, T-shirts, or badges. Chants of "Anna is India, India is Anna" imitated the 1970s slogans for Indira Gandhi at her demagogic height.

Hazare fasted for weeks, protests spread, and the words of the great Dalit leader B. R. Ambedkar, who drafted India's liberal constitution, suddenly seemed prescient. He had warned of the "grammar of anarchy," meaning the threat of angry populists using Gandhi-style fasts to impose their will on an elected government. In fact, Hazare was not interested in a political career. It was instead his lieutenant, Arvind Kejriwal, the man campaigning in east Delhi, who took advantage. Short, with a moustache and eyeglasses, Kejriwal had the air of a modest clerk. Yet he was skilled at attracting publicity, worked crowds well, and performed deftly on television. After Hazare whipped up public fury, Kejriwal launched a movement for the "common man," the Aam Aadmi Party (AAP). Its symbol was a broom, to sweep away corruption, and he appealed to urban families of modest means. Rickshaw drivers were handy promoters, strapping brooms to their roofs. Just like Imran Khan in Pakistan, Kejriwal offered himself as an "anti-politician" for the urban masses.

On that sultry summer evening in 2013 we had squeezed inside his tiny blue car, a Suzuki WagonR, as he canvassed in east Delhi. He had been shunned by television broadcasters—previously enthusiastic—after he made accusations against the head of Reliance Industries, Mukesh Ambani. (Journalists and television channels would not dare to say anything critical about the firm or its leader.) "The media almost entirely blacked us out; Mukesh Ambani has controlling interests in many media houses," grumbled Kejriwal. On the streets he was surrounded by crowds, and explained how he was inspired by protesters in the Arab Spring who had used cellphones and the Internet avidly. "Egypt was amazing, social media played a very big role and brought people together," he said, explaining that millions subscribed to a text-message service of his party. He also pointed out that he had studied Barack Obama's online campaigning to reach donors, volunteers, and voters.

There was an air of insurrection. Kejriwal and his party eventually triumphed in the Delhi elections, turning the anti-corruption movement into a successful electoral machine within a few months—a remarkable development. His first stint in office lasted only forty-nine chaotic days, but in 2015 he won a landslide victory, taking 67 of 70 seats in Delhi elections and confirming that many voters wanted not only a change of faces in power but a cleaner political system overall. Congress, which had run Delhi's local government for fifteen years, was obliterated. Kejriwal understood—like Modi—the growing power of India's urban middle-class voter.

Yet the sorry postscript in Delhi was that Kejriwal's own party, once in power, became bitterly divided and leading figures were accused of corruption, even as administration in the city became chaotic. For example, as chikungunya, a viral disease spread by mosquitoes, took hold in the city late in 2016, Kejriwal's responses were inadequate and amounted mostly to denying any problem. The government was accused of using state funds for party ends, and the responses of the party's leaders to criticism at times looked authoritarian. Even so, the AAP hoped that it could spread its message as an anti-corruption movement into other states, aspiring to emerge into space vacated by Congress— for example, in Punjab. The party understood that corruption was still an invigorating political issue—but this did not necessarily mean it would do much to tackle it.

ELECTIONS NEVER END, BUT THEY IMPROVE

ELECTIONS IN INDIA ARE SO ENTERTAINING THAT IN THE 2010S tour companies started bringing foreign visitors to watch them—just as sports tournaments or great religious events draw crowds. In 2014, for example, private operators brought Europeans, Americans, and Middle Easterners to attend public rallies, witness campaigning, meet politicians, and hear from officials of the Election Commission at lively spots around the country. Commentators routinely compared bold and glitzy elections in India to a great circus, so perhaps it was no surprise that holidaymakers had as much fun as journalists in witnessing the show. The voting itself was spread across many weeks, but for the best part of a year beforehand the contest had gripped the country, dominating social media, television, and much conversation—just as surely as an American presidential poll overwhelms public discourse in that other big democracy.

In Delhi, at any time, political conversation predominates. Elsewhere in India there are more discernible seasons. Fly two hours south, to Bangalore, and residents have other obsessions, usually to do with technology. Many in that city, even high-fliers, cannot name their chief minister and seem unfussed by national affairs. Yet it was in cosmopolitan Bangalore, in 2014, that an ex-businessman launched an experiment: trying to win a parliamentary seat without breaking rules, overspending, or bribing his voters. He said he would instead trust in data analysis of voter habits, technology, and idealist volunteers. It sounded like a crazy idea—as entertaining to witness as the electoral tourist offerings elsewhere in the country.

The candidate, Nandan Nilekani, lacked certain obvious attributes of a successful politician. A cerebral, gentle man, he did not demonstrate low cunning, nor did he belong to an established political family or show the hunger for power that characterizes many successful party figures. He also had a poor sense of timing. He picked the worst moment to dive into electoral politics, naively signing up as a Congress candidate just as public disgust with that party reached new highs. On the other hand, he had some real advantages: name recognition as a co-founder of the IT firm Infosys, a global corporate giant; a billionaire's deep pockets; and public admiration for his role in government, where he had built the enormous biometric identification system, Aadhaar. He also attracted throngs of volunteers—youngsters who were inspired to win by efficient, high-tech, ethical methods, and to improve how elections were fought. They studied data published by the Election Commission, assessing trends at individual polling booths with just a few hundred voters each. Over one thousand volunteers criss-crossed Nilekani's constituency and knocked on doors, creating a buzz among reporters and on social media. The campaign was run by text message and online. The candidate's wife, Rohini, a popular philanthropist who was well known in the city, had a prominent role.

For a moment it seemed possible to imagine electoral politics becoming more idealistic, clean, and honest. Yet near the end of the campaign a senior member of Nilekani's team confided to me that real political life had a nasty habit of pushing in: "Dirt in politics is a reality, the journalists come demanding cash, they talk of what 'package' they will get," he complained. A photographer had refused to transfer pictures to his publication because Nilekani's team would not bribe him. TV cameramen demanded "envelopes," payoffs, to produce attractive shots for broadcast. Middlemen approached Nilekani's manager and offered to sell wholesale blocks of votes. "You see groups of voters bargaining for what they want, individuals with micro bargains. Then people do come and offer to deliver us a big chunk of votes," he said. "We don't say no. We stress-test the claim: How many of these people really exist? Is he a leader of them?" he said, out of earshot of his boss.

Nilekani knew he faced a tough fight against an incumbent skilled in old-school electoral methods. "I'm constrained by my ethical frame," he said. "So I'm my own guinea pig. I'm trying these things on myself. I'm trying to see how to change the system. I want to do it to know the pain points." He called the process "physically and emotionally punishing," and looked drained as the campaign went on. Mostly canvassing in wealthier corners of a middle-class, urban constituency of leafy avenues and educated voters, he could charm small rallies of admiring office workers and business leaders. But Nilekani was soundly beaten. As another losing candidate said to me (one who had failed as the face of an anti-corruption party in a nearby constituency), "we are all air-conditioned people, we don't know about campaigning."

Indians have immense experience with elections. Since independence theirs has been the world's largest democracy: the first general election in 1952 already had an electorate of 173 million voters. At some point in the 2020s, India's electorate will become a billion strong. The country's impressive constitution is more liberal than the society it has served, and more liberal than those found in much of Asia and many other parts of the world. India's fortunes as a democracy matter as an example to others, even if Nilekani's experiment came too early. He was right to think that the way elections are fought—along with voter attitudes about corruption—are beginning to shift.

Politics has always been fiendishly messy in the continent masquer-
ading as a country. It has never been easy to get a grip on the place,
especially for outsiders. In 1858 a predecessor of mine writing for *The
Economist* grumbled that most people at home in Britain were "ignorant
of the very alphabet of Indian politics." Nearly a century later Winston
Churchill, among many others, misread the alphabet. He wrongly said,
in a speech to the British parliament in March 1947, that "[i]n handing
over the Government of India to these so-called political classes we are
handing over to men of straw, of whom, in a few years, no trace will
remain."[1]

In fact, India's national leaders have largely turned out to be moderate, performing mostly within the rules of a political system modeled on Britain's Westminster parliamentary one, in a hybrid with an
American-style federal structure that leaves much power to states. The
country has avoided most of the ruptures and violence that beset, for
example, Pakistan next door.

By 2014 India was divided into twenty-nine states with elected assemblies and governments, plus seven smaller union territories ruled by
representatives sent from Delhi. The states' chief ministers—like governors in America—had great clout. A strong prime minister could try
to shape national laws and policies but lacked the individual heft of,
say, an authoritarian Chinese, Russian, or Turkish president in deter-
mining events. Modi, who made a rare move from being chief minister
to prime minister, and who had a big electoral mandate, found that at
times he had less direct power to implement changes, or boss around
civil servants, than he had enjoyed at the regional level.

Regional politics mattered enormously, not least because some
states in India had populations larger than most countries. (Uttar
Pradesh, with well over 200 million people by 2016, was more populous than Brazil or Pakistan, for example.) Relics of the past also
lived on. Not many parts of the world still have a lively Communist
Party that wins elections at the state level, as India did as of 2016. The
entrance to its party headquarters in Delhi offered a holy trinity of

lefty icons: a white marble bust of Lenin, a portrait of Karl Marx, a plate with a picture of Ho Chi Minh in a dusty cabinet. Attending a rally of the Communists in Kerala, I felt that I had tumbled back into mid-twentieth-century history: men waved wooden poles with twists of red cloth, murals showed hammers and sickles, posters displayed white-bearded candidates dressed in red—Santas bearing lectures on the glories of the proletariat. The Communists won state elections in Kerala but did worse in another state, West Bengal, where they had previously ruled nonstop for thirty-four years, until 2011. Voters there were no longer intimidated by Communists' hoodlums, thugs linked to political parties, who were notorious for sometimes fatal clashes. Nor did electoral jiggery-pokery pay as it had done before. The Communists had long worked to block opponents from voting, a practice known as "scientific rigging" in Bengal, but such meddling was proving less effective than before.

Electoral politics was changing, and largely for the better. It was getting harder to rig outcomes. Old, colorful ruses included impersonating other voters, notably dead ones. My landlord in Delhi recalled that a cousin, an Indian National Congress agent, reliably appeared at his home on election days in the 1960s to organize relatives to don different clothing and take turns casting ballots on behalf of long-dead individuals. However, the Election Commission was learning to shuffle names of the dead off the electoral roll more quickly: a former commission boss said his officers once counted 530,000 dead voters on the rolls in just one state, Uttar Pradesh. Eliminating zombies also lifted overall voter turnout: in 2014, a record 66.4 percent of Indians voted in the general election. Another rigging method, "booth capturing," was also almost extinct. It had involved armed thugs who overran polling stations and stuffed ballot boxes. But the practice all but ended once voters and party agents got cellphones to film attackers, and after electronic voting machines were rolled out.

Politicians still tried schemes to confuse voters. One ruse was to field a dummy candidate who shared your opponent's name in order to divert votes. A popular regional figure in Andhra Pradesh, Y. S. Jagan-mohan Reddy, broke from Congress in 2011 and in his next election faced six rival candidates with identical names. He still won. In 2014 a candidate called Lakhan Sahu in Chhattisgarh also confronted several namesakes—a mason, laborer, lawyer, and builder. His opponents in Congress called it mere "coincidence" and the original Sahu won. Puppet candidates could have another role: to help hide excessive campaign spending by candidates who sponsored them. Prior to the 2017 state election in Uttar Pradesh, a gang of politicians and a company were exposed for putting up fake candidates over the previous fifteen years, and for sending out apparently rival candidates who would really campaign for their sponsor. Anyone could be bought, one of the men involved reportedly told an investigative journalist who exposed them. A similar trick was to field a candidate of the same sub-caste or religion as your main rival, to split the block of Dalit, Muslim, Yadav (or whatever) votes going his or her way. Another was to create a party with a symbol similar to your opponent's, to confuse illiterate voters. Parties proliferated: 1,687 of them contested in 2014, and each picked a symbol from an official list, including drawings of a broom, toothbrush, nail clipper, cauliflower, cricket bat, carrot, flashlight, badminton shuttlecock, pen-and-nib, and hundreds more.

The tried-and-tested way of shaping Indian elections, however, was by overspending, bribing, and generally dishing out as much cash as you could—the practice Nilekani shunned in Bangalore. In 2014 S. Y. Quraishi, a silver-haired former Election Commissioner, listed forty ways he had found politicians cheating, and all involved money. You might bribe a pollster to invent an encouraging survey result, for example, then pay a television or newspaper editor to report on it. Quraishi described a pollster ready to found an entirely new company to give a party a favorable, but fake, forecast. Some voters expected to be paid, or to have politicians pay their electricity or water bills. The proportion who asked for bribes was probably falling, but the amounts dished out kept rising. Amarnath Menon, a veteran journalist in Hyderabad, estimated that in his city, "around 20 percent of voters want sops, something in advance of voting, some goodies or cash, but it used to be a higher figure earlier and especially in rural pockets." A candidate had to put on a show, he said, at least providing voters with food and drink at lightly disguised campaign events. He estimated in 2014 that a candidate needed 50 million rupees, some $750,000, "to fund and feed the voters," some ten times more than the legal spending limit for a constituency. Nonetheless, the money had to go a long way. An average constituency was enormous, with around 1.3 million voters (the biggest had 3 million), and some were physically immense: for example, the territory of Ladakh constituency, in the Himalayas, was bigger than all of Bangladesh or North Korea.

Bribe-giving sometimes went wrong. In 2004 at least twenty-two women were killed in a stampede in Lucknow, in north India, after BJP workers threw cheap saris to a crowd in a park. Candidates learned to be more discreet and, for example, dressed up campaign events as weddings, where they would give guests booze and food. In Tamil Nadu politicians folded money into newspapers distributed to households at night. In one state election, voters near Madurai reportedly each got cash worth $100. Party agents were known to haul around rice sacks stuffed with wads of rupees. Some in slums distributed bricks for those eager to build solid homes; others paid to credit voters' cellphones. An American diplomatic cable, published by WikiLeaks, once quoted an MP, Asaduddin Owaisi, in Hyderabad, who said what everyone thought, that official spending limits were a "joke." He admitted to having funded voters' projects during a recent campaign—digging wells, paying for weddings—and said he probably broke spending limits for an entire election on "polling day alone."

Candidates might not have known for sure how much money was splurged on their behalf. Enterprising academics noted that the construction industry fell quiet and cement sales dropped around elections, because so much cash got diverted to campaigns. Builders were often hand-in-glove with politicians, funding them to win access to land and permits. The sums that officials seized in elections rose in each electoral cycle: in 2014, 3 billion rupees (around $50 million) in cash were nabbed, much in Andhra Pradesh, but only a fraction of all the "black money" that was being thrown about. Hyderabad police said they seized so many goodies—bundles of cash, bags of gold and silver, cricket kits, local rum and whisky—they could not store all the loot. They found rolls of rupees stuffed behind car dashboards and booze in milk vans. Unassuming men were discovered with tens of millions of rupees to be used for "transactions" in the election. Officials said tycoons were ever more involved in elections, trying to buy political clout. As the economy expanded, asset prices soared—for telecom spectrum, natural resources, land near cities—and stakes rose for those who controlled political office.

Some voters wanted bribes in the form of booze or drugs. A Sikh businessman friend of mine, with a trimmed beard and a sky-blue turban, once explained how he volunteered in campaigns for the Indian National Congress in Amritsar, in Punjab. Drugs flowed there—for example, from Afghanistan, a few hundred miles away, smuggled via Pakistan, or from producers within India. During "party weeks" before voting, stimulants were in lavish supply. "An individual comes to the office and claims he can deliver a number of voters. Maybe he is the head of a large family, or a ward boss, or has influence over neighbors," said my friend. "The local guys, they decide if he is credible, and negotiate what he gets." In return he handed out paper slips—"chits"—to be traded for plastic pouches of alcohol, or for a thick black opiate paste that was drunk with tea or chewed. Politicians of several parties promoted drug use. A prominent party, the Akali Dal, was accused by its opponents of being in league with the biggest drug dealers in the state. During the 2014 election, across India, officials seized 16 million liters of liquor and roughly 18 tons of drugs. The lion's share was in Punjab.

Politicians spent heavily, with no guarantee of an electoral return. Party agents monitored polling booths to check who turned out, but surveys suggested 85 percent of voters trusted that the ballot was secret. In theory, voters could collect bribes from many candidates at once, but politicians nonetheless had a degree of trust in those they bribed. Those keenest on election gifts were poor, living in a slum or a village, and ready to defer to someone in authority such as the head of a large family. Voters were also keen on backing a winner and assessed candidates' prospects in terms of the money they threw around. They might assume, for example, that only a confident candidate would bribe a lot, certain that he would recoup his "investment" through subsequent corruption in office. Those who failed to bribe, such as Nilekani, unwittingly sent the message that they did not really expect to win. Dishing out money was a form of signaling. Not every politician relied on it: in Delhi, where some of the most educated and better-off voters reside, the anti-corruption movement, the Aam Aadmi Party of Arvind Kejriwal, eschewed most of the old dirty tricks and won in state elections. Perhaps Nilekani might have succeeded with his ethical methods in Bangalore, if only he hadn't been saddled with Congress.

Police could have done more to stop electoral graft. But they mostly did the bidding of politicians, and as my Sikh friend said in Punjab: "They know who is likely to be in charge after the election, and don't want to piss them off." Election bribery was also so deep-rooted that it was seen by many as semi-legitimate. A predecessor of mine who reported from Uttar Pradesh in 1971 for *The Economist* once found a "local leader pledging his whole village's support to the highest bidder." Such old habits died hard.

Yet Indian general elections were changing, improving, as voters' expectations rose. More voters tired of direct sops and small bribes, understanding that a few hundred rupees once every few years was poor compensation for misrule. Some of the best-known efforts, such as a plan by one political party to hand out 15 million color television sets to households in Tamil Nadu, became notorious for falling well short of their targets. A more educated electorate—as Delhi showed—was becoming better informed and caring less about cheap saris or gifts of kitchenware and more about what politicians promised and delivered. Bold promises of material gains to come were mostly what got Modi into power in 2014. He ran the most expensive election campaign in Indian history: the BJP admitted to spending 712 crore rupees, well over $100 million, though unofficial estimates put the total much higher. Modi made the point that voters' expectations were changing. In a conversation in Gandhinagar one rainy day, at a time when he was still Gujarat chief minister, he said of elections: "We consider there should be no vote-bank politics," meaning that it does not pay to pander to, or bribe, groups defined by caste or religion. He said he pushed for economic growth, without favoring just one bit of society, adding that this was a "new way of seeing politics." He argued that poor voters as much as rich ones were turning against freebies and populist policies.

Modi told me an anecdote about meeting a poor, elderly couple in a rural spot waiting for a bus, who waved on the first one that came along, preferring a lengthy delay and to pay more to ride in a cleaner, air-conditioned vehicle. He said this taught him that the poor cared about quality of service and would not settle for low standards that come with free handouts. He scorned rival politicians who "to get the political mileage, give the free electricity," adding, "these free things that I don't follow."[2] Indian voters were changing: more would judge politicians by their performance, not by a 500-rupee note wrapped in a newspaper.

Modi's claims would have set off any journalist's bullshit alarms. He denied appealing to vote-banks but also rallied sections of the Hindu majority against minorities, and in some states—such as Bihar and Uttar Pradesh—he whipped up nasty caste divisions. In others—Assam, West Bengal—his campaign was flagrantly anti-Muslim. But his broader point—that voters were best understood not as groups of people with a shared identity but as individuals who increasingly scrutinized the overall performances of those in office—was relevant, especially in cities, and it will become increasingly so in the future. Evidence accumulated that voters judged there to be better government when economic results were better overall. That counted as a profound shift in Indian politics: the country's democracy would become more effective at delivering broadly good outcomes—policies to generate faster economic growth and jobs, rising prosperity, and improved public services—only if voters rewarded the politicians who delivered them. Many Indian elections since independence had pointed to the opposite: Congress, for example, presided for decades over miserably slow economic growth and bad state services, but it kept getting reelected (thanks to its history, the charisma of its leaders, vote-bank politics, and more). Only in the past couple of decades did voters begin to insist on better economic outcomes.

Two researchers—Milan Vaishnav, at Carnegie, and Reedy Swanson, at the University of Virginia—tracked this crucial change.[3] They first looked at state assembly elections in the 1990s and found that ruling parties that presided over faster economic growth were, counterintuitively, likely to lose votes at the subsequent election and thus be turfed out of office. Presumably the rulers, at that time, would have been better off focusing on directing rewards instead to favored groups of voters rather than creating conditions for general improvements. In contrast, parties that had overseen slower growth did better at elections. What seemed to matter especially, in the old days, was how well one could appeal to different groups of voters defined by caste.

But then the researchers looked at the results of elections in the 2000s, and they found a big change: politicians who oversaw faster economic growth gained votes and were more likely to be reelected. Modi in Gujarat was one example, getting reelected repeatedly as he presided over fast growth. This was also true of others in Bihar, Madhya Pradesh, Odisha, Delhi, and elsewhere. Vaishnav told me he concluded that "[t]he trend is deepening in seeing economic voting. The growth rate seems to matter more for voters than it did in the past. Caste and patronage plays itself out, the identity phase of voting moves on to an economic phase. It is not that caste logic is over, but it is now caste-plus. Before caste was the text and the subtext, now it is only the subtext to everything."

The election in 2014 showed this, too. As Vaishnav argued, "the economy was the motivating factor in a way not seen before. It was a time of scandals, high inflation, billions allegedly stolen. And you had an easy villain in Congress, a party that reeked of ancient regime, lacking new ideas."[4] An opinion poll found that 57 percent of voters were most concerned by matters like growth, inflation, or their incomes. Only 3 percent admitted that the caste or other identity of candidates mattered most. Even if the poll overstated things, the message to politicians was getting loud: voters wanted policies to bring broad economic gains, not just sops for favored groups.

Modi cottoned on to that, promising *vikas* (development) and *acche din* (good times). One evening at twilight, eight thousand of his supporters gathered in a field near Delhi airport as snipers patrolled the roofs of surrounding buildings. People talked of Modi's strength and his promise of material progress for all. A property developer in a purple-brown shirt said that "Modi-ji is absolutely flawless, he is a development man." A woman said he would "control inflation, give people employment, and end our water problems. Modi will care about everybody." When the candidate appeared, in a red Nehru coat over his usual kurta-pajama suit, many in the crowd filmed him with their smartphones. In his stump speech he promised to extend his Gujarat "model" across India. He talked of his state: "Soldiers used to employ 900 camels to deliver water. Now we have built a huge pipeline to bring water; 9,000 villages now have clean drinking water. The pipe is so big that you could drive a Maruti car inside it," he said. The crowd roared with laughter at the image. "I am a village man and I have done it," he added. "If your intentions are right, if you are attached to the happiness of the people, solutions will come." His speech boiled down to a claim that as a tough leader he could deliver. "A humble person knows the real problems. If he gets to power, he will try to solve them," he said.[5]

Urban voters, especially, liked development promises. And before long, town-dwellers—especially young, well-connected ones—would shape elections more than rural voters who had decided outcomes in the past. As of this writing, in 2016, India has fifty cities at least 1 million strong, plus industrial and residential corridors that link sprawling conurbations. In the next quarter of a century those cities will gain some 300 million residents—and the existing 646,000 towns and villages will grow into something truly urban. In short, India's town-dwelling population will roughly double. As demography shifts, within a few years the political balance will also tip in favor of cities over villages. As of 2014 more than 150 of the 543 constituencies were already "totally or substantially urban," according to a BJP strategist. That figure will only rise, bringing less party loyalty, inasmuch as urban voters look readier than rural ones to swing between parties. Congress, under Manmohan Singh, won the most urban seats in 2009, but Modi swept them in 2014. Urban voters want jobs and material gains. As one aging journalist grumbled, from his grand but slightly worn gentleman's club in Kolkata, "the post-liberalization generation, the twenty-two-year-old, thinks there is only one God, that is GDP."

Such voters in fact exist far beyond city centers: big towns have influence that radiates deep into the countryside, changing the attitudes of rural Indians. Kamalpur village, 45 miles east of Delhi in Uttar Pradesh, is typical. It has long been desperately poor, badly connected, and rural. But by 2014 it had a tarmac road, a row of tiny barber shops had sprouted between wheat fields, and decent mobile-phone coverage had arrived. A highway passes nearby, and along it are concrete towers and housing blocks, rising for a future generation of commuters. A villager told me that "you cannot earn from farming, so everyone wants to get educated and find jobs in factories near Delhi." Those who have remained sell milk, flowers, and other goods to urban consumers. The villagers are Muslims, once natural Congress supporters, previously swayed by handouts such as subsidized rice. They complain about corruption and say that the welfare "doesn't reach here," so why should they care for more promises of it? A good road to the city has helped them more.

Around 100 million new voters have been added to the electorate between each national election, many in semi-urban places like Kamalpur. Modi expects to keep appealing to such urban-minded, young, and well-connected types, who in turn influence a wider circle of voters. A journalist close to him, Swapan Dasgupta, explained the focus on youth, estimating that 40 percent of voters are younger than thirty-five: "They ask what their future is likely to be, that is more important than their local identity," he said.

Rising incomes have also begun to change voter behavior. Modi has talked of a "neo Middle Class," whose prospects are modestly up but who fear they could fall back into poverty. His talk of *vikas* was mostly aimed at reassuring them. Rahul Gandhi, slower on the uptake, recited Congress's "regime of rights," meaning dole from government; yet he later admitted in a private chat that people had lost interest in talk of rights, and he even spoke about a "new class" of voter. Nilekani understood, telling me "the new, aspirational young voter, the professional, educated, who doesn't look to the state for benefits" would matter more as Indian democracy changed. His manager added to me that "an earlier generation was content to be ruled and lorded over. Young Indians now expect more."[6]

Rising literacy and better communication have also lifted expectations. Whereas Kamalpur's houses were mostly built with mud walls in the past, more are made of concrete today. A village teacher said that 70 percent of households have a small motorbike or some other vehicle. Everyone has a cellphone: "They're for girlfriends," a boy said, grinning. Text messages from relatives in town rapidly spread news and opinions. A young man showed his smartphone and said proudly "we are connected." His three words summed up the change. Around half of the homes in Kamalpur have a television. The spread of smartphones and the Internet has grown apace: India got its 200 millionth Facebook user in 2016, and every minute another 100 people got online for the first time in the country.

What will be the effect on politics of these changing trends in the electorate? If voters become better informed, more literate, but also more likely to respond to economic conditions, then it is possible to imagine that elections will bring more decisive outcomes in the future compared with those in the past. More dramatic swings of fortune between parties also look likely. The decisive BJP victory in 2014 was due in part to effective campaigning, especially in states like Uttar Pradesh, but it was also the result of many Indians fearing that the economy was badly run and beset by corruption. The message should have been clear for future politicians: if you fail to deliver on promises of jobs, rising incomes, and cleaner politics, then voters will reject you, too. The old patterns of deference among some voters, the buying of blocks of voters by crooked politicians, and other shady behaviors might not disappear entirely. But if voters grow consistently more demanding, they will give politicians stronger reasons to find ways to deliver better economic outcomes for as wide a portion of the electorate as possible. Ideally, this will be a process in which India's rulers increasingly dare to push for bolder economic reforms, as the only way to meet the electorate's rising demands. If they do so, India's political and economic future might just improve in tandem.

INDIA'S WOMEN, INDIA'S MEN

ILLIONS WERE MISSING. BIRTH RECORDS, CENSUS DATA, AND child sex ratios and other data analysis revealed who the victims were. In parts of the north of India, in 2015, 120 male babies were being born for every 100 female ones—not at all what nature intended. Heavy societal preference for boys, combined with new technology such as ultrasound scanners, together explained why millions of girl fetuses were being aborted. By one estimate, 12 million girl fetuses had been discarded—because they were girls—in the three decades before 2010. Fatal discrimination continued after birth. An analysis of seven- to fifteen-year-olds, counted in the 2011 census, suggested that another 11 million girls were lost, in addition to those aborted. They had died from neglect, or worse. An expert in the field added a grim detail, explaining how some mothers in Bengal rubbed salt on their breasts to kill newborn daughters, in effect poisoning babies as they tried to feed.

Such statistics and details were appalling, but they did not explain why ill-treatment happened. South Asia was arguably the worst place anywhere to be born female, by the 2010s, at least if you were born poor. Statistics showed that malnutrition, stunting, and other public health–related problems—especially in north India—were especially dire for young women and girls. India had fallen behind almost everywhere on this score. For decades China had done a much better job than India of keeping women alive as they gave birth, for example. For politicians eager to improve well-being, this should have been an obvious area for public spending: devoting an extra billion dollars a year to improving maternal health clinics would have been a far better choice than subsidizing losses at Air India. Getting women better educated and fed, economically stronger, healthier and more powerful: these were obvious paths to raising human capital in India. After all, the well-being of future generations, literally, depended on it.

If India were to enter into its political prime, it needed to achieve dramatic gains by focusing on its women. Women were well represented at the very top of politics, as leaders of some of the largest parties, as a president of the country, and were active in sport, television, art, dance, culture, journalism, academia, and business. The first female voters (though they, like men, had to own land) were enfranchised in Madras, as early as 1921, and universal suffrage came shortly after independence. But by 2014 only 12 percent of national MPs were female, and in regional assemblies the average fell to just 9 percent. Nor did politicians, male or female, make the prospects for Indian women much of a priority.

Schools need to be improved for girls. The first decade or so of this century saw almost all girls get to classes at the primary level for the first time, which counted as welcome progress. Manmohan Singh's government had rolled out free midday meals and enshrined theoretical rights and minimum national standards in schools. But it did too little to get teachers to turn up and give quality instruction. Modi's government did even less. Basic shortages, such as schools that had no toilets, discouraged older girls from sticking with formal education. Corruption, whereby teachers took bribes and let students cheat, meant that many millions of students dropped out or learned little. Girls were especially vulnerable if their parents chose to pay bribes on behalf of sons, who were expected to go to work, rather than for their daughters. A huge number of families, including poor ones, paid for private education, as at least 40 percent of Indian households made some use of private instruction. But because many families favored boys over girls, spending on education for boys was bound to be higher than for girls.

A root problem was that many families simply valued girls less than boys, or women lower than men. Indian society (and many others) over the centuries had a way of measuring this: dowry payments. These became illegal in 1961, but continued anyway in much of Indian society, sometimes disguised as extravagant wedding presents from a bride's family to the parents of the groom. Dowry amounted, in effect, to paying another family to relieve you of the burden of having a daughter. It seems likely that having to pay a dowry was also one reason why some parents much preferred male babies. As in many other countries, sons were favored because they conferred higher social status; brought a higher income, because men were more likely to get jobs beyond the home (plus a dowry); and, by tradition, were supposed to care for parents in old age. By contrast, tradition deemed that a daughter would leave for another household.

Some brides were ill-treated when they arrived in a new family. In 2013 India's Supreme Court lamented "emotional numbness in society," saying that daughters-in-law were sometimes kept as near slaves or attacked over dowry. The judges said "life sparks are extinguished by torture, both physical and mental, because of demand of dowry and insatiable greed." At the time, nearly seventy thousand trials were pending over dowry violence—brides who had been attacked, even killed, because payments were late or low.

Of course, most Indian women did not suffer in this way, and the problems were not unique to India. It is also true that, for many women, India was an enabling place, especially in more educated, urban, and well-off communities. Yet in some instances even the better-off suffered. One way to get a glimpse into many families was through the eyes of Ajit Singh, who had launched a private detective agency in the 1990s and specialized in the flourishing business of premarital investigations. That gave him an unusual vantage point from which he could trace the changing position of women in society. Investigation of brides (and grooms) was "increasing like anything," he explained. "Now everyone relies on matrimonial portals, websites" to find partners, he said, twitching his moustache a little in disapproval. "Twenty years ago it was only the higher-income group that would hire us. Now people from the weaker section also do," he said. "In the past the poor had their own relatives and sources, now people send each other their resumes and don't tell the truth," he said. "And if you are not telling the truth in relationships, it is much more serious than in business. You are cheating two families."

Extended families of several generations in a single household were growing less common than before, but remained more widespread than in most other countries. A census in 2011 found that 18 percent of homes in India had more than one married couple; barely 1 percent of households in Britain fell into this category. The wider family remained intensely important, and it did much to define what opportunities— social, economic—were possible for women, especially when a bride went to live in her new husband's household. Marriages arranged by parents for their offspring remained the most usual, but even with "love marriages," where the couple already knew each other, the parents of the bride or groom might hire a detective to check out the other family. A simple investigation, for about 20,000 rupees (roughly $300 in 2016), provided basic information about reputation and "general character," plus details from the workplace. Some clients spent as much as

300,000 rupees, said Singh. "Then we will follow the subject. We put more energy into checking the financial status. We offer detailed financial analysis, detailed information into the extended family, monthly income, circles of friends, behavior and habits—for example, whether they are into drinking and partying, what is their weekend style, do they like going to pubs, do they take beer all the night? We talk to maids, drivers, gardeners, nearby persons, neighbors."

Parents of a bride wanted most information about the groom's mother, the future mother-in-law, said Singh. "They ask about the nature of the lady. Is she God-fearing, quarrelsome, friendly with the neighbors? How does she deal with the maid, is she going to temple, does she spend all day in the markets, at kitties [parties], and at the parties is there any drinking? Because the girl who is going to marry [into] that house, she is going to spend a lot of time with that lady. Every day she is going to face the mother-in-law," said Singh. The parents of the groom, however, were most likely to judge the bride, said Singh. The investigator was asked to lay bare the bride's previous "behavior and character, their upbringing. If she is living a lavish life, will there be a difficulty to adjust to the house? What is their temperament? The majority of the girls have a very high expectation of marriage—and it doesn't meet reality. They ask what expectations she has. What friends? Her upbringing, standard of living, the kind of car she has, the brands she wears. If someone is in a Mercedes, shops in malls, buys big brands, will it be a problem when she comes to the in-laws?" Most important was whether she is *gharelu*—literally, "homely," but meaning subservient, timid, hard-working. It all sounded intimidating—families studying each other's women, paying Singh to help them to assess whether the union would raise or diminish social status.

Singh's clients were urban, from Delhi especially, though his agency was spreading nationally. If a woman kept working for a salary after marriage, as became more usual, she would probably be expected to "deposit her salary into the house, to share her income with the husband," said Singh. Double standards were obvious in judging sexual history.

"Previous affairs is a big subject," said Singh, because a young woman's past "matters to mothers. We check at the office, we ask about affairs at college, or in the neighborhood, or school even." Lying was common. Around a third of Singh's pre-marriage cases "trend negative," meaning he found that somebody had been dishonest about something serious, perhaps a previous marriage or a falsehood about one's income. It was surprisingly common to be hired by parents of a bride who doubted the sexuality of the groom, he said.

After marriage, the often difficult relationship of brides and their mothers-in-law was a bumper source of extra business. Singh described a woman who had recently asked him to investigate her husband's mother. The client was from Mumbai—"girls from there are very fast. It's a reality. We here, in Delhi, we cannot keep up with them. Life is fast." The woman had moved in with the groom's family in Delhi and things soon went awry. She continued working, but broke convention by sending money to her own parents. Relations soured until she left and each side launched a legal case, accusing the other of deception, abuse, even sorcery. "The daughter-in-law wrote in her FIR [a police charge] that the family were doing tantric worshipping, wrong pujas, against her," he said.

Changing relations between mothers-in-law and daughters-in-law— the *saas-bahu* relationship—were a subject of intense interest because the domestic household was a rare domain in which women dominated. "It is the toughest relationship across the families. In a very rare case the mother-in-law treats the daughter-in-law as her daughter. In the majority of cases the mother-in-law is wrong," suggested Singh, talking of his clients. He saw young women growing more assertive. More were educated, employed, and financially independent than before. "Now they don't tolerate the bullshit," he said. Walking away from an abusive relationship had become possible, something hard to imagine in the past. Books about mothers-in-law offered blunt advice, such as: "Run, she is trying to kill you." Online discussion threads let women share horror stories under titles such as, "I've got a mother-in-law from hell."

A popular soap opera had run with the clunky title *Because the Mother-in-Law Was Once a Daughter-in-Law Too* (Kyunki Saas Bhi Kabhi Bahu Thi). The star, Smriti Irani, an ex-model-turned-actress (who later became education minister, bizarrely), explained to me that, for seven years, viewers—at one point over 20 million nightly—tuned in for its lifelike family drama. It was "the longest-running, biggest-grossing serial in India," she said, describing how her character progressed from being a daughter-in-law to a mother-in-law. It dwelt sympathetically on how a mother-in-law, in a time of changing mores, managed the young women who entered her life. It also tackled previously neglected topics—"for example, the issue of marital rape, it was the first-ever discussion of that on television, and our audience was a family audience. I never projected a girl or a lady as a hapless victim. Everyone recognizes it was a soap, but the soap became a medium for projecting certain ideas," said Irani.

Veena Venugopal, a journalist who turned a sharp eye on Indian society, wrote a study of brides and mothers-in-law.[1] She found educated, prosperous, English-speaking women—with just about the best opportunity of any in India—whose lives were made miserable by their mothers-in-law. "I hadn't expected how bad the stories were going to be," she said, blaming the "unhealthy" joint Indian family "as the source of both the greatest closeness and stress." She described a fabulously wealthy family of nine in Mumbai, whose matriarch wore "diamonds the size of bird's eggs"—a family that feuded for years ostensibly over who controlled the kitchen servants. The daughter-in-law fled when the conflict turned abusive. Venugopal generally blamed the elder women, saying they mistreated the younger ones, and described what she said were elder women's near "obsessive" control of "sex and shame" as a way of keeping a grip on the household. Mothers-in-law "don't trust her to be faithful, so they try to desexualize the daughter-in-law," locking her up, fattening her up, phoning her several times a day. Women competed for attention from the shared man in their lives: the mother's son, the wife's husband. My assistant, Indrani, from

Kolkata, explained how in Bengali wedding ceremonies much of this was made explicit. A groom on his wedding day repeated to his mother, three times, "I will bring you a servant." Meanwhile, the burdensome daughter, leaving home to join the new household, would take a handful of rice and tell her own mother, "Your debt is cleared." The message was pretty blunt: a new bride was considered little better than a skivvy, or servant.

But for all the gloomy stories about women in India, there was some progress being made. At least their prospects were being debated intensively in the press, on television, in magazines, on social media, and beyond. For India to tackle the various threats to girls and women, these threats first had to be talked about: a broad cultural change could follow. Some signs pointed to improvements. Divorce rates appeared to be rising (though they remained low by international standards), from almost nonexistent to about 13 dissolutions per 1,000 marriages. Family courts in larger cities, especially, reported a big increase in applications for divorce. That suggested more women were able to leave unhappy or abusive marriages, resulting in increased independence for at least a portion of the female population.

Progress on these scores can be seen in relation to the decline of older, unappealing, practices. One place to hear of old practices that were becoming rarer was in Vrindavan, a pretty town near Agra, a favorite for devotees of Lord Krishna as well as backpackers seeking joints and spiritual highs. The town was famed for its many elderly homeless women who lived out their final years there while begging for alms. At a soup kitchen for the elderly I met Renubala Dasi, a Bengali who had a bent back, a grey smear of mud on her forehead, and oval spectacles. She told a story of years of neglect and toil. It was typical of those told by several elderly women who attended the kitchen. Married at the age of twelve, Dasi had moved to her husband's farming family in Tripura, in northeast India, initially sharing a bed with his widowed mother. She recalled being "very scared of my mother-in-law" and respectfully calling her *ma-goshai,* or "God mother," and "worshipping her as a goddess." She rose at 4 a.m., prepared a hookah for her *shashuri* (the Bengali term for mother-in-law) to smoke, fetched water, and cleaned. "After she had taken her bath, I would wash her clothes, massage her head and body, tie her hair. Whenever she came in[to] sight I would bend and touch her feet to show respect," she said. Submission brought order and Dasi could at least hope that if she produced a son, she would graduate as a mother-in-law herself, and get similar care.

Years later, when it came to arranging a wife for her own son, she said much had changed. She complained that her own daughter-in-law was a "tigress," a woman already thirty years old who had ideas of her own. The younger woman never called her a "God mother": "She calls me nothing, just orders me to sit or stand." The younger woman grew hostile, "denied me food, stopped me speaking to my son," and eventually her son drove her 870 miles to Vrindavan and abandoned her. Resigned to it, she took up singing devotional songs and reciting the 108 names of Krishna. Her son won't light her funeral pyre when she is cremated, she said sadly. Did she think her story reflected a change in the family, and in the place of women in Indian society? She saw only her own sorrow. "We are living in the time of Kali Yuga," the end of civilization, when humans live only for lust, greed, broken vows, and violence, she said. Another widow spoke tearfully of her broken leg, and lamented that "brides arrive in the house prepared, they can't be abused, they do the abuse." A third complained about the influence of soap operas, like Smriti Irani's one, saying: "I blame TV for daughters-in-law being like this. From the age of five they watch TV and learn about money and families."

In fact, though the widows' stories were sad, they reflected a more hopeful turn in society: that many younger women no longer accepted being exploited, shaking off habits that were more common among previous generations. They were less weak than those of an earlier age. Bitter fighting between generations was a welcome sign of power shifting. As women got more paid work, earning income outside of the household, they could dare to assert themselves, leave bad marriages, and defy repressive traditions. Old attitudes—captured in the Hindi saying that "once you go to your in-laws' house, only your dead body should come out"—were fading. The head of a "mother-in-law protection forum" grumbled once to me that "the main problem is that today's women are educated, but not in the proper way. Parents are incapable of teaching the daughter how to stay in her in-laws' house." But the sooner regressive views like hers declined, the better for India.

By 2016 or so, there was mounting evidence that more women were standing up for themselves. Many rejected the old practice of *sindoor,* wearing vermillion at the hair parting to signify devotion to one's husband, for example. Debates also arose over another traditional practice, Karva Chauth, in which women are supposed to fast for a day, each year, to bring their husbands long life and safety. Women were marrying later: at twenty-one or older, on average—up from fifteen years of age in the mid-twentieth century. Later marriages, in turn, gave more women a chance to get educated and to control when the first birth would follow. The more educated expected paid jobs, to work after they wed. Women also had more of a chance of knowing whom they were marrying. Before 1960, fewer than 20 percent of women had any communication or interaction with their future husbands before marriage. By the 1990s that figure had risen to 60 percent of urban women (and about half of rural ones). No doubt, by 2016, it was higher yet.

Change had to come on several more fronts. Only when girls and women were better fed, for example, would fewer underweight babies be born. And only then would India start to be rid of its dreadful record on malnutrition. Surveys showed that bad nourishment persisted even among some wealthy families, suggesting neglect of girls. The grim tendency, especially in north India, to abort female fetuses remained roughly as prevalent in towns as in villages. Modi spoke well, a couple of times, on the subject of horribly skewed child sex ratios in India, but his government did little to change behavior and opinions.

As one consequence of this, northern states including Haryana, which is relatively wealthy and close to Delhi, began to experience a shortage of women (as happened in parts of China). This led to the trafficking of brides from other parts of the country, some tricked or forced against their will. Evidence of this was easy to find. Not far beyond the glass towers of Gurgaon, Delhi's business-satellite suburb, were villages set among wheat fields of Haryana. Dung cakes on the roadside were artfully stacked into house-like structures, drying for use in cooking fires. On one dung stack stood a satellite dish, for receiving cricket games, soap operas, and TV news. Here were mud-built homes and paths thick with people walking from school or leaving fields in chattering groups, a reminder that rural does not always mean lightly populated. In one village, Kotla, in the courtyard of a home where children clambered over walls, Sakina, a mother in her thirties, explained how she had been tricked into marriage while still barely a girl, in the 1990s. She had been brought more than 800 miles to the village by a middleman who trafficked young women as brides. Her husband's family had mistreated her. Sakina explained that "it was when I started having children that I realized I had no time to be upset." She produced nine offspring, eight of them boys—and by producing so many male children, she was elevated in status within the village.

In the dying years of Manmohan Singh's government the mistreatment of women became an issue of national, even international, debate. The spark was the gang rape and murder, on a bus, of a young physiotherapy student, in December 2012. The victim, in Delhi, came to represent an emerging, aspirational group of Indians. Huge protests erupted, helped by intense television and press coverage. Seething crowds appeared, some chanting that they would torture and lynch the attackers. At times, police resorted to tear gas and curfews to restore order. The rape and murder of poorer women never got such attention, but there was a widespread push for more debate over the ill-treatment of women in general. Official rape statistics did not prove that India had a worse problem with sexual violence than other countries, but such statistics were not widely trusted and opinion polls suggested that 90 percent of Indians thought rape was a "very big" concern, and most said it was getting worse.

People in authority mishandled their responses. Some blamed the girls and women who were assaulted for wearing supposedly immodest clothes or for daring to go out after dark. Mulayam Singh Yadav, a leading politician in Uttar Pradesh, said that rapists were treated too harshly—that "boys make mistakes"—and vowed to "revoke the anti-rape laws." A policeman in the same state was seen on television in effect telling villagers to murder a fourteen-year-old girl who had been abducted by older men, saying that if his sister had "eloped" he would have killed her or killed himself in shame. A Bengali politician, the son of Pranab Mukherjee (who became president), scoffed at women protesting against sexual violence, calling them "highly dented-painted." The police chief in Mumbai, where a female photojournalist had been gang-raped, blamed youthful "promiscuous culture."

Thankfully, others promoted women's safety. Ranjana Kumari ran an organization to help women on the edge of a slum in Delhi, for example. "I deal with rape cases on a daily basis." she said. "It is very difficult to believe anything will improve because there is a lack of political will." But at least, as with corruption, democratic India was beginning to confront this enormous, complicated problem. The rise of cities was one reason to be optimistic, because police there were more likely to respond to complaints of sexual assault than those in villages. Kumari dismissed Hindu nationalist commentators who claimed that "Bharat," implying rural India, never saw attacks on women. It was just that such attacks were far less likely to be recorded or publicized than those in town. In cities a new sort of debate was also becoming possible. A decade or two earlier it was almost taboo to utter the Hindi word for rape (*balatkar*), let alone address the problem of how men behaved. But more people in modern India said they refused to be treated as victims.

The photojournalist who was gang-raped in Mumbai said she would keep working, and refused to be shamed by the attack. What needed to change, argued Kumari, was that men and boys should start to have a "fear of law, or at least the semblance of the rule of law." Police have to take the attacks more seriously. It would help, too, if more youngsters got to talk frankly about sex, she said, complaining about "fundamentalists who won't allow sex education in school, and teachers who won't utter the word *sex*."

A judicial commission set up after the Delhi rape and murder received thousands of public suggestions for tackling violence against women. It proposed sensible laws—such as tougher punishment for those who disfigure women by throwing acid at them—which parliament enacted quickly. At least the perpetrators of the Delhi gang rape, men from a nearby slum, were arrested and jailed (though one died in prison) after a swift but fair trial that involved 130 hearings and nearly 200 witnesses. Extra courts—a plan called for 1,800 eventually—helped to speed other prosecutions for rape, to clear a backlog of 23,000 cases. The democracy showed it could function when pressed. The media also got better at discussing sexual violence, dropping euphemistic terms such as *Eve-teasing*, a reference to men's taunting, abuse, or groping of women in public. And although rape statistics in Delhi worsened, that was paradoxically encouraging, suggesting that women there were more willing than before to report attacks and the police were readier to record them.

Growing public anger about the issue at least encouraged those who campaigned to change attitudes. Activists tried to shift opinions. In south Delhi, off a narrow alley, was Maitri, an outfit for battered women. The organizer, Winnie Singh, sporting round tortoise-shell glasses and cropped grey hair, said "our laws are among the strongest in the world," but police and judges failed to implement them. She spoke of being attacked during her first marriage and got only unsympathetic reactions from police. She created her group, one of many, to help battered women lodge legal cases against attackers, though that often proved difficult.

Prospects should improve for women, especially if politicians do more to speed up gains. India spends far too little on public health—1.4 percent of its national wealth, compared with over 3 percent in China. The burden of that is felt hardest by women and girls. Putting more resources there would lift their prospects in general. As of 2014, combined private and public spending on health, per year, averaged $75 per person in India. Even in Delhi, one of the wealthiest corners of India, only one in five women have a midwife or other skilled person present when giving birth, and barely half of the children get a measles jab.

Modi as prime minister, to his credit, did talk about Indians' preferences for sons over daughters as a "psychological illness of the entire country," saying that "we don't have a right to kill our daughters" and "in our neighbourhood, girls are commonly killed in their mothers' wombs and we don't feel the pain."[2] It was welcome to hear him address the difficult subject. But wider efforts are needed, across both political and economic realms. Only if more women are paid for the work they do, for example, will their clout rise. Labor done by women is said to account for only 17 percent of the output of the formal economy, whereas in China it accounts for over 40 percent.[3] Nearly two-thirds of women in China are in the formal workforce (even if many do drudge jobs), vastly more than in India. If manufacturing were to boom in India, even to the level achieved in Bangladesh, with big textile and other factories, then more women would surely start earning salaries. That could have widespread social effects. According to McKinsey Global Institute, India could have an economy 60 percent larger if women were in the paid workforce and more productive—meaning better educated, better fed, and healthier. That is a tremendously hopeful goal for Indians to aim to achieve.

10

TACKLING THE TRAGEDY OF THE COMMONS

THOSE WHO COULD, FLED. EACH SUMMER, AS THE NORTHERN Gangetic plains sweltered and temperatures reached as high as 124 degrees Fahrenheit (51 degrees Celsius), the mountains grew intensely appealing. Hindu pilgrims, for example, found this the ideal time for a devotional walk, or *yatra*—in effect, a delightful hike in the hills of Kashmir. Throngs of devotees—600,000 each summer—ascended to a valley for a three-day walk to a holy cave called Amarnath. One year the walk was briefly delayed as soldiers checked for landmines or infiltrators from Pakistan; then a mass of happy pilgrims lurched on. Barefoot and bedraggled *yatris,* including some scrawny men who were near-naked and puffed on pipes of cannabis, walked while tinkling bells. They passed far larger numbers of city boys and middle-aged men with pot-bellies who lurched ahead, then sagged down for frequent rests. This was a friendly sort of religious stroll, an extended picnic for the masses. Chattering blended with the hiss of wind in the trees. Chaucer, a millennium or so after writing his *Canterbury Tales,* would have reveled in the scene.

Young couples walked hand-in-hand, pausing for a smooch or a selfie in the shade of a tree. One man staggered in such tiny, agonized steps it was hard to imagine he would get far before the snow returned. The landscape was serene: white peaks above intense green valleys with glacial lakes.

As a reminder that this was also a war zone, soldiers were everywhere. Cliff-faces were daubed with painted instructions—"slow and steady," "respect nature"—and the names and insignia of army battalions. Marksmen crouched in nests of sandbags, atop ridges, their red communication wires thrown upward along cliffs and around waterfalls. Even at fifteen thousand feet, soldiers guarded field kitchens that turned out noodles, fried food, tea, and starchy sweets. Militants, trained in Pakistan, had previously attacked the walkers, but in most years the threats were more mundane: altitude, bad weather, poor health. Some 130 of my fellow *yatris* died that year, victims of accidents, heart attacks, exhaustion, complications from altitude, or sudden flooding rain. Many were ill-prepared, in T-shirts and flip-flops, unconcerned about the mountain weather, trusting fate for their well-being.

The walk was a delight, shared with both pilgrims and the Kashmiri men who rented out tents, convivial in one another's company. It was a thrill to be a part of it and to reach the cave at Amarnath. Revered by Hindus, especially by couples ready to start a family, the cave contained a lingam, a phallus-shaped lump of ice that symbolizes fertility. Only one thing marred the expedition: the valley around the cave was all but trashed. It was a puzzle hard to explain, a wider problem for India: the disregard for public goods, shared spaces, air and water. The last approach was up a narrow valley to the cave, surrounded by jagged peaks, beside a rotten glacier-turned-rubbish dump, on a path strewn with plastic, paper, tins, drinks cartons, and mounds of waste half-buried in the ice. Pilgrims, some atop donkeys or ponies, scattered plastic potato-chip and candy packets, empty bottles, and other litter as they plodded on. Almost nobody worried about soiling a place considered sacred, or that they visited because it was—or had been—pristine.

A few Kashmiri men had been hired to gather some trash. They filled sacks with it and hurled them into streams, or partly buried rubbish in the snow. Near the cave itself, the valley was crowded with tarpaulin-covered shacks, stalls, ponies, and pilgrims. It had the despoiled air of a refugee camp: paths were slippery with mud and excrement. The sky filled with acrid smoke from damp, smouldering piles and half-burned plastic on cooking fires. Helicopters buzzed noisily just over-head, whisking the wealthy and unfit back and forth. After years of pilgrimages the effect was to leave this part of the valley as an extended rubbish dump, some of it melting into the river.

What was true near Amarnath applied in much of India, where the environmental strain was often overwhelming. China's experiences of ecological ruin, along with soaring rates of cancer, asthma, and other woes, constituted a stark warning of what India—much more densely populated, on average, than China—faced as it tried to industrialize. It was quite possible Indians would suffer even more than the Chinese from pollution, shortages of fresh water, and the effects of climate change. One sorry example was a site even more revered by Hindus: the River Ganges, the holiest, longest, and probably filthiest river in India. The faithful dunked themselves in it, sipped its murky water, called it their mother, offered it flowers and rose petals, set afloat on it little oil lamps, and generally celebrated it as a life giver. In its upper reaches it remained relatively clean. In the foothills of the mountains the water could seem icy and clear, as fish and other wildlife flourished. But downstream, in the densely populated flatlands, rivers that fed the Ganges were almost literally sewers, with darkened, sludgy liquid, as farmers extracted huge quantities of water for their fields. What re-mained was topped up with mostly untreated industrial and human waste. Any boat trip along the Yamuna River in Delhi left you gagging at the smell of feces as untreated effluent spilled from pipes into thick, black water that bubbled and fizzed. A yellow, foamy scum gathered atop the river, creating an apocalyptic-looking bubble bath. Not too far downstream, at Agra, the white marble of the Taj Mahal temple began to turn green—the result of clouds of insects from the nearby pesticide- and sewage-infused river defecating on a great symbol of India.

Equally striking was the poisoned Ganges when it reached Varanasi, farther downstream. An authority on the river, a man in white kurta pajamas, a brown waistcoat and square glasses, was Dr. Vishwambhar Nath Mishra, the priest of the Sankat Mochan Temple. His temple was on a *ghat,* a built-up riverbank, in the old city. For decades Mishra's foundation had conducted daily tests of the contents of the river water that were both more accurate and more worrying than official figures. Mishra's assistant dropped a garland of orange marigolds over my head and presented a sheet of paper with statistics describing a water sample gathered, just outside, a few hours before. Mishra leaned forward and tapped the paper: "These show the septic conditions of the river, the fecal count today is at least ten times above the safe level, our river has become a sewer," he said. "You should not treat the Ganga as a flush-toilet."

The river accepted much of north India's waste. Tens of millions of people lived near its banks, hundreds of millions in the territory it flowed through. At best only a tenth of their sewage was treated. The national census in 2011 found nearly five thousand towns and cities without even a rudimentary sewerage network. Streams, small rivers, and the land were all polluted. Varanasi was also the most auspicious place for many Hindus to be cremated: every year thirty thousand corpses, many only partly burnt, were dropped into the Ganges at this spot alone. Upstream were industrial cities: run-off and heavy metals from leather tanneries, discharges from factories, paper mills, and chemical plants all ended up in the same coffee-colored water. Farmers' pesticides and fertilizers sloshed in, too. During the monsoon, when the river burst its banks, the few sewage treatment plants were swamped. In the long dry months, when even the mighty Mother Ganges became a more modest waterway, the stench could be overpowering.

Modi had pledged to Mishra, and then to the public, that he would clean the Ganges. He then launched a campaign to improve hygiene in the rest of India. He appointed a minister, Uma Bharti, to take charge of the sacred river. Some mud was cleared from the *ghats* on its banks, in a token gesture. Experts and donors offered help: Australians would relate their experiences of cleaning the Murray River; the British talked of the Thames, in London, which once stank so badly parliament had to close. An expert on water, Asit Biswas, described how Singapore successfully cleaned its waters and told of his frequent requests from Indian political leaders to repeat that process in India. But Modi offered mostly gestures. He appeared on television wielding a broom, sweeping streets in a corner of Delhi, urging celebrities—in politics, sport, movies—to set similar examples. He bragged in the most vainglorious way about what he would achieve. "Ma Ganga has called me," he said shortly after winning the election in 2014. "She has decided some responsibilities for me. Ma Ganga is screaming for help, she is saying I hope one of my sons gets me out of this filth," he said. "It is possible it has been decided by God for me to serve Ma Ganga." He pledged that $3 billion would be spent to clean the river.

Some personal behavior changed because of the overall campaign. In Lodhi Gardens, a beautifully tended park in New Delhi, you might see a well-dressed young man stoop to pick up an empty plastic bottle, discarded by someone else, and drop it in a bin. The railways, notoriously dirty, were spruced up somewhat; the stations were kept a bit cleaner. Modi used his first speech as prime minister from the ramparts of the Red Fort, in Delhi, to tell each individual to take responsibility and reduce filth. A moment of hope existed. Yet after the applause at the end of that speech, the crowds dispersed and revealed a carpet of litter—empty bottles, snack packets, candy wrappings, rags—discarded even as the listeners cheered his words about a clean India.

Private homes were almost always pristine, even in poor areas. But unlike villages in rural Africa, where the shared areas are often neatly swept and cared for, Indian villages were often unclean. Overcrowded cities were routinely filthy. The cost of this was evident. Awful hygiene was a big reason why nutrition levels in north India remained just about the world's worst, with Indian children skinnier than those in poorer countries. It was not unusual to see human waste on pavements, railway tracks, and in parks. UNICEF, the United Nations agency for children, launched an animated campaign song titled "Take the Poo to the Loo." Others campaigned to improve public hygiene; for example, politicians said that building toilets was more important than putting up more temples. Yet there were times when India seemed to be buried under a layer of trash and waste. In one dispiriting visit to a northern town, Gorakhpur, I saw children playing cricket in a field that looked entirely covered by plastic and other junk, where cows chewed on plastic bags. The rubbish at their feet, lifted by gusts of wind, flapped like the beating wings of dying birds.

Arun Jaitley, India's finance minister, pledged that by 2019—to mark 150 years after the birth of Mohandas Gandhi—nobody should be defecating in the open. It was a wildly ambitious goal (and undoubtedly would not be met), but also a dismally basic one. Politicians made occasional strong speeches on public hygiene, but few came up with any detailed policies or described how effective implementation would fix the problem. The fate of the Ganges told the broader story. Those foreign advisers and experts soon said they doubted that progress on cleaning India would happen any faster than it had under previous governments.

As late as 2015, around 130 million Indian households lacked toilets. Nearly three-quarters of villagers still relieved themselves behind bushes or in fields. Even in towns, near the plushest homes, latrines were missing—or were not maintained—for the poor. Immediately beside the American embassy school where my children went daily, in the swankiest part of Delhi, a slum existed without sewerage or any proper housing. Children in rags defecated on the roadside. Wealthy parents at the school would have helped to pay to improve the slum, in the interests of their families, but for decades the slum-dwellers had been denied legal status to stay. Installing basic infrastructure was apparently forbidden, in case it conferred to slum-dwellers the right to remain. If the problem could not be fixed there, it was hard to imagine the rest of north India tackling it quickly.

Campaigners kept attention on the problem. Of the many splendid tourist sites in Delhi, for example, none quite matched the eccentric brilliance of the International Toilet Museum. The founder was Bindeshwar Pathak, a toilet enthusiast with round glasses and frizzy dark hair, in his seventies, who described himself as "a missionary of sanitation." Pathak headed Sulabh International, a non-governmental organization that promoted public hygiene. He displayed diverse contraptions in his sprawling museum: solar-powered solid-waste incinerators, waterless flushers, cooking stoves powered by bio-gas, human-sized statues made of plastic-coated excreta. Most striking was a photo of a Harappan water closet—a modern-looking toilet, with piped water, from the nearby Indus Valley. The civilization that built it existed 4,500 years ago.

Pathak wanted every policymaker to study that history and said Indians should get to work digging basic latrines, not fuss about space missions: "We are trying to go to Mars, yet we have no money for public health," he said. Attitudes changed slowly. Occasional articles in the press claimed that women in villages were refusing marriages until their fiancés provided a toilet in their family home. But poor understanding about basic procedures like hand-washing meant that children were ingesting bacteria and worms that infected their intestines. Around 120,000 of them died yearly from diarrhea, an entirely preventable cause of death. Far more suffered problems such as enteropathy, which prevents the body from using calories and nutrients from food; the resulting poor nutrition, in turn, hampers brain development. Fixing the problem, as China did decades earlier, should have been a priority for India's government officials. But few seemed interested.

Individuals could have done far more to take it upon themselves to dig and use latrines, or at least to maintain those that had already been built by the state. Yet by 2010 or so, more Indian families owned mobile phones—and more would eventually have smartphones—than had toilets. That suggested the most pressing problem was to educate and change attitudes. It was a sensitive topic, one of culture and religion, about behaviors notably seen in poor Hindu households. Ordinary Indians could be urged to change simple habits, especially those who might be influenced by tradition: the *Laws of Manu,* a text from two thousand years ago, had encouraged defecation far away from the home—to avoid impurity, for example, at a cooking place. Surveys by excellent institutions, such as RICE (Research Institute for Compassionate Economics), an economics think-tank in Delhi, suggested that many rural Indians still had a lingering preference for defecating outdoors, even if a latrine existed at home. North Indian and Nepalese villagers talked of relieving themselves in the open as wholesome, healthy, and social. Men sometimes scorned the idea of using latrines, implying it was unmasculine to do so, and suggesting latrines were for use by the infirm or the elderly.

Culture and religion mattered, and a lingering belief in caste played a role. By tradition, society's lowliest, the Dalits, had cleared away human waste, helping to generate a taboo among some in confronting the problem. A clear difference in behavior also existed between religions. Since at least the 1960s Hindu families had suffered from higher rates of child mortality than Muslim ones—even though Muslims typically were poorer, less educated, and had less access to clean water. By 2014, for every 100 children, 1.7 more Muslim than Hindu ones survived to be five years old, a big gap. Dean Spears, a researcher at RICE, argued that this could be explained only by differing sanitation habits. A 2005 government survey found that 67 percent of all Hindu households practiced open defecation, compared with just 42 percent of Muslim ones. (In the rare places where there was more open defecation among Muslims than Hindus, the mortality gap was reversed.) The most urgent priority was not to order more concrete latrines to be built but, rather, to tackle attitudes and education.

Other problems reflected a lack of individual care for the common good, as in Amarnath. Progressively more foul air choked Delhi and many northern cities; the smog was often even worse than in China's cities, and brought a high human cost. If you rubbed your skin after a short walk, your fingers were left coated with sooty black smudges, an indication of what you had also breathed in. During a shower, black water ran off your body. By one estimate Delhi smog was killing 10,500 people a year by 2015; others put the figure closer to 50,000. Studies of the air suggested that 200 tons of arsenic, black carbon, formaldehyde, nickel, sulphur dioxide, and nitrogen oxide were falling on Delhi every day. That fug triggered heart and asthma attacks, including among the young and apparently healthy; tiny particulates caused cancer in lungs. Winter brought the sootiest air, milky yellow light at noon, a carpet of grit and dust that settled on everything. Even in cabinet ministers' offices, grand government rooms with high ceilings, the smog was visible indoors. Flying over north India—or Pakistan and Bangladesh—in winter, I noticed that the entire territory was trapped under a blanket of brown, wet air, the product of cooking fires, stubble burnt in fields, brick kilns, factories, coal-powered plants, and millions of vehicles. Winter inversions meant a lid of cold air that pressed the blanket low and unmoving.

Yet India had shown it could act. For roughly a decade after 2001, some hope—and blue skies—came to Delhi after courts forced 100,000 buses, taxis, and auto-rickshaws to switch from diesel engines to ones run on liquefied gas. A daytime ban on lorries within the city cut pollution. The annual average level of sulphur dioxide fell from 14 micrograms per cubic meter to just five in 2016. Much else got worse, however. Levels of nitrogen oxide almost doubled, from 29 micrograms to 55. A measure of the average level of particulate matter known as PM 10 (dust with a diameter less than 10 micron-meters) rose from 120 to 261, far above the supposedly safe limit of 100. It was not unusual to see PM 10 levels of 750 in winter. (By comparison, PM 10 levels in Los Angeles were considered terrible when they averaged 88, in 1988.) Even scarier were the really tiny particles, PM 2.5, which settled deep in the lungs. The agreed-upon safe limit for these was 60, but official Delhi monitors at times indicated levels of 900 or higher.

The huge annual holiday of Diwali, the festival of light each autumn, is greeted with deafening firework displays that continue for days. The result is sulphur and gunpowder smoke that also lingers for days and marks the start of the worst season of pollution. Meanwhile, Punjabi farmers, west of Delhi, burn stubble. NASA one year released pictures showing thousands of orange dots, blazes over much of north India late in the year. In November 2016 thousands of schools in Delhi were closed because air pollution had reached exceptionally dangerous levels. Indoor smoke is probably more deadly yet: fumes from cooking fires, often burning straw-filled dung cakes, kill hundreds of thousands of people a year.

The government could fix some of these problems while also making India richer. Rolling out a reliable electricity grid, and getting more people to cook on gas stoves rather than on dung, wood, or coal fires, would improve human health (depending on how the power was generated) and bring about a cleaner environment. Brick kilns could be powered by electricity instead of charcoal. Shifting more goods from overloaded lorries to trains would also help. Paying farmers to stop burning stubble would make sense, too. In 2016, the Delhi government experimented with limits on the number of cars on the road, to little effect. But what really mattered were heavy vehicles: Delhi's biggest highways, in the middle of the night, carried immense lines of juddering trucks, all belching sooty, sulphurous diesel smoke. Often the fuel was adulterated with cheap kerosene, causing it to be even more polluting. That helps to explain why, in 2014, India had thirteen of the twenty most polluted cities on Earth, according to the World Health Organization (WHO)—and four of the remainder were in Pakistan and Bangladesh, making South Asian air exceptionally polluted.[1]

The WHO reckoned that almost every Indian was breathing unsafe air. A study published in 2012, but drawing on data gathered as long as a decade earlier, found Delhi children's lungs to be unusually small and filled with sputum.[2] Children also showed high blood pressure and other worrying symptoms. Outdoor and indoor pollution causes an estimated 1.6 million early deaths of Indians every year. Drawing on work from China, Michael Greenstone of the University of Chicago said that the cost of air pollution is immense.[3] He reckoned that 660 million Indians breath the dirtiest air, in the north, and live on average five and a half fewer years than if their air were clean. Greenstone calculated that pollution limits working lives, too, and thus could be said to have already cost 2.1 billion life-years in India—something economists usually do not measure. Other direct costs are slowly being understood better. One study of agriculture in India from 1980 to 2010 suggested that soaring ozone levels and other air pollution explained why wheat yields were one-third lower than would have been expected.

Official plans exist to improve the air quality, but Modi has also proposed to make India an industrial powerhouse, a workshop of the world. Manufacturing requires energy, and much of that would inevitably be generated by more coal-powered plants. Despite talk of cleaner supplies, the reality is that as of 2016 India relied on coal for at least half of its electricity, and many of its power stations lacked even the most basic scrubbers on chimneys to remove particulates. As for transport, fuel standards were kept low because raising them would have made engines, and cars, more expensive for consumers—thus affecting sales. Various states also failed to cooperate. Delhi enforced higher fuel standards than nearby states, but as a result many drivers bought cheaper and dirtier fuel outside of the city.

India has some good laws (though these are badly implemented) on protecting forests and wildlife. Tree plantations are growing, though more important old-growth forests have shrunk. Some impressive activists and academics have insisted that more attention must be paid to these issues, but India's government, especially under Modi, has bullied groups like Greenpeace that protested. Huge wind farms did get built—for example, in Tamil Nadu and in Gujarat. Producing solar electricity in sunny India has become almost as cheap—about 9 US cents per kilowatt-hour in some places, and falling fast—as importing coal to burn for electricity. India has cut subsidies on some fossil fuels, such as petrol and diesel, and on cooking gas, and plans to do so for kerosene. That would bring real environmental gains. Some 115,000 mobile-phone towers once powered by diesel generators were ordered to be changed to clean energy. In Uttar Pradesh, in 2013, in remote areas you could see phone companies fitting solar plants for their towers instead, and then selling surplus clean electricity to light up nearby homes and businesses using micro-grids.

But the pace of action on protecting and cleaning the environment is too slow. Nor has India been especially responsive in tackling climate change. Individual Indians have a low impact on the Earth's climate, but as of 2015 the country as a whole was already the third-largest emitter on the planet. Each Indian, on average, dumps just 1.6 metric tons of carbon into the atmosphere yearly, the same level that China had reached in 1980. China, per person, dumped five times more carbon than India in 2015. Americans, per person, emitted ten times more. But as India gets richer, it will inevitably emit more carbon and add to processes that make the climate less stable. By 2030 India is likely to triple its total emissions of carbon dioxide, to about 5.3 billion metric tons a year, with each person on average dumping 3.6 metric tons. As a result, India is on track to becoming the single biggest emitter of carbon dioxide on Earth. The consequences are likely to be tragic.

One fear is that the annual monsoon in South Asia will get less predictable—a dire prospect when roughly half the farmland in India still uses no irrigation. More rain may drop on India in a warmer climate, but it also might come down intensely or in unpredictable periods, bringing floods and damaging crops. Heavier bursts, combined with storms, would be devastating for the poorest. Between the heavy downpours, long periods of drought could become the norm. In 2016 an early-summer drought and heatwave in parts of India turned out to be the worst experienced in decades: several big reservoirs were almost entirely empty by May that year, leaving over 300 million people with little water. Record temperatures were set. A heatwave the year before had killed over 2,500 people. Those events might have resulted from an

unusually strong El Niño effect in the Pacific rather than from a changing climate. But it is possible that they were compounded by climate
change—and they gave a hint of the uncertainty to come. As the Indian
landmass became warmer in the summers, the way it drew moisture
from the oceans showed signs of changing. Given the water scarcity in
India, already one of the thirstiest countries on the planet, that bodes
ill for the future.

There is more that India can do to improve its environment. Nothing
has made a tragedy of the commons inevitable in India, however big its
population. Incomes can rise alongside improvements to the environment. Investing in—or persuading outsiders to pay for—a high-quality,
efficient national grid and getting all Indians access to reliable electricity
would be crucial for the country's further development. These measures
can also help to clean up the country, if people are diverted from dirtier
forms of heating, cooking, and lighting. Getting clean sources of energy to power the grid will also be essential. Many cities have set about
building decent public transport, including excellent metro systems,
as in Delhi. Most important is raising awareness about what problems
have to be tackled. One test is whether the country will become cleaner
for *yatris* hiking to the Amarnath temple or for pilgrims trekking to the
Ganges.

India can avoid the sort of environmental disaster that China inflicted on itself as it entered its primetime years—specifically, as incomes rose and education improved. In theory, the rulers of a democracy
should be far more responsive than those in an authoritarian state, as
citizens grumble and NGOs stir up anger about pollution. In the next
decade or two it is perfectly likely that opposition politicians, probably
beginning in Delhi, will take up such issues—for example, the need to
tackle smog—as a way of winning wide support. As scientists produce
ever more convincing evidence of the costs of air pollution, those who
live in Delhi—including foreigners who have moved there for work—
increase their demands for action. Unlike in China, where officials try
to deny the severity of pollution by hiding data about it, in India the

facts will be made public. India began with a clean-up campaign in the mid-2010s that can be followed by higher fuel standards for cars, the spread of more public transport, and higher standards for factory and kiln emissions. Because India developed its industry and transport systems later than many countries, it has a chance to avoid some of the worst mistakes made by others before it.

Efforts to clean up the environment, like those intended to improve prospects for women in India, will no doubt come more slowly than would be ideal. But politicians will act more quickly if they hear that voters care about such issues. The reshaping of Indian democracy is possible, especially as voters in towns and cities get increasing sway. Indeed, if the influence of old, feudal-type dynasties really can be reduced—if politicians (and crony-capitalists) understand that outright corruption will be punished more severely than before, and if voters demand better outcomes for all (not just for favored voter blocks)—perhaps it will make sense to talk of Indian democracy as entering its Primetime.

PART 3

ULTIMATE—ABROAD

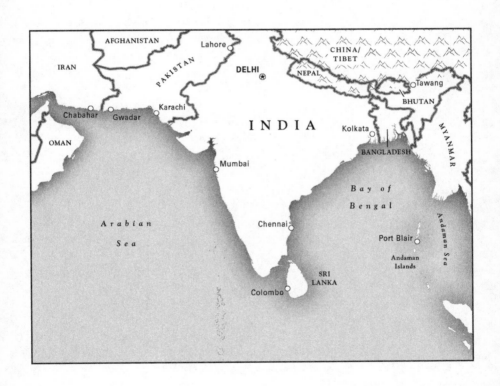

LIFTING AN OLD CURSE FROM PAKISTAN

NARENDRA MODI APPEARED TO BELIEVE THAT HIS PERSONAL-
ity and activities were the embodiment of foreign policy, or of
the state. His predecessors, by tradition, took office with a relatively low-key ceremony, indoors at Rashtrapati Bhavan, the president's
cream-and-red sandstone palace. Modi organized a much grander affair
in 2014, with a huge crowd and a high-kicking show. Bagpipers played
and twirled, trumpeters tootled from balconies, tall men in white uni-
forms lined red carpets. The event had a Disneyfied air of a coronation,
set in the sprawling grounds of the palace, the Lutyens centerpiece of
colonial architecture from 1929. Sitting near the front in the chuckling
company of Gujarati MPs, I was told by one of them how astrology was
the best guide for politicians and that "Modi will make India a hundred
times stronger."

Clouds of starlings swooped across the pale evening sky. Men
with pikes and knee-high riding boots stood to attention as ministers
pledged their loyalty. Most striking, however, were the foreign guests.

Leaders from South Asia had formed a group in 1985, SAARC (the South Asian Association for Regional Co-operation), which by 2016 accounted for over one-fifth of the world's population. But they rarely attended each other's inaugurations, nor did they act as a meaningful regional body, encouraging trade, cross-border travel, or coordination. There was nothing like the routine gathering of leaders in the European Union, for example. Yet all but one of SAARC's heads of government came to this event. Mahinda Rajapaksa, then Sri Lanka's president, flashed a Cheshire Cat grin and Hamid Karzai, the Afghan leader, offered an obsequious bow, followed by leaders from Bhutan, Nepal, and the Maldives. Modi and his guests signaled that the neighborhood was a priority and foreign affairs had become a more pressing concern.

The most notable guest was Nawaz Sharif, Pakistan's prime minister. Modi was reviled by most in Pakistan as a virulent Hindu nationalist. A Pew Research Center poll in 2015 found that only 7 percent of Pakistanis would trust him. Yet Sharif came, defying both Pakistan's public opinion and, more significant, its powerful army. Both India and Pakistan had leaders ready to explore a new sort of relationship. As ceremonies wrapped up, Sharif strode toward Modi through a swirl of presidents, royalty, and heads of state and shook his hand demonstratively. The two held their first bilateral meeting the next day. That meeting and subsequent ones in the next two years, in Nepal and in Pakistan, showed them exploring how to move on from decades of awful relations. The men had to get beyond the bitterness of a winter of war in Kashmir in 1947 and 1948, a month-long border war in 1965 (which killed perhaps three thousand Indians and nearly four thousand Pakistanis), war between the countries in 1971 over Bangladesh (during which ninety thousand Pakistanis were forced to surrender and the eastern half of Pakistan seceded), and a brief war in 1999, again in Kashmir. If Pakistanis, especially, were sore about the cost of launching and losing most of these conflicts, Indians were furious over the many years of cross-border terrorism launched by groups based in Pakistan. Yet Modi, a right-winger with a big mandate, had the rare domestic freedom to extend a hand—as Nixon had done in relation to China, for example—without being called a sellout. Modi could also cite a precedent: Atal Bihari Vajpayee, the only previous Bharatiya Janata Party (BJP) prime minister, had signed a declaration in Lahore in 1999 promising warmer ties with Pakistan. Sharif, coincidentally, had also been Pakistan's prime minister at that time.

For India, fixing relations with Pakistan would be one key to wider progress abroad. Foreign affairs—the topic of the chapters in the "Ultimate" section that follows—is an arena in which India has the chance to gain far more influence in the coming decades. Mostly that is because India's global heft, in the first seventy years after independence, proved little more than puny. India boxed far below its weight in military, diplomatic, and economic arenas. Much of what preoccupied India concerned its land borders: foreign affairs was Ultimate in the sense that it dealt with events at or just beyond the limit of its land borders, meaning disputes with Pakistan and with China over their shared (and disputed) frontiers. On the northwestern side, India faced a nuclear-armed state that looked fragile and at times on the verge of failure. On the northeastern side (and beyond), India faced a huge, authoritarian and nuclear-armed state that had already grown into a great power. How it deals with these two challenges will be the ultimate questions of Indian foreign policy in the coming decades. But the key to doing so, and for India to advance along a much broader range of policy challenges, would be to get the right relationships farther afield, especially with another power active in Asia: the United States.

Foreign policy for India began with Pakistan. Animosity between Pakistan and India was just about the most futile and prolonged of cross-border confrontations anywhere. It achieved nothing useful for either side (other than for a few self-interested men in uniform). Border clashes, frequent terrorism, disputes over territory in Kashmir, rows over water sharing, propaganda barrages, and other miseries persisted for decades. From the 1970s onward the two countries pursued a nuclear-arms race, even as violence sputtered on their borders.

That combination of hostilities led various commentators to judge the India-Pakistan border to be the world's most dangerous.

Some theorists believed that nuclear arms worked as a deterrent to a large-scale conventional war. Their existence did not prevent a Pakistani military incursion into Kargil, in Kashmir, in 1999, which could have escalated. In any case, there were enormous costs to the perpetual low-level confrontation. Those costs mounted in different forms: decades of forfeited trade and prosperity, lives lost, families divided, and huge public spending on armed forces that could have been used more productively. Many millions of Pakistanis and Indians were poorer and more insecure as a result of the mutual hostilities. Yet, over decades, despite occasional peace efforts, it was rare to hear either side seriously talk about negotiating a resolution.

Relations were poisoned from the start by Partition—the midnight furies unleashed as formerly British India won independence, in 1947, splitting simultaneously and with little preparation into two countries. Many Indian Muslims had said they feared domination by the majority Hindus, so they demanded a homeland. Secessions, geopolitical divorces, are never happy events—as North and South Koreans might testify, or Eritreans and Ethiopians, or Bangladeshis (East Pakistanis) who split from western Pakistan. Pakistan's break from India was certainly bloody, with hundreds of thousands killed and millions displaced as many Muslims shifted to Pakistan, while many Hindus and Sikhs were uprooted to India. Religion played a big and destructive part: almost the only unifying idea of Pakistan, which would prove close to disastrous because it legitimized those who pursued ever stronger forms of religious fanaticism, was to create a Muslim-majority homeland. Many of its leaders, civilian and military, resorted to stoking up ever stronger Islamic identity after independence. Grappling for a way to bind together an ungainly territory, they launched appeals to religion. At the same time, Pakistan's army was quick to suspend democracy and grab the lion's share of national resources for itself. India, to its enormous credit, instead defined itself as secular and democratic and proved vastly more stable and moderate as a result.

Partition was horrific. At least 14 million people were displaced, in one of the biggest forced migrations in history. In some cases, human caravans of trudging refugees stretched more than 50 miles. Moments of dramatic horror followed in terrifying succession: Sikh nationalists blew up a train in Punjab and massacred its Muslim passengers; Muslim thugs bombed Hindu-occupied homes in Lahore and relished hearing the panicked screams of victims burnt alive; neighbors slaughtered each other. Less well known, in 1948 Hindu extremists, the Indian army, and others massacred perhaps forty thousand Muslims in Hyderabad as rebels were defeated there, part of the process of incorporating former princely states into Indian territory (in this case, against the wishes of its last ruler, the Nizam, Osman Ali Khan).

The man most responsible for Partition was Pakistan's founding leader, Muhammad Ali Jinnah, an urbane lawyer who, ironically, had tried to avoid whipping up religious sentiments in politics until, late in life, he resorted to doing just that. He fell into a bitter rivalry with Mahatma Gandhi over India's independence campaign. It was Jinnah's call for a separate homeland, and the irresponsibly hasty retreat of Britain, that did most to unleash murderous religious tensions. Jawaharlal Nehru shouldered some blame, too, mostly for arrogance toward Jinnah, feeding his rival's fear that India might "strangle Pakistan at birth" by denying it the economic means to prosper or to defend itself militarily. Pakistan's reckless first invasion of Kashmir, using proxy fighters soon after independence, ensured that bitter confrontation would continue for many years.

Seven decades on, what prevented India and Pakistan from ending their confrontation? If those who had the power to make decisions wanted to end the conflict, there appeared to be no impossibly great obstacles to doing so. At issue, in effect, was where the shared border should run and whether Indian-run Kashmir should have a chance to hold a referendum for independence. Delineating the border should have been possible, and nobody thought a referendum in Kashmir was remotely likely. Pakistanis occasionally alleged that Indians wished to undo Partition and seize their country, or that India hoped to break apart Pakistan (for example, by stirring up rebellions in Baluchistan), citing the example of India helping the secession of Bangladesh from Pakistan in 1971. Such claims were not convincing. Yet some groups benefited from the persistence of cross-border clashes, sustained threats of terrorism, or instability, even if nobody wanted to trigger outright, general war.

India's foreign policy thinkers usually said that normal relations with Pakistan were desirable and possible, one distant day. Strategists in Delhi imagined peace as appealing in itself, and as a means to an end— for example, to allow future trade with central Asia, via Afghanistan; to import oil and gas; and to export agricultural, industrial, or mineral goods, even overland to Europe. Trade with central Asia was well remembered from Mughal times, notably involving much-fancied grapes that were brought each season to Delhi from Afghanistan. Those pondering rivalry with China also imagined binding central Asian states closer to India.

Until relations with Pakistan improved, however, India would have to find ways to leapfrog its neighbor. Since the early 2000s India had been developing an Iranian port, Chabahar, in the Gulf of Oman, linked by road—Route 606—to Afghanistan. The idea was to use Chabahar for trade (and potentially military purposes), and Indian officials said that extension of the port would come without delay. Modi visited Iran in 2016 and pledged to spend $500 million to make Chabahar a large-scale cargo port, part of a $1 billion renovation, though one official grumbled about painfully slow-moving Iranian bureaucrats. (When Indian civil servants say that their counterparts are slow, you know progress must be glacial.) Pakistanis claimed not to care too much about the Indian activities in Iran, though these were parallel to Chinese building activities in Pakistan, notably at Gwadar port, less than 100 miles east of Chabahar. A veteran defense analyst in Lahore, Hasan Askari Rizvi, once explained to me that "Chabahar is seen in Pakistan as an attempt by India to increase its influence in Iran. It is seen with concern, but not anxiety." In fact, leapfrogging was difficult for India: large-scale, overland trade with central Asia depended on making up with Pakistan.

India had other reasons to crave stability on its western frontier. Pakistan was a distraction from dealing with looming concerns over China's growing capability and significance in the region. As of 2016 an estimated 300,000 Indian soldiers (no official figures were made public) were camped in Kashmir to deter Pakistani invaders and respond to Pakistani-trained insurgents. For decades India's strategists had been preoccupied by the threat of land wars over the western border. But the growing military might of China increasingly needed attention to other borders, notably in the northeast of India, as well as more investment in naval, air, space, and cyber power. The more India was bogged down by its western border, the harder it was to pay attention in the east.

Warmer relations with Pakistan would bring India other benefits. Open trade with Pakistan's 180 million people, a handy neighborhood market, would boost both economies. It was revealing to be in Amritsar, in India's Punjab, which had less buzz than many other Indian cities. It had small industry, decent hospitals, and an airport, plus tourist attractions including the Sikhs' Golden Temple. Tourists flocked each evening to a border ceremony at Wagah, where Indian and Pakistani soldiers goose-stepped in a pantomime of confrontation, seemingly choreographed by Monty Python. But Amritsar had a melancholy air of forgotten glory, stuck at the end of a blocked road. Small traders in its scruffy Liberty Market huffed about Pakistan ("a dirty country," said one cellphone seller) but also complained that they suffered because of limited border trade. Barely an hour's drive away was massive Lahore: with 11 million residents in 2016, one of the biggest cities in the world. An exporter in Amritsar, munching on a plate of buttered chicken, talked wistfully of profits he would make if only he could get his galvanized steel to Lahore. Others dreamt of selling car tires, farm machinery, and pharmaceuticals to Pakistan. In fact, few goods crossed. Goods worth just $165 million flowed over the border in 2001, rising to more like $2 billion by 2016. Economists suggested that the potential value of trade was some ten times higher.

India had incentives to improve relations. Yet few among its politicians, soldiers, policymakers, diplomats, and analysts expressed urgency in doing so because of the domestic political risk. Indians did not trust partners in Pakistan after too many bitter setbacks, notably in the form of recurrent terrorist attacks that were launched from Pakistani soil, almost certainly with the support of (at least parts of) the Pakistani army. Indians said that their previous gestures of reconciliation, such as granting Pakistan the status of a favored trading partner, had not been reciprocated. And any warming of diplomatic ties over the years was routinely followed by new violence from over the border. Not long after Modi paid a surprise visit to Lahore on Christmas Day, December 2015, for example, well-trained suicide fighters from Pakistan attacked a military base in Indian Punjab, killing fourteen people. In September 2016, militants killed nineteen Indian soldiers in Uri, Kashmir, the worst such attack in more than a decade. India's government accused Pakistan of being a "terrorist state," saying it supported that attack and others. India retaliated by launching a brief military assault across the line of control, just into Pakistani-controlled territory, claiming that its soldiers had hit camps that housed terrorists. The main purpose of the operation, it appeared, was to reassure India's chest-thumping television hosts that some sort of military retaliation, widely called "surgical strikes," had taken place.

India was cautious about reaching out to Pakistan for other reasons. As a "status quo" power, occupying almost all the territory it wanted, the most valuable bits of the Kashmir valley, India's policymakers felt no urgency to act. Indians knew they were growing stronger than Pakistan, with an economy already eight times larger by 2016. Indians were getting richer: average incomes had been lower than Pakistani ones in the twentieth century, but from early in the first decade of the new century Indians were the better off. By 2015, according to the World Bank,

Indian incomes averaged $6,200 (measured by what their money could buy), whereas those of Pakistanis averaged more like $4,900. That gap promised to widen, as India's economy consistently grew more quickly than Pakistan's.

India's government generally functioned better, too, as symbolized by the eradication of polio there (the country was certified free of the disease in 2014), even as cases persisted in Pakistan—just about the last reservoir of the disease that existed anywhere in the world. UN comparisons of health, schooling, and other social trends showed India nudging ahead. Terrorism, an occasional horror in India, had become a steady scourge in Pakistan, where extremists killed 49,000 people in the decade from 2003 to 2013. Responses to natural calamities were also revealing of the relative capacities of the two states. When the Indus River flooded much of central Pakistan, in 2010, its then president, Asif Ali Zardari, took off on a diplomatic tour in Europe, including a brief holiday at his private chateau in northern France. He was accused of abandoning his people. Indian authorities, by contrast, reacted relatively well to natural calamities—for example, giving prompt aid to Nepal after an earthquake killed 9,000 people in 2015.

The bigger country had other advantages as well. Western powers increasingly aligned with India, especially as evidence grew that some in authority in Pakistan were promoting Islamist terrorism beyond its borders. (In 2016 two lawmakers in America's Congress proposed that Pakistan should be designated as a state sponsor of terrorism.) Westerners paid close attention to Pakistan as a partner that helped in some counterterrorism activity, plus as a nuclear-weapons power. But India was courted in a far more substantial manner: for wider trade, investment, diplomatic, and strategic reasons. America, decisively, had struck a civil-nuclear deal with India in 2005, trusting it not to share nuclear materials or information and in the hope that India would develop more nuclear power stations in cooperation with American investors. Under successive presidents from the 1990s onward—Bill Clinton, George W. Bush, and Barack Obama—America's policy grew more explicitly to bring India into a broadly pro-Western camp. Donald Trump, the incoming American president in 2017, also appeared to be pro-Indian. He had told a group of Indian-American donors during his election campaign that he was a "big fan" of India. He and Modi spoke the day after Trump's election. However, some analysts, such as Tanvi Madan of the Brookings Institution, warned that foreign policy under Trump could prove more "transactional"—with America more aggressively demanding support from India in return for help—and more withdrawn from Asian affairs in general.[1]

Because Indian strategists understood that their relative clout over Pakistan would grow, it might have seemed rational to wait to make peace overtures when its advantages were even greater. That was not, however, the calculation made by Modi, who craved a place in history for ending a prolonged conflict. For him, there was more pressure to act. Modi's attitude toward the neighborhood had evolved, and softened, the higher he rose in politics. In the 1960s, as a young Hindu nationalist volunteer, he had patrolled his home town, Vadnagar, in Gujarat, to guard against imaginary Pakistani invaders. At a time when his views had been shaped most by those Hindu nationalists, he absorbed the idea that Partition, the loss of 20 percent of British Indian territory and over 17 percent of its population, was a historical abomination. As a spokesman for the BJP when al Qaeda terrorists struck America, in 2001, he chose to condemn the entire religion of Islam, calling it especially violent because since the fourteenth century it had tried to "put its flag in the whole world and the [terrorist] situation today is the result of that."

By the time Modi was Gujarat chief minister, in 2012, he told me that having normal relations with Pakistan would be impossible unless Pakistan prevented groups on its soil from attacking India: "We must have a close tie-up with all our neighboring countries, but not at the cost of our national security. We must have very good relations with Nepal, Bangladesh, Sri Lanka, Myanmar, everywhere. But Pakistan should stop the terrorism activity," he said. Asked if India could encourage moderate Pakistanis, he batted away my liberal idea, saying that to "encourage means I have to interfere in their domestic politics of Pakistan" and "first they have to hand over the terrorists, these are the basic issues." The people he particularly had in mind were those handlers in Pakistan responsible for directing horrific terrorist attacks on railway stations, hotels, and other soft targets in Mumbai in 2008. Before the election in 2014, he also talked tough on securing India's borders, executing convicted terrorists, and crushing any infiltrators from Pakistan, while condemning Manmohan Singh for his moderation and caution.

But in subsequent discussions with him about Pakistan, in 2015, Modi the prime minister had softened. Rumors by then swirled that he yearned to get a Nobel Peace Prize. (A member of the relevant committee, in Oslo, once told me, later, of visits he had from Indian lobbyists who made the case.) His policy on Pakistan looked somewhat incoherent. Bonhomie with Nawaz Sharif at the inauguration gave way to snarling hostility over the border late in 2014. Attempts to hold diplomatic talks had been scrapped by Modi on a pretext, because of a state election in Indian-run Kashmir that autumn. The worst violence between the two countries in a decade erupted. Modi blew hot and cold, weakening the hand of potential partners, notably Sharif, along with any moderate voices inside Pakistan's army. In the summer of 2015 Modi said that his approach was simple, only to seek "friendship." "I keep trying to find new pathways, new avenues, to reach out to Pakistan," he said. Some pathways, dealing directly with Sharif, were followed outside of public view. A year later, however, relations were once again dire.

One big concern, though Modi waved it away in discussion with me, was Pakistan's relationship with China. China had helped Pakistan get a nuclear bomb, and was the biggest supplier of military equipment to Pakistan. China was also building civilian nuclear reactors for Pakistan. In 2015 China promised to invest $46 billion in Pakistan as one part of its immense "one belt, one road" infrastructure expansion, to boost Chinese trade especially with Europe and the Middle East. But Modi, chatting on the eve of a visit to Beijing, said blandly that India could not object: "In today's world, economic relationships are quite globalized. Each country seeks its own matrix of economic and commercial relations. As far as China and Pakistan are concerned, it is for them to decide the direction and speed of their economic engagement."

Modi found reaching out to Pakistan difficult. In December 2015 he paid his surprise visit there to see Sharif in Lahore—only three other Indians knew of his plan to go. It was a significant act, the first visit by an Indian leader in eleven years—a typical piece of Modi diplomatic theater, yet also the sort of gesture that his predecessor had yearned to make for a decade but never managed. However, policy changes did not follow quickly. Expectation rose, for example, that Pakistan would finally move to open up for more trade over the shared border, but movement was glacial or nonexistent in the first half of Modi's term.

Few Indian politicians showed strong interest in foreign affairs—a fact that would have to change in subsequent decades. Even the foreign minister of India, in 2012, S. M. Krishna, then nearing eighty, had seemed only dimly aware of some aspects of foreign affairs, such as whether India and Afghanistan shared a border (he told me, accurately, that they did not, whereas it was official Indian policy to claim that they did). Hardly any Indian politicians actually visited Pakistan, nor did many Pakistanis get to India. As a visitor to each country I was often asked to describe life just over the border, just as I imagine East and West Germans used to crave information about the lives of their former compatriots during the Cold War, and as North and South Koreans might do today.

One love affair was shared by both countries: cricket. Passion for the game overrode almost everything else. At times, cross-border relations were so bad that the national teams refused to meet on the field, and—to India's shame—even the most dashing Pakistani players were refused entry into the Indian Premier League, the most lucrative league in world cricket. Cricket could surely be a force to help to unite people across the border. Politicians from either side did try to use the game to manufacture excuses to meet, a process dubbed "cricket diplomacy." India hosted a cricket world cup (with Sri Lanka and Bangladesh) in 2011, and its team met Pakistan in the semi-final at Mohali, a venue in Punjab, close to the shared border. The atmosphere in the stadium was electric, and fans from both countries mingled happily. I sat beside an extended family of nine visiting from Karachi, in Pakistan, who spoke warmly of the welcome they had received in India, and who exchanged only light-hearted banter with the local crowd. Bollywood songs set the crowd dancing every few minutes. Nearby, two young Indian fans, wearing face paint, held up a placard that read earnestly: "Our aim is to bring peace, so please co-operate." Celebrities appeared, such as Sonia Gandhi and Rahul Gandhi, who sat among the fans for a time, in the blazing sunshine. Pakistan's prime minister, Yousuf Raza Gilani, also appeared, having accepted an invitation to visit from Manmohan Singh, India's leader. The two men earned cheers as they strolled together on the grass before the game, and hundreds of millions of viewers watched on television. For a moment, at least, it was hard to remember why the two countries opposed each other.

Specialists set much policy in India. Under Singh, starting in 2010, the national security adviser was Shivshankar Menon, a bright man and former high commissioner in Islamabad, who doubted that progress would ever be possible with Pakistan. He saw too many internal problems—notably Islamist radicalization, including of Pakistan's armed forces—for Pakistan to make good on its diplomats' promises. Nor would closer ties between India and America help to make Pakistan more conciliatory, he said. India could not expect a third party to fix its problems. Menon had a sophisticated, subtle grasp of foreign policy and was risk-averse. His successor, under Modi, had a different outlook and character. Ajit Doval was an action man, assertive, expecting to shape circumstances. He believed, like Modi, in bold gestures and leadership, but appeared less sure of strategy. Discussing Modi and foreign policy, he said that "personalities are policies" and stressed "leadership quality" to solve most problems, calling Modi "a tremendous communicator [who] is strongly trying to raise India, he is passionate about India acquiring its economic and political potential." Doval was also ambitious, lamenting that "India punches below its weight. India has its geographical position, resources, [financial] capital, human capital. India has not achieved as much as it can."

Doval believed that force of personality could achieve more for Indian foreign policy than any number of quiet institutional changes or diplomatic interactions. It was unclear whether he and Modi calculated that dramatic elements of foreign affairs—surprise meetings of leaders, state visits, grand speeches—were the means to more substantial change (such as settling disputes over who should control which part of Kashmir and agreeing on the border line between the two countries), or whether such gestures were the sum of policy. Modi did install as his top diplomat a Tamil who was quick and aggressive in conversation, but who, like Menon, was more cautious in his style, while wanting substantive changes. Subrahmanyam Jaishankar said India had to become quietly stronger in the region, to be a "leading power, not just a balancing power." He talked of getting much friendlier relations across South Asia, watching to see if Pakistan "gets worried," and, later, negotiating from a position of greater strength. This meant persuading skeptical neighbors that India was a benign presence. "You cannot be a leading power if your neighborhood is not with you. You need a neighborhood that roots for you," Jaishankar said. For him, progress in Pakistan began with settling borders and tensions elsewhere, specifically Bangladesh; warming relations with Sri Lanka; and generating more economic activity across South Asia.

I was able to report from both sides of the India-Pakistan border, and to hear how strategists, politicians, diplomats, and soldiers talked about one another. In May 2013, a year before Modi came to power, Pakistan held an election that propelled Nawaz Sharif into office. Immediately afterward he invited foreign journalists to his glitzy home near Lahore to discuss his plans as prime minister over an enormous lunch. The host—portly, in a blue suit, grey waistcoat, and shoes with large golden buckles—had won an unusually big mandate from Pakistani voters. His story somewhat prefigured Modi's rise. As a right-winger, with a record of building infrastructure in his state, Sharif once favored religious extremists but had become more moderate and now hankered to make history by promoting trade and peace with the old rival next door. He had campaigned by promising closer ties with India to generate economic recovery at home.

Sharif's efforts were complicated by one big factor: the army. The generals, almost since the birth of Pakistan, had undermined democracy and kept most control over its foreign and security policy. Sharif had to win support from factions of the army that might accept warmer ties with India. The last time he had tried to reach out, as Pakistan's prime minister in 1999, the army chief of the day, Pervez Musharraf, destroyed a putative peace initiative with Vajpayee, India's then prime minister. Musharraf ordered soldiers to infiltrate Indian-run territory in Kashmir and to seize a mountainous area called Kargil. This provoked a short and worrying war that Pakistan lost. The war eventually was followed by Musharraf, the reckless general, toppling Sharif in a coup. He ruled as dictator of Pakistan for the best part of a decade, a particularly dire period in the country's history. An obvious risk for any future India-Pakistan peace effort would be that another Pakistani general might emulate Musharraf.

But democracy went on to grow somewhat deeper roots in Pakistan. For the first time, in 2013, an elected ruler completed a full term and handed power to an elected successor. It became possible to imagine the army getting less adventurous and less influential. One factor was the economy. Some in the army were persuaded that more trade with India would boost their own resources. Another factor was the chastening of the army, in 2011, after American special forces killed Osama bin Laden, al Qaeda's leader, in Pakistan. For years, as America searched for its most-wanted enemy, bin Laden had been living comfortably in a compound in Abbottabad, a pleasant military town near Islamabad, Pakistan's capital.

My visit to bin Laden's home, number 25 on a (normally) sleepy street, in Abbottabad, the day after Obama said Navy Seals had killed him there, in May 2011, was a revealing experience. Clambering along bin Laden's garden walls to peer into the compound, ringing his door-bell, and speaking to neighbors and other residents helped me to build a sense of how he had lived there—and of what transpired when he-licopters arrived during the night raid. Some neighbors said they had feared that India was invading. A few discussed the reticent, long-term occupants of number 25. It was reasonable to conclude that bin Laden had enjoyed some sort of protection from military spies who had known of his presence in Abbottabad. Bin Laden's home was a few minutes' walk from a military academy where the army chief regularly visited. A neighbor said police swept the area weekly, checking resi-dents' IDs and sometimes looking into homes. Police also maintained networks of informers among guards and others. It was hard to believe they would have not stumbled on the world's most-wanted man unless ordered to avoid number 25 by someone in authority. The reportedly small number of weapons at the site, at the time the Americans at-tacked, also suggested that bin Laden relied, perhaps not by choice, on others to guard him.

Some in office in America concluded Pakistan's military spies had known about bin Laden (though America's public stance was firmly otherwise). One indication of this was the dramatic deterioration in bilateral relations that began shortly before the killing of bin Laden and then continued for more than a year. In November 2011 America's army in Afghanistan shelled and killed twenty-four Pakistani soldiers, supposedly allies, on the border. Terrorist attacks on Western and In-dian targets in Kabul, the Afghan capital, were traced to groups backed by Pakistan's army. Because Pakistani generals felt squeezed, and were unsure whether American funds and weaponry would continue to flow to them, as they had for decades, more space opened for civilian leaders to influence foreign policy. It was even possible to hope that a more chastened Pakistan would reduce its traditional hostility toward India. Around this time, Pakistan's generals did start saying that the greatest military concern was no longer from India but from domestic, Islamist, terrorist groups—a big change in outlook.

When Nawaz Sharif took office in 2013, hosting foreign correspondents in his enormous drawing room with heavy chandeliers, gold-trimmed velvet curtains, and wall-sized mirrors, he had reasons to believe he could shift Pakistan's policy on India. Sharif sounded sincere in talking of trade and warmth toward India, seeking cross-border visits by leaders and more economic ties. In 1996 India had granted Pakistan "most favored nation" trading status, but Pakistan, some two decades on, had failed to reciprocate. Under Manmohan Singh India rebuilt and expanded its customs post at Wagah, to handle one thousand lorries a day. Constructed in pink and yellow stone, it remained mostly empty when I visited in 2015. A truck driver flicked at flies; tannoy speakers played elevator music in a big, almost deserted vehicle park. But at least the post stood ready, should trade one day grow. Pakistan had done nothing to prepare its side of the border.

More trade would encourage lobbies for peace in both countries. Sharif's main foreign policy adviser, Sartaj Aziz, a twinkly-eyed man who believed in free markets and remained spry in his late-eighties, said that all of South Asia needed economic revival and that "the peace constituency in Pakistan is stronger than in the past." Aziz said he planned to open a back channel for negotiations with Modi, "away from the glare of the cameras," just as Sharif and Vajpayee had done for eighteen months before their Lahore declaration in 1999. But would Pakistan's army chiefs accept serious talks? Aziz was optimistic, saying, "the army is ready to go along, but it will also watch the size of India's defense budget and we cannot accept military imbalance." Some in the "establishment on both sides of the border" had no interest in peace, he added, blaming India's nationalist media for antagonistically stoking "sensation, drama, and intensity."

On the Pakistani side, the "establishment" meant hard-line military men and spies, plus old business leaders who feared foreign competition. Sharif's brother, Shahbaz Sharif—sometimes referred to as the brains in Pakistan's government—once said in conversation that "security agencies on both sides need to understand, a security-led vision is obviously driven by economic security." He meant that the army could get more money if trade grew with India. Imran Khan, a populist opposition politician who expected one day to become prime minister, said he wanted warmer relations with India, too.

The sticking point was—as always—inside the army, especially among military spies, and those with conservative, religious leanings. Talking to them or to the ISI (Inter-Services Intelligence) was difficult. Previously an ISI spokesman, a man with a ponytail, would meet for tea in hotel lobbies in Islamabad, to spell out how foolishly Americans were behaving in Pakistan and Afghanistan, to claim that India fomented violence in Baluchistan, or to deny any wrongdoing by his employers. He naturally denied that the ISI had harbored bin Laden. He also denied that the ISI beat to death a Pakistani journalist who had investigated the ties between officials and Islamist extremists including al Qaeda.

Once with two colleagues I chatted, in the basement of a house in Islamabad, with an ISI colonel and a junior officer. Over a breakfast of sliced fruit and black coffee I asked whether military spies would scupper the civilians' efforts to reach out to India. The colonel was trim, clean-shaven, well-spoken, and Western educated. He was hardly encouraging. He claimed that "India promotes insurgency in Pakistan," undermining the whole region, and alleged that "India sends finance to mafia, who help to support insurgents in Baluchistan. A lot of criminals are involved." He admitted that finding evidence was tricky, but said India stirred violence in northern Pakistan, specifically in Gilgit Baltistan, where Sunni and Shia Muslims clashed. He accused India of trying to block China's expansion of the Karakoram highway, which links Tibet to the Indian Ocean at Gwadar port: "The invisible hands, the third party," he said, "somehow they spread sectarian disharmony. Some invisible hands do mischief to create sectarian bloodshed. There are killings in that area, law and order problems, international players are active." He alleged that agents paid by India had been kidnapping Chinese workers, claiming that America had ordered India to do this. He added that "if the Americans want to pinch China, why should they use India on us?" As for India in Afghanistan, he said, "India can do anything, but don't disturb the balance. Don't pinch us from the West. I see clear traces of involvement by India, interfering in our affairs."

Such paranoia was not encouraging for stability in the region. Pakistani diplomats were usually, but not always, more sophisticated than the men in uniform. But at times they made similar allegations, presumably under orders. Pakistan's high commissioner in Delhi once suggested to a room packed with journalists that Indian money and backing was behind a horrific massacre by the Taliban of 141 people, mostly children, at an army school in Peshawar in December 2014. Over the years Pakistani officials claimed that India was somehow behind gang violence in Karachi, separatists in Baluchistan, sectarian killings all over Pakistan, and bombings such as at the Marriott hotel in Islamabad. The allegations seemed outlandish and lacked evidence to back them up.

One reason why Pakistani military leaders were quick to allege conspiracies by others was that they found conducting their own operations in the shadows attractive. Leaders from Pakistan's army admitted they had sent jihadi fighters into India, in effect confessing to being state sponsors of terrorism. Musharraf, for example, said in 2010 that training jihadis to attack in Indian Kashmir was legitimate, claiming: "It is the right of any country to promote its own interests when India is not prepared to discuss Kashmir at the United Nations and resolve the dispute in a peaceful manner." Underlying the claim was a justification of asymmetry: Pakistan is so much smaller than India it needed to "bleed" Indian resources and somehow stir sympathy and attention from elsewhere in the world. Yet such groups mostly killed a few low-ranking recruits or civilians, spread fear, provoked repression, and achieved no serious military goal, beyond tying up Indian soldiers in Kashmir.

The Mumbai terrorist attack in November 2008 saw 166 people—including Americans and several other foreigners—killed in a train station, luxury hotels, and elsewhere. It was the more horrifying for being televised and protracted, spread over four days, a "spectacular" terrorist attack. It would later be emulated, in method, by terrorists in Nairobi (in a shopping mall, in 2013) and in Paris (at cafés, a football stadium, and a concert hall, in 2015). The Mumbai attack was organized by a group based in Pakistan and conducted by ten young Pakistani men recruited by Lashkar-e-Taiba (LeT), an extremist Salafi outfit. It was probably guided by an officer who had been in Pakistan's military spy network, the ISI.

Groups such as LeT were tolerated, even supported, by Pakistan's army, which dared not (and did not wish to) confront all Islamist extremists in the country. Some in the army sympathized with extremist groups, especially the LeT and its goals and methods. The result was that extremists grew stronger inside Pakistan, spreading violence there and abroad. As America's ambassador to Islamabad, Cameron Munter, said to me in May 2011, just after bin Laden was killed, "if you grow vipers in your back yard, you're going to get bitten."[2] An academic in Islamabad suggested that army men would never stop using extremist groups, as they "slap the jihadis with one hand and feed them with the other." That pointed to a persistent threat for Modi and Sharif, as they sought ways to improve relations. Such groups—encouraged by some within Pakistan's army—could launch spectacular terrorist attacks, like that seen in Mumbai or the many in Kashmir, whenever they wished to scupper peace efforts.

The men in uniform in Pakistan remained extraordinarily powerful, not least by controlling parts of its economy. Many in the army "are businessmen in protected industries, and some are propped up by the cement industry, textiles, and all fear the cold wind of competition with India," said an ambassador in Islamabad. "The military runs bakeries, big landlords have agricultural interests, old families fear being smashed by competition," he added. Christine Fair, an American academic who wrote a biting history of Pakistan's army, called it an extraordinarily successful machine for extorting resources, including aid from America, for private benefit of the generals. She summed it up as a massive "self-licking ice-cream cone."[3] The world's sixth-largest army, it extracted roughly a fifth of all public spending, more if you counted the costs of military pensions and the country's fast-expanding nuclear arsenal. Pakistan produced, in 2016, roughly 220 pounds of highly enriched uranium a year, enough for four or five new nuclear warheads, to add to a stockpile of warheads some 100 strong. The only way to justify such spending, given widespread poverty, was to whip up fears of India. "We have become delusional, psychotic, fearing how to protect ourselves from the rest of the world," said an academic in Islamabad.

Would Modi and Sharif find some sort of reconciliation, and overcome this? Modi yearned to do something historic, but as of this writing in 2016, no evident progress had been made since he came to power. In Sharif he faced a man with a similar personality, a willing partner, but who was politically weakened by years of protests and as the army regained the upper hand. Pakistan's army retained its sway on foreign and security policy, and appeared to be vetoing any big improvement in ties. Until moderate voices in Pakistan's army spoke out for the benefits of peace with India, it was hard to see anyone else being able to force a deal. For that to happen, the army had to see a strong enough incentive to change its anti-India stance. The gradual decline in American aid to Pakistan might be one factor to encourage that. But then another big power had a role to play: China.

12

A SHADOW CAST FROM THE EAST

THE DALAI LAMA WORE A BURGUNDY ROBE AND TINTED GLASSES
that he might have borrowed from John Lennon. He laughed at
everything, including the prospect of his own death. A colleague
and I asked if he planned to be reincarnated. "My own rebirth, definitely! You two, too!" He chuckled, saying, "I want to be born where
there is more suffering, where I can serve. I pray, I am determined, to
be reborn where some opportunity of serving is." We were at his residence in McLeod Ganj, Dharamsala, in the Himalayan foothills, as
spring sunshine dappled the courtyard outside. Later, listening to a re-
cording of our long conversation, I noticed that almost every sentence
had concluded with giggles. The Dalai Lama's laughter was contagious
even then.

He spoke clearly, but at times his sentences back-to-front seemed
as if uttered by Yoda from *Star Wars*. He was playful, energetic, a little
wizened, cryptic, with as much enthusiasm for science as for anything
spiritual. He talked of a plan for his fifteenth incarnation: "When I

reach around ninety, I will convene a meeting of religious leaders, then decide. The best is like the Pope system. The very institution of the Dalai Lama should continue on." He laughed again, saying he was delighted that Pope Benedict XVI had decided to retire. As much as any Pope, the death of the Dalai Lama and his supposed rebirth would be a matter of geopolitics. China's government despised him, because Tibetans who revered their giggling Buddhist leader also rejected rule from Beijing. Tibetans also opposed the mass arrival of Han Chinese settlers who followed new roads and railways into the mountains, filling their towns, especially Lhasa, the capital. The Dalai Lama also appealed to an unknown number of non-Tibetan Chinese who were rediscovering interest in Buddhism. For these reasons, China's government hoped to influence who becomes the next Dalai Lama, though it would probably have been better off negotiating with the existing one—a moderate, peaceful, and conciliatory man who remembered dealing amicably with the most senior Communist leaders in the past. A successor could prove more confrontational.

His fate matters to the broad relations between China and India, with two-fifths of the world's population between them. A moment of tension is likely after he dies: within a couple of years monks will divine which small boy, somewhere in greater Tibet, is to be his new incarnation. That could be in Tibetan territory on the Indian side of the disputed border with China, perhaps in Tawang, a remote town where an earlier one was born. Tibetans in exile have a government, in Delhi, regularly elected by émigrés, which would throw its support behind the new Dalai Lama. India's government would presumably do so, too. Meanwhile, China's rulers, through their own proxy monks, might pick a boy on the Chinese side, in the hope of dividing the spiritual leadership of Tibetans.

In recent years Indian officials and politicians, increasingly under Narendra Modi, have taken to emphasizing the country's Buddhist heritage and its cultural, religious, and trading ties with much of Asia. They assert India's cultural importance to the wider region for more than two thousand years. Scholars have noted Indian influence on much of Southeast Asia, such as the four-century-long Ayutthaya kingdom in Thailand that existed until the late 1700s. It was probably named after the Indian city of Ayodhya and influenced by Hinduism. The twelfth-century site at Angkor Wat, in Cambodia, began as a Hindu temple and only later became Buddhist. In Odisha, on the east coast of India, an annual festival of *Bali Jatra* celebrates mariners who traded with the Indonesian island of Bali and elsewhere: children float paper or bark boats, at a moment reckoned auspicious for traders. The many Hindu temples of Bali, Indonesia, are testimony to influence from Indian seafarers and settlers.

India's influence went wider. Vietnam has ruins of Hindu temples, such as one at My Son dating from between the fourth and thirteenth centuries. At Hampi, in southern India, stone carvings depict the trade of horses from Mongolia and central Asia, half a millennium ago. In Quanzhou, a coastal town of China, archaeologists in the 1930s found statues of elephants, inscriptions, and Hindu and Buddhist artifacts. These included temples built for traders from southern India, probably Tamils, in the Song and Yang dynasties, stretching from the tenth century to the fourteenth. More recent influences are obvious elsewhere in Asia: Fiji, Malaysia, Australia, and Singapore, for example, are home to substantial Indian diasporas. American diplomats talk up India's cultural-religious soft power, as when America's ambassador to Delhi, Richard Verma, said that "[a]s the birthplace of Buddhism and a historical center of Sufi Islam, India's cultural influence extends from Southeast Asia to Mongolia and from Indonesia to the steppes of Central Asia."

India's claim to regional influence is not just about history. It takes place amid rumbling rivalry with a much more powerful neighbor, China. The two countries have competing interests in greater Tibet, with its many rivers, large territory, and rich culture. The Dalai Lama spoke of his early memories there, and said he was desperate to return. As a young leader he had warm relations with China's Communist rulers, including Mao Zedong: "When I was in Peking in 1954, 1955, Chairman Mao and other leaders emphasized unity and harmony, equality for different minorities. Chairman Mao said he was against Han chauvinism, at the same time he was against local nationalism. He was quite balanced. While I was in Peking I learnt of Socialism and then Marxism, also the history of the Chinese revolution. I was very much impressed as far as socioeconomic theory. I'm still Marxist, not capitalist, that is not a secret!" He said he met Mao "twenty or thirty times" and began what he believed, wrongly, was a sincere friendship: "At that time I really trusted Chairman Mao Zedong. For a few months in Peking we really developed trust, I thought."

He said he had met other leaders whose families were again powerful decades later. Xi Zhongxun, the father of President Xi Jinping, gave the Dalai Lama a gift of a watch. Official policy in China, later, was to revile the spiritual leader and call him a devil. The Dalai Lama laughed at that and posed as an impish sprite as I took his photo: tipping his head playfully, crooking the fingers of both hands above his forehead, forming "horns," and joking that he was a demon. The moment was surreal, and it was hard to imagine what many in China would make of his performance, or his early closeness to Mao and to Xi's father.

Tension was not inevitable between India and China, but relations have never been warm since the Dalai Lama fled to India in 1959. Polls in the 2010s showed that Indians saw China—even more than Pakistan—as the most serious military concern this century. A great imbalance existed between the countries. India had the demographic edge: its population would be larger than China's as of the early 2020s, and would long remain the more youthful. India's cultural exports—such as Bollywood films and television soap operas, which were watched all over the world including in China—constituted a form of soft power. The Dalai Lama believed that India, in the long run, had the upper hand because a democracy is inherently superior to an authoritarian state, and a democracy could cultivate more allies: "China is an economic power, a military power, it has manpower. But from Japan, Vietnam, India, neighbors have some distrust, suspicion. [If] all the neighboring states fear China, that is not good. If there is full freedom in China, then development can be much faster. For its own future, China has to change something." By 2015 and 2016, India's economy also grew faster than China's.

Yet China had more obvious, concrete advantages. It was two decades or so ahead of India in terms of development; its economy was five times larger than India's. As of 2016 India had a gross domestic product of just over $2 trillion, about the same as China's soon after this century began. Average Chinese incomes, in 2015, were equivalent to $14,240 (if you assessed them in terms of what a person could buy), compared with $6,200 in India. China was far ahead on indicators of health, literacy, nutrition, education, and other social conditions. Chinese visitors to India voiced dismay over the poor state of roads, railways, and other basic infrastructure they found. Whereas India was home to about one-third of all the people on the planet who counted as extremely poor, China had only 13 percent of them, said the World Bank. Many Indians certainly felt they were lagging.

An Indian journalist, Reshma Patil, based in Beijing early this century, offered a revealing memoir about observing the "strangers across the border." She found two countries for which "extreme ignorance and nationalism illustrate their mutual relations." Once she discovered a few Chinese sportsmen learning cricket, known as *shenshi yundong*—the noble game—in case it one day became an Olympic event. She suspected they would rather be battling at a ping pong table. At universities she came across students, the few supposed to be learning Hindi, who dismissed India as dirty, poor, and irrelevant. She was frequently told that India suffers an "inferiority complex," and that there could be "nothing to learn" from it. Perceptions of India as backward would take years to shift—in part because India did not rank highly as a trade partner for China, and trade favored China: it imported raw materials and sent back manufactured goods, in much the same way that China did with African countries and other less developed economies. That was not accidental: China blocked firms involved in pharmaceuticals, IT services and the like, in which India excelled.

Only a few individuals the Indian journalist met had countered ignorance about India. A dissident artist, Ai Weiwei, lauded freedom of speech in India. He also said that Chinese security agents cited Indian chaos and backwardness as "proof" of the general inferiority of democracy. Some Chinese business travelers and reporters praised what they had seen of Indian openness, or claimed to have seen "inner peace" among even its poor. Others were impressed by Indian courts, mass protests against corruption, and the fact that rural migrants had some access to schools or hospitals in towns, unlike in China. And Patil found a few traders who saw opportunities in export markets in India: factories in Quanzhou that churned out millions of Ganesh statues and other Hindu figurines, trinkets, and gifts—especially for Diwali, the Hindu festival of lights.

The economic gap between China and India would begin to close, at least a bit, in the twenty-first century. Although Kanti Prasad Bajpai, an Indian analyst in Singapore, once said it was "fanciful to think India will nip at China, it is an idea mostly promoted by the West and the media," in fact it was more fanciful to imagine that China, struggling to shift from being an export-led economy to one driven by domestic consumption, would sustain its rapid growth as exports sagged and its population aged. It was just as likely that China, as happened with many mid-income countries with aging populations, would see growth tapering off. Assuming India, growing from a poorer base, managed to get its economy ticking along fast into the 2020s, the wealth gap would start to shrink.

But China did appear set to keep a large military advantage: by 2016 its armed forces had a budget at least four times larger than India's, and nationalist Chinese bloggers were mocking Indian aspirations to military strength as "loud thunder, tiny rain." Geography had left India permanently disadvantaged because its disputed border with China—some 2,100 miles long in the Himalayas—was near Delhi and the heavily populated Gangetic plain but far from China's capital and its largest cities on the eastern coast. When China's army invaded Tibet in the 1950s, it seized territory that Indians had long considered their hinterland: trade routes from Lhasa once reached Calcutta. Independent India, along with the CIA, had supported Tibetan resistance against its occupiers. That failed, and in March 1959 the Dalai Lama ran to India with a retinue of eighty. Chased by China's air force and soldiers for two weeks over mountains, across plateaus and valleys, he and his supporters spoke of magical clouds that hid their escape. He reached a southern corner of Tibet inside India, in Tawang, before moving west to Dharamsala, where he drew other Tibetans who claimed asylum. His presence let India flaunt its status as a democratic, more tolerant country.

Before his arrival, India's leaders such as Jawaharlal Nehru—preoccupied by colonialism—had talked of China and India as brothers. Some in China in the mid-twentieth century had been impressed by Mohandas Gandhi's peaceful campaign to be rid of the British. Some in China said they admired Rabindranath Tagore, a Bengali who won a Nobel literature prize in 1913. Nehru, though seen as insufferably arrogant and patronizing by his Chinese counterparts, managed to generate respect for India, too. But a painful border war in 1962, then Nehru's death, followed by further border scraps, led to growing hostility. Two cases of Chinese infiltration, near Sikkim, in 1967, led to fighting that killed 88 Indian soldiers and 340 Chinese ones, before the Chinese withdrew. Decades of edgy confrontation followed, though Rajiv Gandhi, by visiting China in 1988, helped to ease these. In the current century, military rivalry has remained low-key, but antagonism on the border—as in China's other frontier areas—occasionally flares up.

Indians are wary of China for strategic reasons. China is a firm ally of Pakistan, a nuclear-armed power that has launched several wars on India. Pakistanis play this up, as when its ambassador to China once described relations as "higher than the mountains, deeper than the oceans, stronger than steel, dearer than eyesight, sweeter than honey, and so on."[1] Another favored term used by both countries is *iron brothers*. In Islamabad, think-tanks that specialize in China studies are mostly vehicles for the well-connected to win stipends and take official jaunts to China. Indians say one reason why bad blood persists with Pakistan, seven decades after Partition, is that China encourages it in order to weaken India. China had provided Pakistan with civil-nuclear reactors, helped it develop nuclear weapons, and sold it military gear including fighter jets and frigates. In 2015 China's President Xi visited Pakistan and said his country would invest $46 billion there, mostly for an economic corridor running 1,850 miles from the border in the mountains to a Chinese-run harbor, Gwadar, on the Arabian Sea.

India tries to respond in kind. It seeks close ties with Vietnam, which has frosty relations with China. Modi also paid a state visit to Mongolia in 2015, the first by an Indian prime minister. India's relations with Japan—another rival to China—have been warming for years, notably under Shinzo Abe, Japan's unusually assertive prime minister. India is trying to adopt a strategy long employed by its rival, finding allies in the wider region. China's influence as a trading partner, investor, creditor, diplomatic power, and, sometimes, intelligence and military partner has risen in South Asia. Bhutan is probably the only South Asian country where India has no serious worry about Chinese influence, but even there, on a visit to Thimphu, its sleepy, low-rise capital, one hears of Indian anger at perceived Chinese meddling.

Indian analysts had dubbed growing Chinese activity as a "string of pearls" approach, whereby Chinese military bases, plus economic and other influence, grew among countries that encircled India. China retorted that it was legitimate to want more say in the Indian Ocean ("it is not India's ocean," quipped a Chinese academic)—a vital route for China's container ships sent to Europe and America, and for imports of four-fifths of its oil. China also pushed for a role in South Asia's regional organization, SAARC, to Indian dismay. Any trip in the region showed a growing Chinese presence. Chinese tourists flocked to the Maldives, where a new Chinese embassy was the tallest building on the island capital, Male. A resort operator described having to adjust to the habits of his new visitors, as Chinese visitors collected crabs from beaches and boiled them in kettles in their rooms. Hotels in Sri Lanka saw influxes of Chinese guests. At a casino in Colombo, its main city, almost every table was occupied by Chinese gamblers, most smoking. Chinese state-backed firms had funded and built new highways and artificial harbors, reclaimed land in the sea beside the capital, and thrown up an airport and other big new projects in Sri Lanka. The process was almost always opaque, stitching up deals of uncertain benefit through local politicians who became extremely rich. All this left Sri Lanka's taxpayers indebted to China by an estimated $8.4 billion. India worried when a Chinese military submarine twice docked in Colombo harbor, in 2014. That happened soon after Chinese soldiers camped in Indian-claimed territory in the Himalayas, an early test for Modi as prime minister.

In Kathmandu, in Nepal, rumors spread of China gaining influence. A Nepalese man, a Chinese-speaker who managed the city's Confucius Center—China's official cultural outreach program—grumbled at length to me about meddling by his employer. He said China was trying to send staff along the low-lying Terrai, on the border with India, to influence the local population against the neighbor. Trade and investment from China were rising, as China helped to build dams to generate electricity from Himalayan rivers and sold manufactured goods. China also did deals with Nepal's police to prevent Tibetan refugees from fleeing through Nepal to claim asylum in India.

One place to see where China and India meet is Tawang. The drive I took up a mountain road from the northern plains to the town took two back-breaking days. The track twisted up a steep valley, where teams of Bengali and Bangladeshi laborers, many of them women, chipped at boulders with hammers and chisels. India's border defense forces patched mud and rocks into a path. At times, fog cut visibility to a few feet; my jeep could barely crawl along the cliff-side track. A river rushed in the valley far below, and gaps in thin vegetation revealed spots where an unfortunate bus or a car had previously gone over the edge. At higher altitude the land was exposed and unstable; rockslides were frequent. A bulldozer had to be dug from under a landslide and then a huge, fallen rock blasted before traffic could flow. When monsoon rains arrived, they carved deep new ravines in the soft hillside. The road coiled extravagantly back and forth, snaking up the steep mountain.

At a roadside monastery, monks spun cylindrical, tinkling prayer wheels, and gardeners snipped at perfect lawns with tiny sheers. Soldiers from a military camp walked hand-in-hand to a dairy, clanking tin milk churns. More hours of driving brought a traditional Tibetan gate at 13,700 feet and the Se La pass, once the northern extent of British rule. Beyond was Tawang, with a white-walled Tibetan monastery, an impressive, if smaller, version of the fortress-like city in Lhasa, decked with fluttering prayer flags and banners. Autumn flowers decorated the roadside. Local people had high cheekbones, jet black hair, and round faces—more Tibetan than typically Indian. Many were dressed in traditional red and purple clothes, with yak-wool hats, as they sat under parasols to listen to a revered Buddhist leader. A tree-covered valley fell away to one side of Tawang; great peaks rose behind. Young monks walloped cricket balls on a patch of grass; street markets were crammed with Chinese crockery, plastic toys, and other trinkets smuggled over the border.

It was impossible to forget that the frontier between India and China lay nearby. Military helicopters thudded past. On a walk around town an individual who was unmistakably a plain-clothes policeman, in an ill-fitting shiny suit and sunglasses, asked if I had a permit to visit. But Tawang's residents were welcoming. Elders recalled China's invasion of India in 1962 and the panic among Indian forces who had burned bridges and houses as they retreated. The invaders behaved reasonably well, some helping to gather the harvest. Older folk at the monastery, too, related this historical event—once again, to the chimes of spinning prayer wheels and the steady murmur of recited prayers. People said the Indian soldiers, though some were brave, had been easily swept aside. The defenders were ill-equipped with weapons dating from World War I and dressed in thin cotton shirts suitable only for the warm plains below.

Indian soldiers' incursions into Tibet had provoked China. An elderly man, Karma Wangchuk, in Indian intelligence in 1962, recalled how he hid in long grass to count the approaching tough, young Chinese soldiers, "some in white hats," pouring south. He fled when his tally got beyond 500 and bullets flew at him. The Venerable Lobsang Norbu, a seventy-seven-year-old monk who presided over a hilltop monastery nearby, described a "very horrible" war, remembering how flares lit up the night and gunfire erupted. Terrified villagers and monks fled through forests of pine and rhododendron to Bhutan. Many of India's outgunned soldiers ran just as quickly. Some weeks later, late in 1962, China's soldiers withdrew again across the line-of-actual-control, with China fearing it would be seen as an aggressor by neutrals. In any case, it had taken, and still holds, the mountain territory it cared about most: land farther west, in Kashmir, called Aksai Chin that connects Tibet proper to another remote region, Xinjiang. The 1962 war, which killed over 4,500 people, remained a painful scar for India and a reminder that China could pose a threat again. In China, however, the clash is barely recalled.

In India the war is better remembered because it could be repeated. On maps and in newspapers China still claims Tawang and much of the state of Arunachal Pradesh—around 31,000 square miles of land, an area it calls "south Tibet." Its diplomats once offered India a deal for each country to count territory it already controlled as legitimate. India foolishly declined, reluctant to legitimize the seizure of Aksai Chin. Chinese diplomats in Delhi said they doubted that the offer could come again. Though the two countries held regular talks on border management, they made no progress on settling their dispute, leaving India vulnerable. China remained the vastly stronger, occupying higher territory, with better roads and even a railway near the border, allowing much faster mobilization. On the Indian side the only choice was to follow the steep, difficult roads or rely on air travel. Some Indian strategists also worried that China would exploit Tibet's rivers intensively, upstream of India, where perhaps 200,000 megawatts of energy could be generated. A Chinese academic once described how engineers "could send power from Yarlung Tsangpo River in Tibet to east or southern China."[2] That river becomes the Brahmaputra in India, and any talk of diverting it, though an unlikely engineering prospect, sent jitters downstream.

Indian politicians in the northeast complained that China prevented investment in their remote bit of the country. China could be capricious: it blocked the Asian Development Bank from funding a big hydropower project in the area, and by issuing visas to residents of Arunachal Pradesh only on stapled pieces of paper it signaled that it did not recognize Indian authority over the state. (India might have chosen to retaliate—for example, by saying it did not recognize Chinese authority over Tibet—but did not.) Modi said he would boost the army and improve border infrastructure, and he promised a more muscular frontier border policy. Four new divisions, some 70,000 extra soldiers, were supposed to be deployed on the Indian side, but progress came only slowly. In total, some 500,000 Chinese and Indian soldiers would be poised to confront each other on this border. Infantry patrols criss-crossed the disputed territory, scattering litter—Indian snack packets, Chinese noodle wrappers—to mark their presence.

Modi considered the relationship with China to be a foreign policy priority. Late in 2014, he welcomed President Xi within a few months of becoming prime minister, first in Gujarat, then in Delhi. He called for Chinese investment in manufacturing, and for a general boost in trade and other ties. The mood of that trip, however, was spoiled when hundreds of Chinese soldiers were found camping several miles into Indian-claimed territory in the Himalayas. They left only after a three-week standoff with Indian forces. Reportedly Modi chided Xi in a personal meeting, saying that his soldiers should not become "like the Pakistani army." Sources in China later said that Xi had ordered his army not to repeat the infiltration, but it is hard to imagine that the Chinese leader had not known of the incursion beforehand, or had not permitted it to continue for three weeks.

The next year Modi visited China, where his hosts organized stage-managed crowds to chant his name. The visit had plenty of pomp, but nothing of substance was announced. Modi, in an interview with me the night before his trip, spoke of his affection for China, recalling that "the first visa stamp on my passport for China was fixed many years ago when I first traveled for the Kailash Mansarovar Yatra. This is a holy pilgrimage site [to a mountain revered by Hindus, Jains, and Buddhists] in China. That was a spiritual journey which will leave an indelible mark on not only this life but also on my next." He spoke of finding inspiration in China for more practical reasons: "I have also visited as chief minister on Chinese invitation a couple of times. If one analyzes China, one can say that it has made a great progress economically. It has definitely modernized its infrastructure, and doing things in the large scale is in its very nature and behavior." He accepted the potential for rivalry: "I think the whole world knows that there is an unresolved border dispute between India and China. Nobody denies that. But I think both the countries, through dialogue and discussion, have chosen a path to address the question. Talks are going on, meetings are taking place. I feel that despite border disputes, there is a good economic cooperation between the two countries. I think we have made successful progress."

Confrontations between China and India at least were restrained. Standoffs between soldiers rarely involved any firing of weapons. Soldiers waved flags, held up banners or placards, and dug in to create forward bases. When friction did occur, it was typically because of domestic factors. A year before the Chinese army incursion into Indian territory that Modi had to deal with, in 2014, it had been Manmohan Singh who had to confront the fact of Chinese soldiers camped on Indian-claimed territory in the Himalayas. In 2013, as China saw a once-in-a-decade change of leadership, tension grew on the border.

When China's new prime minister was about to pay an official trip to India, Chinese troops were found camping 12 miles inside mountain territory that India called its own—a preview of the events in 2014 to test Modi's response. When Li Keqiang arrived in Delhi he talked about "maturing" and "strategic" relations, and spoke poetically of handshakes over the Himalayas. He dismissed the mountain standoff as "a few clouds in the sky [that] cannot shut out the brilliant rays of our friendship." A Chinese diplomat in Delhi argued that the confrontation was really evidence of an internal clash between China's army and its civilian leaders—the army's way of putting pressure on their own diplomats and civilian leaders. "Don't see China as homogenous," he advised. At the time, Modi, in opposition, tweeted that India's government was "absolutely lax in securing Indian borders," vowing that if he were prime minister, nothing of the sort would happen again. It did, of course.

India might have been vulnerable in the mountains, but it had another hand to play—at sea. Its top-heavy, triangular landmass resembles, on a map, a fat arrowhead pointing to the Indian Ocean. Delhi strategists, preoccupied by land borders, often neglected India's strength as a maritime country with an immensely long coastline and near neighbors such as Singapore, Indonesia, and Thailand. But strategic thinkers in Chennai, on the southeast coast, paid the sea more attention. They urged policymakers to promote India's naval power. A useful place to get a perspective on that was from the Andaman and Nicobar islands in the Bay of Bengal, 750 miles east of the Indian mainland. The forest-covered islands—there were 572, mostly uninhabited, with sandy beaches, small bays, and beautiful coves—loomed out of the ocean. These had areas, including on tiny islands, that supposedly protected the last remaining populations of tribal people in India who had little or no contact with outsiders. Indigenous people were extremely vulnerable: of various groups, including Great Andamanese, Jarawa, Onge, and Sentinelese, just a few hundred people remained in 2016. As roads were built, development grew, and tourism spread, those pre-modern lives were disturbed and in some cases destroyed.

The islands almost touch the coasts of Thailand and Myanmar, stretching 450 miles, north to south, across the wide approach to the Malacca Strait, which connects the Indian and Pacific Oceans. In Port Blair, the islands' capital, there were palm-fringed bays and an islet with the ghostly remains of a Victorian-era British town. Its red-brick barracks, ballroom, and Presbyterian church were strangled by monstrous banyan trees. On another shore was the headquarters of India's only tri-service—army, air, and navy—military command. At a nearby wharf, warships formed a line, white ensigns flapping. A frigate passed, heading to the Bay of Bengal.

For natural disciples of late-nineteenth-century strategists who saw geography and sea power as destiny, the Andaman Islands were a great military asset—the equivalent of a huge, moored fleet of aircraft carriers where a navy could in theory block Chinese trade through the Indian Ocean. Some strategists imagined the islands as an anchor for India's broad commercial, diplomatic, and military strategy of reaching out east. "It is geography" that matters, said Ajay Singh, an ex–tank commander who governed the Andamans from a wood-paneled office, with jungle nearby. He pored over maritime charts and discussed how the strait was one of the world's busiest sea routes, with more than one thousand ships running through it every week. "We have a large say in the Bay of Bengal. We have become a net security provider," he said. "The mind-set in the early years was that the Andamans are a liability," he continued. "There was an outpost mentality, which we are changing to a springboard mentality."

Populated for thousands of years by indigenous tribes, the Andamans were subsequently used as little more than a penal colony by British colonial rulers who needed somewhere to dump political prisoners. India also treated the Andamans as a backwater, too costly to supply or defend heavily. But as India's attention turned more to the East, and as it sought closer ties with other Asian democracies, its navy obtained a growing share of India's military budget—some $6 billion a year. In the Andamans the naval force is set to double by the early 2020s, to thirty-two sea-going vessels. The number of soldiers on the islands would also double, to six thousand. None of that would worry China much. The launch, in 2013, of India's first home-built aircraft carrier drew some attention in China, but its own navy, with 150 ships, was already three times larger.

Hawks in India said that a more capable Indian navy, cooperating with American and other ones, could use the Andamans as a "choke-point," disrupting Chinese trade and oil imports in some future confrontation. Some Chinese naval strategists also wrote of Indian designs to drop an "iron curtain" there. Activity was certainly growing. A new Indian air base was opened on Great Nicobar Island, as its prince, Rashid Yusoof, explained to me over dinner in Port Blair one night. Yusoof had smart plans to use tourism to develop his territory, but also watched warily as a military expansion gathered momentum. The runway brought Indian military aircraft several hundred miles closer than before to the Malacca Strait, within striking distance of the South China Sea. Other airstrips were reportedly being built or lengthened to handle big aircraft, such as Hercules transport planes. Airfields for helicopters would follow. Regular naval exercises centered on the Andamans involved forces from America, Japan, Australia, and other democracies in Asia.

It was evident from the mountains to the ocean, and in every neighboring country, that India was growing increasingly conscious of the importance of China as a security presence. Modi, and any successor, would have to combine an economic policy of reaching out to China for capital and trade with a security policy of preparing for future rivalry. For the next few decades, India, despite its nuclear weapons, will remain at an acute disadvantage to China. But its strength would be greater if it took another big step: developing a much closer relationship with an even more dominant power in the region, America.

13

AMERICA CALLS

WHEN THE AMERICAN PRESIDENT PAID HIS SECOND OFFI-
cial visit to India, in 2015, he shortened his life by six hours.
Environmentalists calculated that the three days Barack Obama
spent breathing the foul air of the Indian capital—during which, for
example, he reviewed a Republic Day military parade—would on average trim his life by that much. Perhaps it was time well spent. Obama
spoke eloquently, as ever, pointing out similarities between the two big
democracies, such as the mobility of the people within them, and noting how two figures, political outsiders, each with a relatively humble
background, could reach the highest office in their respective lands.

Strong parallels exist between America and India: both are conti-
nental-sized, federal democracies, relatively isolated by geography, with
big, multi-ethnic and multi-religious populations. Both have populations that are also—compared with Europeans, for example—religious
minded, but do not let any religion entirely dominate public affairs.
Each has a history of being under, then shaking off, British colonial

rule. That helped to produce a legacy of elites (at least) who speak English, laws that enshrine respect for individual property rights, independent courts, a mostly free press, and power divided between various institutions, both in central government and in states. Those divisions of power will, hopefully, constrain any demagogic leader. And large, privately owned and publicly listed companies have clout, including political influence. India's remarkably liberal constitution has drawn inspiration from America's. Meanwhile, an increasingly influential Indian diaspora has grown successful and large in America—one that is taking part in the tech economy especially.

Obama's trip took place in the context of America claiming to be making a "pivot" to pay more attention to Asia—although under Obama, America appeared to be a less assertive, more cautious actor in terms of promoting its military and economic heft abroad, including in Asia. Analysts and politicians in the region talked of this century as somehow "belonging" to Asia, meaning that soaring populations, economic growth, and rising military and other power were all becoming irresistible facts in the region. Just how the South Asian subcontinental part of Asia fitted into this broad narrative of a resurgent Asia was unclear. Those most confident about India took to making bold but vague claims about its coming importance, but details—as ever—were missing. Soon after becoming prime minister, Narendra Modi had told Indians, "I want to take all of you with me to take this country forward," and promised, vaguely, to "make the twenty-first century India's century." In fact, India's main preoccupation was modest—trying to catch up with living standards seen elsewhere in Asia, to become a comfortably mid-income economy sooner rather than later.

To get stronger, India needed closer ties with America. It had to open up more to the rest of the world; draw in foreign capital, technology, and expertise; and raise standards in its industry and beyond. Its foreign policy after independence had been deliberately modest and introverted—it had adopted a semi-ostrich position, turning its back on outsiders. It grew isolated from much trade and investment, especially under Indira Gandhi, though it allowed aid to flow in. Just as most of the rest of Asia began to prosper from more open trade, from the 1970s and 1980s onward, India was banning Coca-Cola (from 1977 to 1993) and other symbols of foreign economic imperialism, imposing high tariffs on imports of most goods, keeping out foreign capital, and restricting who could, for example, get foreign currency. In diplomacy India was "nonaligned," taking no side in the Cold War. It avoided costly international entanglements and conflicts, but also influenced few events beyond its immediate region.

At times India had accepted closer ties with America and the West. After independence India acquired British military gear, including warships, though the Soviet Union became a more important supplier of military equipment. In 1962, when China's army invaded, Nehru asked America for urgent diplomatic and military help and won quick support. In the 1960s relations between America and India remained friendly, as American president John F. Kennedy and others showed affection for India, mostly as a recipient of aid, funnelled, for example, through the Ford Foundation. The Green Revolution, whereby India became self-sufficient in grain, owed much to American scientific help, notably from Norman Borlaug. But in the 1970s, and beyond, relations cooled. Richard Nixon as president favored Pakistan's military leaders over Indian democratic ones. Pakistan offered a means to connect secretly with China and, as Gary Bass describes well in his book *Blood Telegram,* Nixon supported Pakistan's military junta in 1971 as it conducted a near genocide in East Pakistan, now Bangladesh, displacing some 10 million people into India. When Indira Gandhi complained, Nixon and Kissinger dismissed India's leader, in private conversations recorded at the White House, as a "bitch" and a "witch."

One reason for American suspicion of India was that Indira Gandhi had tilted India more closely to the Soviet Union, even after the Soviet invasion of Afghanistan in 1979. Meanwhile, America kept up close ties with India's rival, Pakistan. In the 1980s America and Pakistan together funded and armed Islamist insurgents in Afghanistan to fight Soviet occupiers, and American military aid inevitably bolstered Pakistan against India. After the Cold War, America and Pakistan cooperated against some Islamist extremist groups, but Pakistan's army supported others that attacked India, notably in Kashmir and Afghanistan. Nuclear tests by both India and Pakistan, and the Kargil war of 1999, kept American attention on South Asia. But from the 1990s onward, India's economic openness and its rising economic potential generated warmer relations with America. Meanwhile, India saw less benefit from state-directed trade and close relations with Russia. After successful visits to India by Bill Clinton and George W. Bush, relations improved steadily, continuing with Obama's two official trips.

By the end of Obama's administration, India and America were closer partners than at any point in their history. Despite occasional frustration—for example, over whether America allowed the transfer of enough high-end military technology—the two countries were set on improving ties. Modi, running ahead of his foreign policy establishment, called the countries "natural allies" (Indian policymakers shunned talk of having any ally) and made four substantial visits to America within roughly two years of becoming India's leader. Senior American officials said they had "taken a bet" on India. That meant more military, intelligence, energy, and other security cooperation; closer diplomatic ties; and the promotion of more trade, investment, and other economic links, including the manufacture in India of military gear by American firms. India reduced the intensity of its ties with Russia as it grew more comfortable with close links with Japan, Australia, Israel, and the West, including Europe.

What changed? Personalities mattered. Modi built on initiatives of his predecessors, notably Atal Bihari Vajpayee and Manmohan Singh, just as Obama developed his pro-India stance from efforts begun by Bill Clinton and George W. Bush. In the 2000s Bush's national security adviser, Condoleezza Rice, and others had sought to bring

India closer—for example, by pushing for cooperation on civil nuclear power. Yet the bigger changes were strategic, not the result of individual leaders.

Almost whoever came to office, in either country, was likely to continue the friendly process. American policymakers calculated that India's usefulness as a partner would increase, if from a low base. As long as India stayed mostly poor, closed, and inward-looking, with little military or economic heft (and a big chip on its shoulder about the superiority of its "nonalignment" stance), its wider influence would be modest. India's contribution to wider international affairs had previously amounted mostly to lectures and moralizing, notably by Jawaharlal Nehru. Yet after India showed itself to be an emerging consumer market, a destination for investment and a source of outward capital flows, a partner for trade (one open to foreign firms), a driver of wider economic activity, and a country with influence over neighbors and in international institutions, outsiders started taking it more seriously.

That began tentatively in the 1990s, after the liberalizing reforms of 1991 by Narasimha Rao and Manmohan Singh, and as India developed its telecoms, IT, outsourcing, and pharmaceutical giants. The IT and outsourcing industry in India was worth $100 billion yearly by 2016. At over $2 trillion, its overall economy is bigger than Canada's or Russia's. It is also larger than the economy of Italy or Brazil, and by 2030 it could overtake that of France, Britain, Germany, or Japan. India is turning into a big (if still fragmented) market for outsiders to tap. It is still a minnow in trade terms, accounting for a little over 2 percent of world trade in 2015, but it is growing. In 1991 India's foreign trade was worth the equivalent of about one-sixth of its GDP, low for an emerging economy; by 2015 this figure had risen to about one-half, a big share for such a large country—higher than in China, for example.

Since the late 1990s, India has also emerged as a military and diplomatic power. Previously it claimed to matter because its army had 2 million serving and reserve soldiers, it supplied many UN peacekeepers, and its navy could reach far out to sea. It had emerged as a sizable donor by 2015, with an aid budget counted in billions of dollars (most went to Bhutan, Afghanistan, Bangladesh, and others in its region, plus to Africa), building on an old practice of giving technical help to poor countries. But India had kept its global influence modest. Individual diplomats could be excellent, but they formed a small, closed shop: in 2015 India's foreign service, with around eight hundred diplomats, was about one-fifth the size of China's corps (if you included the staff in Delhi, the number was nearer two thousand). India had roughly as many diplomats as Singapore or New Zealand, hardly a sign of a great power.

Yet India's ambition had grown. It campaigned for a permanent seat on the UN Security Council. Its military and diplomatic heft expanded after it tested five nuclear bomb devices in May 1998, then repelled an incursion by Pakistani soldiers in Kargil. The nuclear tests first provoked hostility from Britain and America (tempered after Pakistan did its own), but over time they meant that India was seen as a more serious military force. Growing expertise with its space program had a similar effect. India and America also began to cooperate against terrorists and Islamist extremist groups in third countries, sharing some intelligence.

The countries worked together in Afghanistan after the removal of the Taliban government in 2001, and India became the fifth-largest donor there. India kept close ties to Hamid Karzai when he was Afghan president, and then with his successor, Ashraf Ghani, and generally had good relations with rulers in Kabul who were suspicious of Pakistan for supporting the Taliban. Policymakers in India and America shared a growing frustration because of violence in Afghanistan blamed on groups loyal to, even directed by, Pakistan's military spies. Extremist Islamist groups, usually Pashtuns, backed by the military spy agency in Rawalpindi attacked the embassies of both India and America in Kabul. The killing of Osama bin Laden in Abbottabad, in May 2011, brought the nadir of America-Pakistan relations—and thus a boost to America-India ties.

Behind the friendlier diplomacy, America became a more important supplier of high-technology military goods to India (as did Israel, France, and Britain). In 2015 an estimated $10 billion worth of American defense goods were on order to India, or had recently been supplied, with a similar quantity expected to follow. Russia remained a big source of more basic gear, but its goods were gradually supplanted by higher-tech ones from the West. As Modi launched a "Make in India" policy to promote local manufacturing, his government raised a cap on foreigners investing in local defense firms. American and Japanese companies were the likeliest to invest. Defense ties grew. Late in 2015 America's ambassador to India, Richard Verma, bragged of a "remarkable expansion of bilateral training, exercises, and sales of advanced weapons systems to the Indian military. Our defense industrial systems are now co-operating on the co-production of new technology that will be used by our respective armed forces." He pointed out that "India engages in more bilateral exercises with the United States than it does with any other country."[1]

Indian and American officials also sought ways for American energy firms to invest in civil-nuclear power stations. A civil-nuclear deal struck in 2005 was the biggest symbol of closer ties, promoted by American policymakers such as Ashley Tellis. He saw Indian relations with America getting warmer. But whether American investment in nuclear power would come to India remained unclear, because of doubts over who had liability in case of an accident like the one in Fukushima, Japan, in 2011. Indian politicians were also sensitive after the chemicals plant disaster in Bhopal, India, in 1984, involving an American firm, Union Carbide (now part of Dow Chemicals). The Bhopal disaster killed at least 3,800 people, and possibly four times as many as that. Obama in 2015 said there had been a "breakthrough in understanding" on nuclear liability, but investors were slow in coming.

The US-India relationship was not all roses. A spat had erupted over an Indian diplomat arrested and ill-treated by New York police in 2013. She was accused of visa fraud and submitting false documents to secure a work visa for her Indian maid. India's diplomats let the fuss overshadow other concerns. In another potential confrontation, soon after Modi came to office, India and America disagreed over a global trade deal previously struck at the World Trade Organization. One of Modi's first international acts as prime minister was to align India with Venezuela in blocking the agreement to open trade, an unedifying start for a man who promised economic progress. India and America later negotiated a compromise.

Such moments apart, the relationship warmed. The diaspora was a big factor: growing numbers of people of Indian heritage grew influential in the West, especially America. Indians had long found inspiration and influence abroad. Mohandas Gandhi studied law in London and found his early vocation in helping fellow Indians fight discrimination in South Africa. One of his fiercest Hindu nationalist opponents, Vinayak Damodar Savarkar, also went to London—the two men met when Savarkar, an enthusiastic meat-eater, disparaged vegetarian Gandhi as feeble and a sissy. Nehru, India's anglophile first prime minister, was educated in Britain, as was his daughter Indira Gandhi. In turn her son, Rajiv Gandhi, met his Italian wife, Sonia Gandhi, in a café in Cambridge, Britain. And their son, Rahul Gandhi, went to college both in Britain and in America, and he worked for a time in London. India's elite, in other words, long had exposure to the West.

A mass exodus of young and educated Indians was more important. Huge numbers settled permanently or worked temporarily overseas. Over 28 million people of Indian heritage were abroad by 2016—as numerous as the population of Malaysia. Indians overseas remitted $70 billion a year, equal to 3.5 percent of GDP, often outstripping flows of foreign direct investment. The migrants helped to fund economic and human progress back home—or at least paid for lots of consumption—in states like Kerala that exported skilled workers, notably to the Gulf. Twice as many Indians as Qataris lived in Qatar. In Dubai around 80 percent of the population were foreigners, roughly half of them from India.

Otherwise, it was notably English-speaking democracies that welcomed Indian students and migrants, in America, Canada, Britain, Australia, South Africa, and Singapore. The diaspora in America, 3.3 million strong, proved to be remarkably successful. In the twentieth century many were of Gujarati descent: Patels dominated America's hotel industry, just as Gujarati traders from western India avidly ruled the roost in Britain's corner shops and a previous generation flourished in east Africa. Modi, a Gujarati though not a Patel, had long hankered for a close relationship with America and was personally fascinated by the diaspora.

He discussed trips to America as a younger man, and was unusually animated when describing travel as a backpacker. In the 1990s he relied partly on Hindu nationalist families in the diaspora. He also spoke of his fondness for Delta Airlines in America: "You could buy a ticket for $500 that lasted a month and allowed you to take as many trips as you like. . . . I used to book long journeys to travel at night, so I could sleep on the plane and avoid the cost of hotels. The conditions were you could bring no luggage. So I traveled and traveled, I explored America. I visited twenty-nine states, I don't think many people have done that." He laughed, proud of getting by frugally, always washing his only spare change of clothes, living up to a Gujarati stereotype of eking out money.

In 1994 Modi took a sponsored tour of America. One photo from it shows him posing in the sunshine, wearing a cream-colored kurta over white trousers, at the railings at the White House. In another he was at Universal Studios, Hollywood, perched on a raised flower bed. A third had him by the wheel of a boat touring a harbor. He traveled with an Indian delegation, brought by a US-government scheme, the American Council of Young Political Leaders. Its aim was to help early- or mid-career Indian politicians to better understand America, and for Americans to forge relationships with rising political figures. In each picture Modi wore a different outfit. A journalist who has known him since the early 1990s said the politician visited America whenever he could, to promote Hindu nationalism among the diaspora, and to learn. "He is a learner, he wants to expand his vision," said the writer in his office in Ahmedabad.

As a rising leader in the Bharatiya Janata Party, Modi addressed Indians abroad and stayed in their homes. A wealthy family in Boston once gave him a flashy computer even though as a *pracharak,* a preacher in the Hindu nationalist movement, he was supposed to refuse lavish presents. Envious rivals at home sometimes grumbled about how he came back from foreign trips with expensive shoes, watches, or gadgets. He craved material things, including pricey clothes, spectacles, and pens. In Ahmedabad his tailor, Bipin Chauhan, said Modi was unabashed, telling him that "for my clothes, my eyes, my voice, and my work I never compromise."

Modi also went with party leaders to America, raising funds for the BJP and getting support from Indians abroad. "He is fond of traveling, he went to America. . . . He is living for himself, he went just to travel, for sight-seeing," grumbled Shankersinh Vaghela, a former party colleague and former leader within the Hindu nationalist movement, who had become a bitter opponent in Gujarat. An American embassy official in Delhi said Modi had benefited again from another trip, thanks to American government funds, in 1999, as part of a program of the Fulbright American Studies Institute. Modi spoke fondly to me of these visits, recalling how he joined a "young diplomat" course for a month and took part in a Congress of World Religions in America. Ironically, the man who did so well from American largesse, as prime minister later cracked down on "foreign-funded" non-governmental groups, such as the Ford Foundation, as his ardent nationalist supporters condemned outsiders' influence on India.

Modi played up his ties with America. He reminisced with Obama, claiming that a biography of Benjamin Franklin had helped to inspire his own rise from a humble background to high politics. He called the American president "Barack" and frequently hugged him (and others, including Facebook's Mark Zuckerberg later and, once, me). He and Obama exchanged anecdotes about standing outside the White House, neither dreaming that each would find his way inside. Modi as prime minister also relished getting among the diaspora. He held rallies at Madison Square Garden, in New York, in 2014, in Australia the same year, then in San Francisco, and he spoke before a crowd of over 70,000 in London in 2015. Many in the diaspora favored Modi, donating to his campaign, staffing much of his social-media efforts, even volunteering on the ground in India. During the 2014 election it was not unusual, even in remote rural areas of north India, to bump into enthusiastic volunteers with North American accents, on holiday from Houston or Vancouver, who believed in strongman Modi.

It helped bilateral relations that, within America, people of Indian descent were getting more influential. The flow of educated young Indian graduates to America has surged during this century. In 2015 alone, 130,000 Indian students applied to study there, 40 percent more than the year before. Not all made it, but if you counted others who traveled for work, it was likely that some 150,000 Indians came to America yearly—and 90 percent remained. Devesh Kapur, an academic who studied the diaspora, described a "flood" of Indian immigrants: over half of all Indian-born people in America had arrived after 2000.[2]

Gujarati motel owners gave way to educated migrants from the big southern state of Andhra Pradesh. The Indian minority in America became recognized as professional, highly qualified, rich, and successful. They began to outstrip other minorities on the usual measures of success such as average income or years of education. One telling sign, explained Kapur after studying census returns, was that migrants (or children of migrants) from Pakistan or Bangladesh often preferred to identify themselves as Indian. Many Indian migrants—42 percent— held graduate degrees or higher in 2012; average household incomes were $99,000, roughly double that of average Americans. Over two-thirds of Indian Americans were in high-status jobs, such as management; over a quarter held the highest-paid, professional jobs.[3]

Indians were self-selecting: it was the most educated and dynamic individuals from the subcontinent's massive population who got to America. And America slurped in highly skilled graduates as fast as India produced them. From 1997 to 2013 half of all H-1B employment visas were issued to Indians. After 2009 the share rose to two-thirds. An estimated 91,000 Indian-born people with PhDs were living in America by 2015—a brain drain from India but also a base for creating stronger economic, cultural, and social ties between the two countries. Such networks had helped before: the 1990s boom in Indian IT was partly thanks to Indian-origin staff in Western companies who persuaded bosses to place back offices in India. Some of the most successful IT companies in India from the 1990s onward, such as Wipro and Infosys, had founders who returned from work or study in America.

People of Indian heritage headed tech and other companies overseas—such as Pepsi or Nokia in 2016—and earned leading positions in America's government. No one suggested that members of the diaspora unduly favored India, but they were certainly capable of showing understanding and cultural appreciation. Sanjay Puri, the chairman of USINPAC, the main political lobby for Indian Americans in Washington, DC, said that people with mixed identities could "push brand India without being disloyal to the country you are in." He also lauded Modi's long history of engaging the diaspora and praised "energy and discipline" in Modi's government. Puri brought Indian American business leaders to India, saying interest soared among a "very successful diaspora in the US, Canada, UK—a highly successful community" that was "looking to engage back again."

The diaspora mattered in American politics, said Puri: "Now we have two governors of Indian origin, senators, a surgeon general, the USAID boss, ambassador to India. This is a big change in the past ten years." He saw India becoming far more pro-Western: "When you look at values, interests, where does India align most? Where do technology, funding, and opportunities come from? It is mostly America or Japan, not China and Russia." Indians expected improved relations, urging relatives in America to emulate the Jewish-Israeli lobby in gaining public clout, donating to political parties, and more. A measure of the diaspora's influence was that schools in New York State closed for Diwali, the Hindu festival of lights. Barack Obama also celebrated Diwali in the White House. In October 2016 he became the first American president to light a *diya*, a lamp of symbolic importance to Hindus and others, in the Oval Office. In November of that year, Donald Trump, president-elect, chose Nikki Haley as US ambassador to the United Nations. Haley, whose parents had migrated from Amritsar, had been the second Indian-American to serve as a governor.

Shivshankar Menon, a former national security adviser, said Indian Americans helped to press America's Congress to approve the civil-nuclear agreement in 2005. Puri said the diaspora could lobby for America to supply more high technology, and natural gas, in the strategic interests of both countries. Indians became bigger donors to political parties in America, as social conservatives who were non-Christian. In Britain, too, wealthy people of Indian background grew politically active, notably in the Conservative Party.

One more factor helped to explain India's warming ties with the West: a mutual concern over the rise of China. Indians saw China as a rival. America was concerned that China challenged its primacy in Asia. When Obama talked of "rebalancing" or of America's pivot toward Asia, he meant that the American and Asian democracies (plus Vietnam) could cooperate to check the spreading influence of China. India and America in 2015 published a joint statement on security in Asia, for example, calling for all countries to ensure freedom of navigation in the South China Sea, where China's armed forces were becoming increasingly assertive. India also forged more intimate diplomatic and military ties with Japan, Australia, and other countries that were allied to, or in a close relationship with, America.

Opinion polls showed that India's public far preferred America over China. A survey by the Pew Research Center in 2016 found that 56 percent of respondents favored America, whereas 69 percent thought

China's growing military heft was a problem. Yet Indian strategists, like others in Asia, said they would refrain from forging an outright alliance with America. A residual fear lingered that China and America, both more powerful, could leave India out in the cold if their greater bilateral interests demanded it. And India would probably stop short of offering military support for America if this were ever demanded, as had happened in 1991 when India would not back the American-led coalition to evict Iraq's army from Kuwait.

Across Asia, India also had much further to go in building friendships. It did not engage in big regional institutions to improve trade and cooperation. For example, it had no part in the Trans-Pacific Partnership trade deal between America, Japan, and several other Asian countries in 2015. It was not a part of APEC, the Asia-Pacific Economic Cooperation. And though Manmohan Singh had implemented a trade deal with Southeast Asia, India's long decades of shunning trade and engagement with other countries left a legacy that would only slowly be undone.

A trend toward closer ties would continue, but the pace proved slower than it might have been, held back by India. Indian membership in the Nuclear Suppliers Group—a gathering of forty-eight powers that traded in nuclear material and agreed-upon anti-proliferation standards—would have been a big symbol of India's acceptance by other nuclear powers. America pressed for Indian membership, among other efforts to bring India into the fold of more open, trading nations. China appeared to veto Indian membership. Though Modi spoke of alliances and used the most pro-American rhetoric of any prime minister in memory, he delivered relatively slowly on the sort of economic reforms that outsiders, including American investors, believed India needed. India slowly opened up for foreign capital to be invested, and brought reforms to create a single market, but it remained a difficult place for foreigners to do business.

Overall, however, India will gain strength in foreign affairs and its alignment with America is likely to grow. The consequences of several broad trends make changes in this "Ultimate" sphere relatively straightforward to predict. Assuming India's economy really does gain weight in the coming decades, India's share of global trade will rise significantly, and it should become more closely plugged into global logistics chains. As a result, the country is bound to matter more to the economic prospects of others. As a big and populous nation, with a long history of democracy, India also will project forms of influence—soft power—that authoritarian rivals, such as China, will struggle to match. China under the authoritarian Xi Jinping is seen by neighbors in Asia, and beyond, as increasingly aggressive. Democratic India, though not especially loved by its immediate neighbors, is perceived as a potential ally, or at least a neutral force, by many in the region and beyond. Finally, India is likely to strengthen its diplomatic, trade, and military ties with Western democracies, in Europe and especially the United States, with the role of the diaspora destined to prove particularly significant. Together, these factors will see India's "Ultimate" power grow. How fast it grows will depend partly on domestic decisions, such as whether India gets around to appointing more diplomats, or how quickly the country really opens up its economy. But India's voice in the world is going to become louder—and on balance, that will be a welcome prospect.

PART 4

NATION—HOME

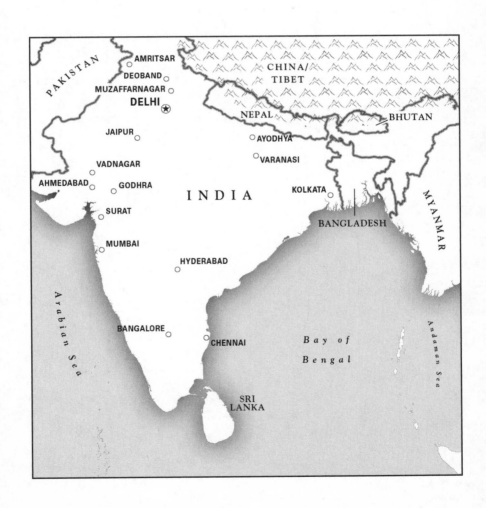

HINDUTVA NATION?

WHAT IS THE IDEA OF INDIA? AMONG SOME INDIANS, EVEN asking the question is provocative. Those closely aligned with the Hindu right grow impatient with others—usually more left-leaning—who talk of the secular values of India's constitution, refer to human rights and universal values, and are more likely to downplay culture and traditions linked to the Hinduism of the majority population. In turn, the more secular-minded worry that politicians who stir up Hindu identity, and appeal to voters based on culture and tradition, risk opening up, irreversibly, dangerous divisions. The idea of the Indian nation is contested, most broadly between those who define it by referring to traditions of its communities and those who refer instead to articles of the constitution and equal rights of all its individuals.

The fourth and final section in this book touches on the idea of the Indian nation. It considers whether the approach of the past seven decades, to celebrate (mostly) secular India rather than to emphasize the culture and religion of the majority, is giving way to something different. It would be a mistake, for example, to see Narendra Modi's 2014 election victory only in reference to his talk of *vikas* and the "ABCD of development." Economics mattered, but not exclusively. Culture and religion counted, too. A clever electoral strategy meant that Modi's message was tailored to particular audiences. In some parts of the country, especially the semi-rural, northern, and central areas, he appealed to religion, nationalism, and identity politics. He posed in front of a big poster of Lord Ram, to cheer Hindu nationalist voters in Uttar Pradesh. In Assam he lashed out against Muslim migrants, a couple of days after violence in which Muslims were killed.

He knew his subordinates stirred up rivalries of caste and religion in places where such things would have the most effect. Amit Shah, a close collaborator and rather sinister figure from Gujarat, delivered an immense victory in Uttar Pradesh, where the Bharatiya Janata Party (and an ally) took 73 of 80 parliamentary seats. More than anything, victory there decided the outcome of the overall election. Shah managed in part by exploiting Modi's identity as a member of the "Other Backward Classes" (OBC) category, urging members of the Jat community to back him. He also made the most of religious tension in the west of the state, around Muzaffarnagar, months after clashes killed sisty-two people there and helped to polarize voters. Shah told Jats to get "revenge" (against Muslims) at the ballot box. The Election Commission said he promoted "hatred and ill will" and banned him from campaigning. Yet Shah succeeded.

Modi's party did best partly because it proved more professional in running its ground operation, aided immensely by Hindu nationalist volunteers. Somewhat like the Christian evangelicals in America who became increasingly influential in the Republican Party from the 1980s onward, Hindu nationalists who were growing more active on the right of Indian politics were made use of by Modi. Ajeet Upadhyay, a graduate student with a smear of vermillion on his forehead, was typical. He and two friends spent months knocking on doors, for hours every day, registering six thousand voters in his corner of a constituency in Varanasi, in 2014. An organizer for a Hindu nationalist movement, he said two thousand activists in that town trooped out for Modi, to restore pride in "what the nation lost in the last one thousand years, the sons of the nation, the Hindus who originally belonged to this country."

The growing influence of the Hindu nationalist right can be seen by retracing the story of Narendra Modi's own life, beginning in Gujarat, in the west of India. A few hours' drive from Ahmedabad, the state's main city, is a small town called Vadnagar. It is scruffy, busy, and growing—three words that apply equally to most urban areas in South Asia. A walled, older corner of Vadnagar had been home to Modi's family. The town had a fifteenth-century temple and was supposedly inhabited continuously for at least the past two thousand years. It got a mention, under an earlier name, in the Mahabharata, India's great historic saga. It has stone archways, handsome carved wooden balconies, and narrow streets that preserve a medieval air. "See how beautiful it is," said my guide, Niyati, rather wistfully. "Somehow Modi's town has escaped from his juggernaut of development."

Modi's father had scratched out a living at a tea stall near the railway station: India's prime minister said, truthfully, he was "not from an elite club, but from a simple family." The day I visited the station, with its single track and corrugated iron roof, it had a solitary customer—a grey donkey, immobile on the platform—and nearby stood an old school friend of Modi's. Dasharathbhai Laxman Patel, who called Modi his "brother," was the town leader of the RSS (Rashtriya Swayamsevak Sangh), the national volunteer organization for Hindu nationalists. Formed in 1925 to oppose both British colonial rule and Muslim separatists, it was modeled in part on Italy's fascists, complete with a paramilitary-style uniform. Members called it the world's biggest non-governmental organization, with millions of adherents. Opponents likened it to other groups of religious fanatics, set on "cultural purification" and hostility to non-Hindus. Modi had been an avid member for almost all his life.

Patel recalled how he and Modi joined the youth wing of the RSS in the 1960s. Modi, from a relatively poor family, one of six children, enjoyed being away from home. The RSS offered distractions, an identity different from being a tea-seller's son, and perhaps it gave him the idea of escape to somewhere less parochial. Male youngsters met in the evenings to discuss patriotic subjects and the exploits of nationalist heroes. The mid-1960s were a time of recurrent tension and war. In 1962 China had humiliated India with its invasion in the north. Jawaharlal Nehru, the prime minister, died soon afterward. Then a border war erupted with Pakistan, in the west, in which India triumphed. Gujarat shares a border with Pakistan, although it is mostly empty desert and estuaries. Modi recalled watching soldiers at a nearby railway station on the way to the front line. The boys' discussions at gatherings of the RSS were often intense, not about frivolous matters like girls but about "doing something for the nation," said Patel. They spent evenings "roaming around the town, to do blackouts, looking for infiltrators," he said. Modi joined the junior National Cadet Corps, said another childhood friend. That involved parades, more history lessons, exercises, plus some rifle shooting. He never considered joining the army.

Life as a youngster in Vadnagar in the 1950s and 1960s was quiet. Patel spoke of street games like *kabbadi,* a team contact sport in which opponents tag and wrestle each other. "We would play 'short go,' a chasing game, '*kho kho*,' which was more like fighting, and 'I am Shivaji,' where boys competed to be the chief," he said, grinning. At weekends they swam in a nearby lake, where Modi once found a baby crocodile that he brought home and kept for a short time. Modi was known for dressing with care, in clothes made of terracotton, a cheap mix of polyester and cotton. He made gestures at community work. Patel recalled how "we once took brooms to clean the town and the Dalits [formerly known as untouchables], who were supposed to do the work, they sat, watched and mocked us." Modi later extended that youthful RSS effort into a national campaign to persuade Indians to "clean India."

The boys made meals together, recalled Patel, gathering curry, seeds, and vegetables before Modi led the cooking. "It was the same with the games, Modi would always be the captain," said Patel. They performed dramas, including one about villagers worshipping a prince's sandal in a temple. Modi always played the prince "and we were his underlings," he said. That fondness for drama and dressing up persisted throughout his career: Modi was intensely aware of how he presented himself, his posture, hand gestures, his tendency to hug others, and his dress sense. Showing off with a purpose was a recurring theme.

Modi's story at times appeared to be inspired by another renowned Hindu nationalist, Vinayak Damodar Savarkar, also from western India. Savarkar was an atheist, brilliant and personally brave, a man who campaigned against colonial rule and caste discrimination and who wanted to create a strong, successful India. But he was also a dangerously flawed, intolerant, divisive, and unsympathetic man. This founding figure of Hindu nationalism was a prolific writer; in the 1920s he invented the political term *Hindutva,* meaning "Hindu-ness," a belief that India, or Hindustan, must be run by and for the majority Hindus. (Hindutva paralleled an idea that eventually triumphed among Muslim hard-liners in Pakistan, that only certain types of Sunni Muslims were truly Pakistanis.) Before independence Savarkar fell out with the more appealing, inclusive figures who built independent India to be a secular, multi-religious, and tolerant place.

The likes of Mohandas (the Mahatma) Gandhi, Jawaharlal Nehru, and Bhimrao Ramji Ambedkar triumphed over Hindu zealots such as Savarkar and other RSS figures. Secular-minded thinkers defined the idea of India as an inclusive country, in which individuals could believe what they wished. They sought change through mostly peaceful methods such as strikes, protests, mass mobilization, and courting arrest. And though many Congress leaders were Hindu, they saw the need to accommodate India's many non-Hindus. Savarkar, by contrast, favored violence as a way of achieving political ends and grew to despise Gandhi's pacifism and tolerance toward India's Muslims. Suspected by the British of involvement in political murders, he famously once tried to escape arrest by diving through a porthole on a ship in harbor. He was jailed on the Andaman Islands (where his cell is now a tourist attraction).

Savarkar later sneered that Gandhi was "mealy-mouthed," a "crazy lunatic" who "happens to babble . . . [about] compassion, forgiveness."[1] He attacked Gandhi as a hypocrite, because the pacifist had worked as a stretcher bearer for the British in South Africa, during the Boer War, and later supported the British in World War I. Furious when Gandhi failed to prevent the secession of Pakistan from India at independence in 1947, Savarkar encouraged followers from Bombay who came to Delhi intent on violence. They went on to murder the Mahatma in 1948. Savarkar was arrested and tried as a conspirator in Gandhi's assassination, though he was found not guilty. A biographer of Savarkar once summed him up as "the first, and most original, prophet of extremism in India."[2]

Yet many Hindu nationalists, including Modi, celebrated Savarkar as a national hero. (A few Hindu extremists also celebrated those who were convicted of murdering Gandhi.) Modi paid homage to his portrait in parliament in Delhi, on his birthday, and in speeches called him an independence hero. Modi was perfectly happy to be associated with a strongman of the Hindu right. He inaugurated a website promoting Savarkar, calling him "largely unknown to the masses because of the vicious propaganda against him and misunderstanding around him," meaning Savarkar's arrest and trial over Gandhi's murder. Modi also tweeted about Savarkar's "tireless efforts towards the regeneration of our motherland."

Savarkar was an unappealing figure to venerate. Hindutva, even in its softest form, meant asserting an exclusive idea of India, drawing on its especially Hindu heritage and culture—rather like Europeans or Americans might talk of their Christian culture as the only legitimate element of their countries. Often, however, Hindutva was interpreted to mean something much harder—namely, the excluding of non-Hindus as illegitimate or incomplete Indians. Extremists tried to convert others to Hinduism or used violence. Modi repeated phrases that were stock Hindutva complaints, drawn over the decades from the likes of Savarkar. For example, during his maiden speech in India's parliament, in 2014, he spoke of ending "1,200 years of mental slavery" in India, a crude (and not entirely accurate) reference to the period in which Islamic ideas and Mughal rule, plus European colonial ideas and rule, came to the sub-continent. Modi was not the only leader in Asia to use history to whip up nationalist fervor—Shinzo Abe in Japan and Xi Jinping in China exploited particular versions of the past to bolster themselves. Europe and America, too, saw notably ugly nationalism rise in the 2010s. But Modi's approach in India, where religious clashes were always possible, looked dangerously divisive.

Savarkar had called Muslims and other non-Hindus alien and separate. He wrote of his delight as a twelve-year-old, in what is now Maharashtra, neighboring Gujarat, at leading a gang of schoolmates to stone his village mosque, smashing windows and tiles, after riots between Hindus and Muslims. He told how "we vandalised the mosque to our heart's content,"[3] before he and his pals wielded knives and sticks to chase off Muslim youngsters who objected. In 1937 he wrote of "two antagonistic nations living side by side in India,"[4] and urged Hindus to adopt what he called Muslims' more warlike behavior. The phrase *two nations* was significant, for it suggested that Muslims and Hindus were irreconcilable. When Muslim figures used it, they did so to call for a separate homeland. When Savarkar used it, it was not clear if he agreed that Muslims should be ushered out of India. He certainly wanted Hindus to dominate: "I want all Hindus to get themselves re-animated and re-born into a martial race," he said.[5] To help this come about, he had become leader of the Hindu Mahasabha, an extreme-right body, from which the RSS emerged.

Modi also called himself an adherent of Hindutva and said he saw nothing wrong in it. However, as a child he was not obviously a rabble-rouser in the mold of Savarkar. Patel told of occasional playground scraps with Muslim children, but called the confrontations a mere *bega*, meaning a verbal clash that turns to blows. An Indian sociologist, Ashis Nandy, writing in 2002, was far more damning. He recalled meeting Modi and concluded he was a "fascist," with an "authoritarian personality," showing a "puritanical rigidity, narrowing of emotional life, massive use of the ego defence of projection, denial and fear of his own passions combined with fantasies of violence." Nandy also saw within him a "matrix of clear paranoid and obsessive personality traits" and described Modi as an individual who saw "cosmic conspiracy against India," and every Muslim as a potential terrorist.[6]

In Vadnagar, among Modi's friends and relatives, there was only evidence of a community relatively at ease with different religions. A street-side Sufi Muslim shrine sat just beyond a beautiful stone gate in the old town wall. Inside the ancient town, a tiny medical clinic had a wall adorned with a poster showing Swami Vivekananda, an even stronger hero for Modi and an early, moderate promoter of Hinduism, depicted as "The Hindoo Monk of India." Another wall displayed the painting of a Hindu God riding on a tiger. Dr. Sudhir Chandrakandhi Joshi, with a brown striped shirt over his thin frame, said he had studied beside Modi for eight years, calling him driven but not bookish. He said Modi mostly read about Swami Vivekananda and about Ramakrishna Paramhansa, the Swami's teacher. Modi's real interests from the age of fourteen, when he won his first class election, were politics and theater. Joshi recalled that Modi won a school prize for performing the story of a nineteenth-century Gujarati, Jogidas Khuman, a Robin Hood–type figure who looted enemy villages. (Khuman was evidently a prudish sort of hero, who once said he doused his eyeballs with chilli powder to "punish my eyes" for looking at a beautiful woman.) As for politics, Joshi said that Modi was "very passionate with the Jan Sangh [another Hindu nationalist group], and then the RSS. There was always this leadership quality."

The town was home to the usual South Asian collection of barber shacks, paan shops, ice-cream stalls, carts laden with onions, and a few solar-powered street lights, plus a stall jammed with tin sousaphones and other instruments for delightfully noisy wedding parties. Few people showed much warmth for their most famous son, however, perhaps because Modi in adulthood had mostly shunned his family and town. At Modi's inauguration as prime minister, thousands of guests were invited, but none of his own family. Officials had urged Modi at least to invite his mother, but the prime minister refused. Though he had made occasional, much-publicized visits to his aging mother, he had spent little of his adult life in her company. Residents of the town recalled a cursory trip he took in order to attend his father's funeral, but mostly the family, including brothers, were kept at arm's length. One interpretation was that Modi wished to show that no relative would get political favors, or pose as a middleman for tycoons seeking opportunities. Another theory suggested he had deeply absorbed the solitary habits of being an RSS *pracharak*.

In one narrow street many households shared the name Modi. The family belonged to the Ghanchi caste, who by tradition pressed cooking oil. In the hierarchy of the Hindu caste system, Ghanchis fell into a broader category now known as the OBC (which, as noted earlier, stands for "Other Backward Classes"). These were by tradition not as deprived as many, such as the sub-caste Dalits, but they were less privileged than, for example, Brahmins, the scholar caste. Modi was only the second OBC to become prime minister. A part of his appeal to middle India was his ability to reach out to other "mid-level" caste groups, like the Jats in states such as Uttar Pradesh, and to suggest that he understood their needs.

His mother lived elsewhere in Gujarat, and others had bought their old home—a narrow, renovated, three-story building with a staircase outside. The immediate neighbor, a grey-haired woman in a green sari, offered a glimpse of what Modi's childhood had been like: her house was unchanged in decades, with walls of faded green paint, a stone floor cool under bare feet, and steel dishes and cups balanced on exposed wooden wall beams. It had the feel of a small stable. A *charpoy*—a bed with a rope mattress—was the main piece of furniture. The place was spotless, though a fearless brown mouse scampered around our feet. Kamuben Modi's voice crackled with age—she was eighty-five—and the two largest toes on her left foot were missing. "The house next door, where the family lived, was not in good condition. They had no attic, no proper roof, just a tin roof," she recalled. Modi was a stubborn and forceful child, she said: "I remember he would never get beaten by other children, he would beat the others." As for helping with his father's business: "He did not work, not regularly, on the tea stall. The mother wanted him to help, but he didn't."

She spoke of Modi's arranged wedding as a teenager. "The wife came from the same community, and the parents had given their word when the children were little. A decision can be taken very early, even with the child in the womb," she explained. "I was at the wedding. He didn't want to get married. It was against his will. She was from a nearby village, from the extended family. It was a full ceremonial ritual at Brahmanwada, the bride's home. I went to the village, it was a summer wedding, it took two or three days." Modi was not defiant during the ceremonies, she said, but soon after, he quit his studies and left his wife in the family home. "His mother used to cry a lot after he went. His wife was here, and he had no contact with her. It was a prestige issue for the family that he had left his wife behind," said Kamuben. She suggested that Modi never slept with his wife. He supposedly told his parents "you wanted me to get married, that's your lot, then keep her." Kamuben concluded that "his ambitions were too big."

Modi's private life was discussed only sporadically in the Indian press. Recurrent press speculation concerned Rahul Gandhi's failure to marry, despite the existence of various girlfriends over the years. But Modi himself was not often the subject of such close personal attention. One discussion centered on his treatment of, and apparent infatuation with, a young woman whose father had won business with Modi's government in Gujarat. There were allegations, known in the press as "Snoopgate," that Modi (and Shah) deployed state resources, including spies, to follow the woman, and later even arranged for her to be married off to somebody else. But beyond rumors that he'd had occasional affairs with women in Delhi, it was widely accepted that Modi was a strikingly solitary man who eschewed meat, lectured others on not overeating, shunned alcohol, and kept his sex life as private as possible.

Modi after all had gone to some lengths to hide his marriage. As he rose in the RSS and became a *pracharak,* he was supposed to devote his life to the cause and not marry. The fact of his marriage did not prevent him from rising but might have left him with a greater sense of being an outsider, already vulnerable in the organization because he was lowish caste, from a poor family and with little education. In public, Modi was a bachelor, but he never divorced or annulled the marriage. As he advanced in his political career, he made a virtue of having no family. Finally, in 2014, when running for national parliament, he was forced to admit he had a wife.

Kamuben did not hesitate when asked about the biggest influence on Modi in childhood: "That was the RSS," she said. The judgment was repeated elsewhere. A few doors along was another elderly Modi, a frail woman with jet-white hair. Her sari and the walls of her home shared the same pale blue—it was natural to wonder, were she to press herself to them, if she would fade away. She had taught Modi and found him unremarkable, but said that "once Modi joined the RSS, that became his life, he never came back or looked back. He was more interested in religion." As a youngster he had dreamed of escaping his small town and found that his passion for the RSS offered a way out: the Hindu nationalist movement would propel him to new places.

The easiest way for an outsider, like me, to see the RSS in action was at a *shakha,* or daily gathering for its members. One steaming morning, in the grounds of a leafy, century-old campus—Banaras Hindu University, in Varanasi—several dozen men stood in a grassy square. The men, in shorts, were enjoying the shade of an enormous mango tree. They saluted the Indian tricolor and listened as a tubby leader in a blue waistcoat finished a lecture and led a rousing song. Indresh Kumar carried off a faintly comical boy-scoutish outfit of sandals, beige shorts, and black cap. So many threads were wrapped around his wrist it looked as if an unraveled cuff dangled there. A national leader of some notoriety, Kumar was quick to lash out at secular softies, and liked to damn Jawaharlal Nehru as a "traitor of the motherland." Oddly, Kumar had the job of trying to attract new members, even Muslims. He advised non-Hindus to emulate Hindus by shunning beef. He was handicapped in his efforts to reach out by years of press allegations, never substantiated and stoutly denied, that he had played a role in the deadly bombing of a Sufi shrine in Ajmer in 2007.

Kumar said his followers had just marked the birthday of Mother Earth, "the day of the first human being on Earth, the first arrival of a human being, every village is celebrating today." They promised "social harmony of different religion and caste" and care for the environment. *Shakhas* brought unity, he said: "RSS daily chants are so we should be healthy and happy, society should be harmonious, above caste, religion, and the world can be without conflicts." That sounded appealing, though it was harmony on the RSS's terms, defined by its interpretation of Hindu culture. No women attended *shakhas*— separate meetings existed for them—and most men here presented remarkably dour expressions.

In the past the RSS claimed only to care for social matters, but everyone knew it also quietly guided the Bharatiya Janata Party (BJP) to promote Hindu nationalism in politics. The pretense was dropped by 2014 and the Hindu nationalist movement became openly involved in election politics, backing Modi and pushing Hindu culture over secular ideas. Its crowds roared for Modi until hoarse; its volunteers brought voters to polling stations. The national leader of the outfit was explicitly partisan. Mohan Bhagwat, a man with a bushy moustache, regularly met Modi and pressed RSS appointments on his government, who turned out to be among its least competent ministers. No government in history had ever been so stacked with current or former RSS figures.

Bhagwat, eager to encourage social division, had all the grace and subtlety of an Indian Donald Trump—far-right Hindus in Delhi even took to demonstrating in favor of the American populist in 2016, apparently fond of his anti-Muslim statements. Bhagwat liked to say that "Hindustan is for Hindus," excluding the fifth of the population who were Muslim, Christian, Buddhist, or something else. Kumar snorted at my suggestion that this was provocative, saying "our country has many names, Aryavarta, Bharat, and Hindustan for Hindus, India, and Indians. These are names for nationality. Hindu is not a religious terminology." Asked if minority religions would see it that way, he bristled: "Why are you branding RSS communal? Christians are the most communal," he said, glowering. He strode away, kicking up dust, his followers huddled importantly about him.

Hindu nationalism had grown more assertive, and the movement helped to shape Modi's understanding of the world. In turn, Modi in power made Hindu nationalism more acceptable among a rising middle class. A senior government figure once said he worried about "the nutty underbelly" of some of his ministerial colleagues, meaning the RSS-nominated ones. As prime minister Modi, mostly, presented its gentler face: he talked up India's devotion to yoga and its ancient Vedic civilization, suggesting that it had invented airplanes, plastic surgery, and more. But Modi also enabled the hotheads, tolerating those who spoke out in more extreme ways.

One RSS figure in the state of Uttar Pradesh, Virendra Jaiswal, once explained from a dingy office over a shopping mall that the "sons of the nation, the Hindus who originally belonged to this country," were reclaiming their birthright thanks to Modi. "At one time India was called Golden Bird, we want to re-achieve that status, as the Teacher of the World," he said. A boss of the national movement, Ram Madhav, said that Modi could only be understood as a "part of our fraternity, a member ideologically of the family," the RSS. Another figure, from the broad association of nationalist groups known as the "Sangh Parivar," regularly lectured me on Hindus as the world's oldest surviving civilization: "It has not happened by accident, Hinduism is our identity and it is a civilizational term. Hindu nationalism is the same as Indian nationalism."

Another RSS leader in Uttar Pradesh was Devendra Pratap Singh, a reedy man with a high voice, white hair, and a black shirt. He joined as a six-year-old, in 1944, and said that "if there is any good in my life that is because of my association with the RSS." He had a smear of sandalwood paste on his forehead and his walls were heavy with portraits of nationalist heroes. He was an old sort of high-caste RSS man who talked up charity work—the group has 150,000 social, medical, and teaching centers—and said "people try to misunderstand the RSS, those who oppose us, but in their heart of hearts they appreciate us." He said of Modi that "the RSS is in his blood, basically he is an RSS person. It affects every aspect of life, it makes a person more disciplined, more devoted to the country. Any action is for the overall development of India." He also lauded Modi as an Other Backward Class figure: "Most *pracharaks* in the beginning were Brahmins from Maharashtra, now it has changed completely," he said. "Only great people can devote all their time to the nation."

The RSS marks its centenary in 2025, at which time it might well be even more prominent in mainstream politics despite its paramilitary uniform and its early fascination with Italian fascism and Savarkar. Modi helped to change its image: keeping its Hindu chauvinism, but appealing to young Indians who craved material goods. Previously an RSS leader had to forget his family, shun the limelight, reject luxuries, and celebrate self-denial, celibacy, and restraint. Modi could not always show restraint, however. As noted, he was known for his fondness for expensive clothing, pens, footwear, and glasses, but also for his bragging about his personal might, his macho poses, and his boasts about supposedly having a "fifty-six-inch chest."

The RSS, with Modi in office, pressed for conversions of non-Hindus, a process called *ghar wapsi,* or "homecoming," though Singh said nobody should fret about that: "If someone had gone over to another religion and come back, it is a good thing." The term *Hindu* encompassed all people devoted to the motherland, he said, and "99 percent are people of this Indian [Hindu] origin. It is because of certain circumstances they have taken up Islam." He warned instead about Muslim Lotharios who seduced and converted Hindu women, a process termed *love jihad:* "It is happening so much. The way Hindu girls are marrying Muslims, everywhere, there is a large trend, from Kerala to Kashmir, a deliberate campaign even in Varanasi, in this neighborhood." He grumbled that liberal, secular types fussed too much when one of Modi's junior ministers called non-Hindus "bastards" at an election rally, or when nationalist right-wingers in Mumbai wanted a statue erected for the assassin of Mahatma Gandhi.

The RSS also tested Modi. In public the prime minister did not disavow the worst extremists in his government (he did not even sack the "bastards" minister), giving the RSS something to cheer about, as other Indians and outsiders looked on, dismayed. But Modi also refused in his first years in office to promote the RSS's core issues, such as its demand to change the special constitutional status for Muslim-majority Kashmir or its wish to be rid of a separate marriage code for Muslims. RSS leaders hoped his delay was tactical, that a red-blooded Modi would turn to such matters once his party fully controlled both houses of parliament.

The most troubling detail about the RSS and similar Hindu nationalist groups was their history of taking part in religious violence. A threat to stable relations between India's religious groups would be a perennial concern even as India's economy grew, its people moved into cities, and modernity spread. Memories of Partition, and of the immense bloodletting of 1947, would not disappear. The threat from the RSS lay in fears that religious violence could one day return. It was a duty of political leaders to do everything possible to discourage divisions, rather than exploit them. To get a sense of Modi's character when put under intense pressure and of some of those around him—notably Amit Shah—it is necessary to understand what unfolded in Gujarat when Modi was in charge.

WHY GUJARAT, 2002, STILL MATTERS

ODI WOULD NOT CONFRONT THE HINDU RIGHT IF DOING
so threatened his own popularity. He calculated that he needed
young, nationalist volunteers to help him to win elections,
though he also hoped to appeal to mainstream voters. So, as one shrewd
commentator put it in 2016, Modi routinely exploited "strategic ambiguity" in failing to confront or curb extremist supporters, even if he
did not offer them outright, public support. The most shameful example of this came relatively early in his career, not long after he was first
appointed as chief minister in Gujarat. At the time he was politically
vulnerable. He faced an imminent election to retain his post. Relatively
isolated and disliked, Modi was threatened by rival factions within his
Bharatiya Janata Party who hoped he would fail in his first post. Naturally, opposition parties also hoped he would stumble. That isolation
perhaps helped to explain—but could not justify—his actions and failures in February and March 2002.

Under his initially impassive gaze, and in the face of inaction or worse from many police, Hindu extremists clashed with Muslims and carried out massacres in his state. At least a thousand people were killed. By some estimates many more died, but police, some of whom were complicit, hid body parts and destroyed evidence. Most victims were in cities such as Ahmedabad, where communication was clear, police were available, and the political control of state apparatus should have functioned perfectly well. Victims were not, by and large, killed in remote villages or out of sight. Murders generally took place in public. Given the advent of rolling television news in India, a horrified country watched on. The pogroms of 2002—and Modi's failures to stop them early, to explain in detail his role as they unfolded, or to express convincing regret for what happened—left many to conclude that, whatever his general virtues, he was a dangerously flawed man.

Not all Muslim Gujaratis disliked Modi. Some people wanted to focus on the years of stability that followed in his state, until his departure in 2014, and they pointed to violence and attacks that happened well before 2002, too. Others said what really mattered was his economic record, and fretting about political violence was a distraction. For example, a Muslim dealer in luxury cars who had long profited from close ties with Modi praised his leader's "iron fist" and said that "Muslims in Gujarat are the best off in India." (He was later rewarded for his loyalty with a government post at a university.) A few suggested that Modi, however culpable for 2002, had learned from the carnage and so would never let it happen again.

But many in Gujarat and beyond were not at ease. An outspoken Californian of Gujarati descent who had lived in Ahmedabad, the main city of Gujarat, for over a decade, said the events of 2002 proved Modi was a monster. Zahir Janmohamed had a goatee and a flop of lanky hair and spoke of his years of working in a Muslim ghetto of 400,000 people, Juhapura, within the city. We walked its streets and he described neglect and poverty, how small manufacturers struggled despite wealth elsewhere in the city, and how residents felt discriminated against. He suggested that "two thousand children in just my area" had no school to attend and told of officials who refused to issue building permits or failed to supply basic services like water or sewerage to Muslim areas. Some officials ordered structures demolished, then collected bribes to leave them standing, he said. Intense suspicion persisted between members of rival religions in a fractured city. Hindu taxi drivers would not enter this Muslim area.

Zahir happened to be living with a Hindu family in February 2002, when trouble erupted. Their biggest concern at first was being prevented from seeing a new *Star Wars* film at the cinema. But in Muslim areas, such as Juohapura, anguish was extreme from the start and continued for years. The killings were not spontaneous, or a "four-day orgy of violence, it was a project, part of a constant pattern of fear," he said, suggesting that Gujarat's government under Modi had continued "intimidating the Muslims and those who would dissent" for years after the pogrom. Though Gujarat had been calm for years after 2002, he refused to see that as progress: "If there is fear, is that peace?" Muslims were 5 million of the approximately 60 million people in the state, he said, and many felt vulnerable. "People fear it could happen again. So they make sure they live near fellow Muslims. This is not a climate where you can criticize." As an activist, when he wrote about Muslim-Hindu relations, how the city was divided between religions, he said he got "death threats and crazy phone calls from Modi supporters." "Good Muslims," he said, were told to be subservient, to "move on" and forget the massacres: "A Muslim businessman would make sure to put up a picture of Modi in his office. Present himself as a 'rational Muslim.'"

If you discussed what happened in 2002 with Modi and his backers, then, naturally, you heard a different view. They did not talk of organized pogroms or massacres, but implied the violence was on a relatively small scale, or was near spontaneous, or even-handed between religious groups. They alleged the existence of a campaign to vilify their leader. When I raised the issue of the killings with Modi, he said he must be judged "in toto" and not only by his response to the violence: "Then you will understand everything, but if you have any problem with 2002 then I am helpless, I can't help you." Yet he spoke about anything but those events. He said his electoral popularity made them irrelevant, as if elections magically wiped away stains of the past. "I always welcome criticism," he said, but "this question has no use. . . . I have faced ten general elections in my state. The people always supported me. So I have completed this examination with distinction marks."

The courts also found Modi guilty of nothing, but then it was extremely rare for judges in India to convict the most powerful of anything. His backers said that even worse bloodshed happened elsewhere and that no other politician had faced the same degree of scrutiny. In 1984, in Delhi and Punjab, mobs linked to the Indian National Congress had butchered several thousand Sikhs as police, under control of politicians, watched or guided the killers. That violence occurred after two Sikh bodyguards assassinated Indira Gandhi, India's prime minister. Congress politicians, including some senior figures active in party politics three decades later, abetted the revenge murders—for example, by identifying Sikh homes from the voters' roll. Only a few junior politicians were ever tried. Rajiv Gandhi, who succeeded his mother as prime minister, sounded callous when asked about the murders, saying that "when a big tree falls, the earth shakes."

Those killings did not make later events in Gujarat under Modi any less troubling, however. As for political parties, the context mattered. Congress was not a movement traditionally hostile to Sikhs or other minorities. By contrast the RSS and Hindu nationalists had long pushed anti-Muslim views—expressed since Savarkar or earlier. Modi as a young politician had helped to organize *yatras* (political pilgrimages) to sensitive locations, knowing that these would stir up tension between Hindus and Muslims. In 1990 he helped to arrange one to Ayodhya, a site in Uttar Pradesh, north India, where Hindus claimed that a five-hundred-year-old mosque was built on a ruined temple. Two years later Hindu fanatics demolished the mosque, provoking religious clashes that killed over two thousand people. That ugly period coincided with the BJP's rise as a national force, as the party whipped up Hindu nationalist support. Vinod Jose, a journalist who studied Modi's early career, argued that this context matters: Congress leaders "don't come from an ideology built on hatred, whereas the civilizational goals of the RSS and Modi imagine an India of two thousand years ago," he said.

No single violent religious clash is simple to explain. It typically involves political interests as much as religious ones, as those with power stoke up and exploit religious and social troubles. Such clashes, as happened in Gujarat, often take place just before an election. The goal might be to intimidate opponents, or to rally and unite kinsmen behind one's party, perhaps in response to a provocation. The first victims in Gujarat in 2002 were Hindus, pilgrims—or *yatris*—who were returning by train after celebrating the tenth anniversary of the mosque's destruction in Ayodhya. At a station in a town called Godhra, some of them reportedly behaved badly; some sources said they were harassing local people. But nothing could justify what followed. A mob from a Muslim area attacked the Sabarmati Express, pelting it with stones, smashing windows as it tried to pull away. A court later ruled that the attackers had thrown burning petrol-soaked rags on board and locked doors from the outside. By one estimate, they poured sixty liters of flammable liquid into the carriages. In the flames fifty-nine people, including children, were killed. The attack appeared to have been prepared in advance, given the availability of fuel. Nine years later, a court convicted thirty-one men for committing a "planned conspiracy" and sentenced eleven of them to hang.

Nothing, in turn, could justify the much larger retaliatory slaughter. Modi rushed to the railway station knowing that he faced a career-defining test of authority. He must have felt exposed, because many colleagues neither liked nor trusted him. A decade and more after the events, few high-ranking participants in this event were willing to discuss Modi's role in detail. But one witness, Sanjiv Bhatt, a stocky man with muscled arms, spoke at length in his home in Ahmedabad. Over tea in a conservatory, an armed policeman at his front gate, he explained that he was the state intelligence officer who had "looked after internal security of Gujarat" before, during, and after the slaughter. "I saw Modi almost daily" at this time, he said, claiming to have "had a window into his mind." He had since turned against his old boss, whom he called "paranoid, very insecure."

Bhatt's account was disputed, but it is worth sharing not least because of the prolonged efforts to shut him up and—since Modi came to national office—to punish him. (He filed an affidavit with India's Supreme Court accusing Modi of wrongdoing that was rejected, and he was forced out of the police service in 2015.) Bhatt said that at the charred scene at the station in Godhra, members of a Hindu nationalist group allied to the RSS, the Vishwa Hindu Parishad (VHP) formed a mob of their own. "Modi was physically beaten at the railway station," claimed Bhatt, saying the chief minister had to be rushed to safety in the car of the health minister as the enraged crowd accused him of failing to crack down on Muslim attackers. "Shaken to the core, Modi thought that with so many Hindus killed on his watch, he'd lose his job," said Bhatt. "He had to deflect their anger."

Modi said publicly that the Godhra attack was an act of planned terrorism, and some newspapers spread false claims of rapes of Hindu women by Muslim attackers or fake stories of Muslims who supported terrorists from Pakistan. (A day after the attack, Modi on state television, exhausted, called those who burned the train "cannibals.") On the night of the Godhra attack, Modi took two decisions that were almost certain to make the situation worse. The VHP had demanded a state-wide *bandh*—a strike-cum-protest—which the BJP supported. Modi should have blocked it to discourage more violence. India's Supreme Court had previously ruled that such strikes were unconstitutional, and Modi's responsibility as chief minister was to preserve order and safety. But Modi, evidently reluctant to confront Hindu extremists, let it proceed. He also agreed to let dozens of train victims' burnt corpses be brought by road to Ahmedabad, in what amounted almost to a public procession.

Bhatt said he was at a meeting with Modi on the evening of the train attack and found him to be "disturbed" and "shaken." (Those who dispute Bhatt's account denied he was there; phone records that would have helped to prove it, mysteriously, disappeared.) Bhatt said he told the chief minister the *bandh* and transport of corpses would be "very likely to mean violence. I warned Modi at the meeting that the lumpen element would feel this was a government-sponsored *bandh* call. I also warned against bringing the bodies from Godhra to Ahmedabad. I told Modi it was a virtual tinder box. Modi heard us out. Then he said 'there is so much anger in the people we will have to let them vent.' He refused to withdraw the *bandh,* or reverse the bringing of bodies. I could foresee what would go on, then I left the meeting."

Bhatt's version was unproven. Modi denied saying that people must "vent," as that would have implied giving permission for retaliatory violence. But what followed was devastating. Especially in mixed religious areas in Ahmedabad, victims were butchered in the street or their homes, attacked because they were Muslim. Bhatt described passing a broken-down car of four elderly Muslims on a flyover and returning to find them all killed soon afterward. He said he saved a Muslim policeman from a mob, as other policemen stood by, inactive. Some police were heroic, and perhaps 200 officers were among those killed. However in many cases police and politicians did nothing; some joined the killers. Over 1,000 people died, at least two-thirds of them Muslims. Around 18,000 homes were destroyed and nearly 170,000 people were displaced, mostly Muslims. Documentary video, recorded days after the killings, showed residents talking about carefully organized violence. One woman interviewed explained that "everyone had a sword in one hand and a mobile phone in the other"; she added that the attackers were members of the RSS, or from the wider Hindu nationalist Sangh movement, and "they wore bands, shorts, and had swords."

The dismembering and murder of a Muslim ex-MP (among many others) at his home in a walled cluster of middle-class bungalows and apartments were especially shocking. Others had sheltered with him at a complex known as the Gulberg Society, hoping that his political status offered safety. A chanting mob surrounded them for hours as the MP desperately phoned fellow politicians around the country, begging them to ask Gujarat's authorities to send protection. He reportedly phoned Modi himself. Modi certainly got calls and reports about the threats at the MP's home. Bhatt said he personally told Modi about the situation and understood from his reply that the chief minister knew in detail what was happening. Yet Modi failed to get the police to help at the Gulberg Society, and he did not prevent the mass murder that followed as buildings were torched and people were chased and stabbed. At that site 69 people were killed. Another massacre, Naroda Patiya, took 96 victims, with some people chased into pits and burnt. Probably more were killed, but police dumped body parts.[1]

Modi, as the man in charge, clearly had some responsibility. He did appear on television a day after the train burning to tell Gujaratis not to "take the law in their hands," saying there was no place for retaliatory violence in civilized society, and that "venting anger is not the solution." He said that the "need of the hour is to maintain peace and self-discipline," to avoid violence, to have "a Gujarat whose future does not get lost, for a Gujarat that does not have to carry the burden of a black moment in its history," and he told people to "maintain peace and harmony." Any punishment must be "through the legal route," he said. Eventually he called for help from the army.

Yet Modi acted late and did too little. He should have ordered an immediate curfew and prevented the *bandh* and the public movement of corpses that helped to enrage public opinion. He should have given the police sufficiently clear, early, public instructions to prevent violence. He should have faced down the Hindu nationalist groups, such as the VHP, despite their fury over the Godhra attacks. Human Rights Watch in April 2002 blamed officials under his direct control, saying they had "actively supported" massacres. India's human-rights commission described a "comprehensive failure" of his government. Sonia Gandhi, Congress's leader, accused Modi's officials of "deliberate connivance" with the attackers. The national Supreme Court in 2004 said Gujarat's rulers were "modern-day Neros" who let killings spread while "deliberating how the perpetrators of the crime can be protected." In 2005 America's government made clear that Modi could no longer travel there, saying he was responsible for the performance of state institutions in the pogroms; many European countries imposed a similar, but unofficial, boycott on Modi.

Shankersinh Vaghela, a bitter rival and a senior RSS figure who defected to the Indian National Congress, blamed Modi personally, calling him "arrogant, cruel, a criminal." As a former chief minister himself, he said he knew Modi had sufficient means to prevent the massacres, or to cut them short once they began, but he did not use them decisively. "If you are chief minister, with all kinds of powers . . . you own the state, the machinery, the police department," he said, in his home in Gandhinagar, Gujarat. He implied that Modi made a political calculation to let violence happen, because confronting the VHP, the RSS, and powerful Hindu nationalist extremists would have ended his political career. Victims, such as the wife of the murdered MP, listed thirty allegations, claiming that Modi told officials they should not stop mobs of Hindu extremists.

Judging only by what courts found later, in Gujarat and elsewhere, was problematic. In long-running cases in India, witnesses are often induced, coerced, or exhausted into giving up on a prosecution. Surabhi Chopra, a human-rights lawyer, and her colleagues have documented how states respond to investigations into mass violence, including in Gujarat after 2002.[2] They showed how badly courts function, and how police, governments, and others can scupper legal processes—police fail to record criminal charges, evidence is destroyed, prosecution teams are deliberately bad, witnesses are persuaded to change testimony, and the process becomes so slow that many participants give up. When police or other state officials are accused, unsurprisingly they are least likely to conduct a thorough investigation or prosecution.

Periods of disregard for the law in Gujarat, as elsewhere, were also well established. Those in power at times approved "encounter killings," when police staged a shoot-out with suspected criminals and executed them rather than go through a tedious legal process. In Gujarat under Modi, high-profile police murders often targeted Muslims, including suspected gangsters. In 2004, for example, police killed four Muslims, including a nineteen-year-old woman, saying they were Pakistani-backed assassins plotting to kill Modi. Five years later, a court ruled that they had been illegally executed and found no evidence of planned terrorism. Modi made little effort to hide his views on such killings. A television journalist, Shekhar Gupta, once asked him about 183 murders by his police: over 100 of the victims were Muslim, a fact he airily dismissed. At a state election rally in 2007, noted Andrew Buncombe, India correspondent for Britain's *Independent* newspaper, Modi bragged about the murders of suspected gangsters. "Does my government need to take permission from Sonia [Gandhi]?" he asked a crowd of BJP fans, apparently referring to the police killing of a Muslim gangster. Buncombe says they chanted in response, "kill, kill, kill."

Modi's supporters called such episodes old hat, no different from events in other states. Yet there was obvious reason for concern that India's prime minister—in his own words—carried the "burden of a black moment in [his] history." Modi also kept questionable company. His nearest ally was a fellow politician, Amit Shah, perhaps the only figure whom Modi really trusted. Yet Shah was one of the most notorious politicians in India. He was arrested in 2010 in connection with the police murder of Sohrabuddin Sheikh, a suspected extortionist. Gujarat's police had detained Sheikh and his wife in 2005, then killed them both. A year later police killed a witness to their murders, Tulsiram Prajapati. It was Shah who ran the home ministry that controlled the police. He was charged with murder, extortion, and kidnapping and told by a court to leave Gujarat, to prevent intimidation of witnesses. Yet his political career did not suffer, thanks to Modi. A journalist friend in Surat, Gujarat, who knows Shah, calls him "Modi's shield," valued because he solved problems, protected his boss, and took control of a "vagabond law machinery in Gujarat." Soon after Modi became prime minister in 2014, Shah was appointed as national president of the ruling BJP. It was the first time someone charged with murder had assumed such a senior post, an unedifying moment in Indian history. In 2016 his position was renewed for three more years.

Courts did eventually jail over one hundred people for murders in Gujarat in 2002, which counted as a high degree of accountability for political violence. In June 2016, for example, twenty-four people were convicted for the massacre at the Gulberg Society. The legal successes were partly thanks to efforts to gather evidence by an indomitable activist in Gujarat called Teesta Setalvad. She was later harassed and threatened with prosecution, over alleged irregularities in how her organization was funded, after Modi became prime minister. Ten years after the killings, a court in Ahmedabad had convicted thirty-two people for the murders at Naroda Patiya. The most prominent defendant was Mayaben Kodnani, a BJP lawmaker who had been seen distributing weapons, urging on killers, and firing a pistol. The trial judge called her a "kingpin of the entire communal riot" and jailed her for twenty-eight years. Kodnani's crimes were extremely well known long before her arrest in 2009. However, a few years after the pogroms, Modi had appointed this "kingpin" as one of his ministers in Gujarat. As for serving her twenty-eight-year sentence, she spent little time behind bars. A couple of months after Modi became prime minister, in July 2014, Kodnani was released on "bail" from prison, on health grounds.

Modi was questioned but was found guilty of nothing. A Special Investigations Team of the Supreme Court cleared him of the thirty allegations leveled by the wife of the murdered ex-MP. Testimony by Bhatt was ruled unreliable. Potentially important phone records disappeared; many presumably had been destroyed by officials to muddy the legal investigation. A minister in Modi's government, who disliked his boss and had been involved in the violence himself, had secretly told activists in May 2002 that Modi behaved just as Bhatt later claimed. But such hearsay carried no legal weight. Nor would the minister ever offer acceptable testimony: two unknown assailants shot him dead in Ahmedabad, one morning in 2003.

Modi became India's prime minister without offering explicit regret or explaining his actions during the crucial days in 2002. Yet, judging by Modi's behavior in the months and years after the killings, he could hardly say later that he lamented the bloodshed. Among the Hindu majority in Gujarat his popularity had soared after the massacres, so he called a state election as soon as possible. At a rally he appeared to mock Muslim victims, once asking his supporters sarcastically about displaced families and appearing to refer to the high birthrates of Muslims displaced by the violence: "Should we run relief camps? Should I start children-producing centers there?" he asked. Many Gujaratis would deny the seriousness of the violence. Footage from a rally in 2002 showed Modi talking of "sixty innocent Rambhakts [pilgrims] burnt alive in Godhra," then asking the crowd, sarcastically, if anyone present had burnt shops in retaliation. "Did you stab or behead anyone? . . . Did you rape anyone?" he called out, earning cheers of "No . . . No." He said those who spoke of violence in Gujarat were "defaming" the state, as "enemies of Gujarat go around saying that each village was in flames. In each village, people were being killed . . . their heads smashed. They have defamed Gujarat so much."

Modi won an enormous victory in those state polls, not despite the killings but because of them. Zahir Janmohamed in Ahmedabad said "nobody here thinks Modi is innocent, they know what he did and they are okay with that." Modi for a time paid a political price beyond Gujarat. Delhi-based television journalist Karan Thapar recalled interviewing Modi in 2007, a rare event, and focusing on the pogroms, saying he was called a "mass murderer" and accused of crude anti-Muslim prejudice—for example, as a "poster boy of hate." Modi pulled off his microphone and stormed out mid-interview. Thapar later said "2002 was a searing experience for Modi, he became a pariah"—but only for a time. Modi learned to deflect questions about his ugly past and, by refusing to discuss the events, got others to focus their attention elsewhere.

When he ran for national office, Modi addressed the topic only briefly. Asked by Reuters if he had regrets over 2002, he spoke of a general, passive capacity for sorrow, comparing his reaction to the mass slaughter to feeling sad if a car ran over a dog. He said he had done "absolutely the right thing" as chief minister: "Any person if we are driving a car [or] someone else is driving a car and we're sitting behind, even then if a puppy comes under the wheel, will [it] be painful or not? Of course, it is. If I'm a chief minister or not, I'm a human being. If something bad happens anywhere, it is natural to be sad." He had said to me that elections somehow had wiped his conscience clean. He implied that he could not be held responsible because voters liked him. It was a warped logic. Elected leaders are supposed to represent, and protect, all in their state—not just those who support them.

Nonetheless, other actors eventually adjusted to deal with Modi. America's treatment of Modi went through great swings of change. Despite his various trips to America as a young politician, relations cooled after the pogroms of 2002. Diplomatic cables, published by WikiLeaks, revealed intense American hostility over the religious violence. For years, diplomats summed up Gujarat's chief minister as a dangerous demagogue, calling him authoritarian, intolerant, and prone to exploiting hostility toward minority Muslims for political gain. America's State Department scrapped his visa because he was a foreign government official held "responsible for particularly serious violations of others' religious freedoms." Administrators quoted an official Indian report on the pogroms, describing the "comprehensive failure" of his government in Gujarat. Modi called the ban "an insult" and "an attack on Indian sovereignty." Diplomats quoted dissidents from Modi's party who talked of his "dictatorial and arbitrary style of functioning" and called him a "religious bigot." They quoted Indian newspapers calling Modi a "poster boy of hate."

American repositioning toward Modi followed later, as diplomats saw Modi thrive. Early on in Gujarat he did well by stirring up the Hindu majority against the Muslim minority. In 2006 the American consul general in Mumbai said "Modi remains immensely popular among the state's non-Muslim voters," and Hindu voters in Gujarat liked that Modi had "put Muslims into their place." Voters were also pleased by his "Hindutva agenda" and liked that Modi used "administrative tools to marginalize and ghettoize the Muslim minority." The American diplomats accepted that "Modi can be charming and likable" in public, but said he "is an insular, distrustful person who rules with a small group of advisers. . . . He reigns more by fear and intimidation than by inclusiveness and consensus, and is rude, condescending, and often derogatory to even high-level party officials. He hoards power and often leaves his ministers in the cold when making decisions that affect their portfolios." One cable added that Modi's "abrasive" style left him isolated, inspired no loyalty, and provoked many opponents because "his friends are his enemies."

Then as Gujarat got richer, and the politician matured and focused on economic growth, America's diplomats warmed up. By 2009 they were asking if Modi would be India's prime minister, calling him a "star campaigner" and "the best 'brand manager' India has seen." The diplomats said "few politicians in India evoke the strength of feeling Modi does, and few exemplify the entwining of two major themes in modern India—communalism and economic development—as him." Those two themes persisted when he was prime minister.

Before the 2014 election, America's ambassador to India was given the task of visiting Modi, in February—an event at which flowers were exchanged and America, in effect, gave its blessing to him as a legitimate candidate to lead the country. That did not bring an end to uneasiness over his past, let alone an assumption that problems would not reemerge in the future. Obama warned him at the end of his 2015 trip to India, for example, saying Modi should do more to promote religious tolerance and respect for minorities.

One lesson for the nation stemming from Gujarat in 2002, from Modi's behavior afterward, and from voters in 2014 was that being counted by many as responsible for political violence does not make one unelectable. Yet for the long-term stability of Indian society, there were concerns. Some, such as people who belonged to minority religions, worried about future instability. Modi and Shah had become the most powerful politicians in India, but they never felt they had to explain their roles in Gujarat, nor that they had fully to disavow what had happened. This circumstance did not guarantee that wider intolerance, or new violence, would rise again. But it raised serious doubts about Modi's character and how he might behave if troubles did recur.

THE POWER OF MINGLING

FTER PARTITION, IN 1947, INDIA AND PAKISTAN TOOK STRIK-
ingly different paths. India chose the much more attractive one.
The way religions rubbed along together, guided by those who
held political (or military) power, varied greatly. In Pakistan, a predominantly Sunni Muslim country, tolerance for non-Muslims and
for Sufis, Shia, Ahmadis, and other minorities gradually shriveled. At
independence over one-fifth of Pakistan's population, including 15 percent of the western part of the country, were non-Muslim. Jinnah, the
country's first leader, had spoken of creating a Muslim homeland where
Christians, Sikhs, and others would also feel welcome. By 2016, however, non-Muslims were less than 5 percent of Pakistan's population,
and many non-Sunnis felt increasingly threatened by the Deobandi,
Salafi, or Wahabi movements, including extremists who used accusations of blasphemy to intimidate members of minority religions or sects
and steal their property. None of this was accidental, or a mere quirk
of history. Politicians had long cultivated extremist groups in Pakistan.

Military rulers had stirred up Islamist groups to use inside Afghanistan and India. From the Middle East came influential Wahabi thought, especially from Saudi Arabia, an ally of Pakistan's government that channeled money for madrassas and mosques. It all helped to cultivate a harder version of Islam in Pakistan.

By contrast in secular and democratic India, with its majority Hindu population, religious minorities mostly looked more secure—despite some bloody exceptions, as in Gujarat in 2002. Hindus predominated and would always do so: census figures showed population growth rates slowing over the decades for all groups, including Muslims. But the non-Hindu population remained robust. A religious census in 2011 found that Hindus were just under 80 percent of India's population and Muslims were nearly 15 percent. (The Muslim proportion will gradually rise this century, perhaps reaching a maximum of 20 percent.) Christians, Sikhs, Buddhists, animists, and atheists, plus tiny scatterings of Jews, Parsis, and others, made up the rest. Nonetheless, because India was massive, its Muslim population was numerically huge. India had some 180 million Muslims in 2016, roughly equal to the Muslim population of Pakistan. Only Indonesia had a larger Muslim population.

One of India's great successes was its survival as a confidently secular, multi-religious democracy—all the more hopeful in contrast to the misery next door. In Pakistan a near-genocide took place in 1971, targeting separatist Bengalis and Hindus (in the eastern part of the country). In India there could be local tensions, but by and large one was free to practice any religion—or none—and even the largest, Hinduism, did not overly dominate public life. India has never had a Muslim prime minister, but Muslims and members of other minority religions have been president and vice-president, as well as cabinet ministers, senior army figures, the boss of national intelligence, and beyond. In sport, in Bollywood, television, art, and literature, performers of any religion have been celebrated as national heroes. India offers a powerful message of inclusivity—a model that other countries troubled by religious strife might emulate. India has not always lived up to its model, as seen in persistent racism toward Africans in India, or ongoing caste and other intolerances, but in terms of its constitution and general practice it has mostly remained inclusive.

Yet India's success was not preserved by accident or a quirk of history, either: it required deliberate work by leaders and institutions to sustain it. You needed only to look at the history of South Asia to understand that the region would be at serious risk of violent confrontation, if divisive political and other leaders were really set on stirring up trouble. Religious persecution and wars had been widespread. Travel to Sri Lanka, to its north, and you saw the aftermath of civil war launched by Tamil (Hindu) secessionists in 1983, after long repression by the Sinhalese Buddhist majority. That war ended after twenty-six years, in 2009, when the UN estimated that perhaps 100,000 people had died. In Bangladesh hundreds of thousands were slaughtered and over 10 million were expelled in 1971. In the Maldives, known to the outside world mostly as a honeymoon destination, the law of 2008 compelled all nationals to be Sunni Muslim. Extremists there smashed old statues in museums, along with other evidence of the country's early Buddhist history.

Inside India, religious clashes occasionally erupted, such as in Assam in 2012, when Muslim settlers and tribal groups confronted each other for control of land. India had its own history of religious strife, especially before independence and at Partition. But under democracy India was relatively more stable and peaceful than most of its neighbors in South Asia. It was typically the country to which refugees fled, not the other way around (although a law proposed in 2016, under Modi, would have discriminated against Muslims from other countries who claimed refugee status, and in favor of Hindus and other non-Muslims seeking asylum).

Keeping India's society stable depended on constant effort from its leaders—political especially, but also religious ones, plus those in the media, in courts, and across many institutions, and including those within its massive, and mostly moderate, Muslim population. Yet radicalization of a minority of Muslims, notably some Sunni sects, as in other parts of the world, was also a concern. For most people in India, personal identity was not exclusively, probably not even predominantly, about religious belief. For many people, differences in geography, or of age, education, sexuality, profession, income, and more, could be at least as important as matters of religion. If you assessed the Muslim population as a single group, you could find distinct characteristics: on average, for example, Muslims were poorer than Hindus and faced worse prospects when measured by housing quality, wealth, employment, and the like. But then, inequality and variety within populations of the same religion were as significant as anything else.

Kashmiri Muslims often supported Pakistan's cricket team, as a way of showing that they resented rule from Delhi. Some Kashmiris, as in the summer of 2016, protested against rule from Delhi. But very few Indian Muslims appeared to sympathize with extremists. A domestic terror group, the Indian Mujahideen, had grown from a student movement, and carried out violent attacks, possibly with help from Pakistan. In Hyderabad, in February 2013, bombs killed sixteen people in a market, for example. In June 2016 police arrested a group of men in the city apparently poised to conduct more attacks. But activity was sporadic. Remarkably few Indian Muslims showed interest in supporting extremists either at home or abroad, or in traveling overseas to support outfits such as al Qaeda or the Islamic State.

Yet as Hindu nationalism rose in India, it did risk provoking some Indian Muslims to become more assertive of their religious identity, too. Some people felt disaffected when Narendra Modi promoted practices closely associated with Hinduism, such as celebrating a national yoga day, over which a Hindu guru, Baba Ramdev, helped to preside in 2015. It was easy to imagine how a more Hindutva-minded leader could stir harder-line responses from some Muslims. One unknown, given Modi's fierce determination to remain in office, was whether he might resort to using religious division to unite Hindu voters behind him, if the economy did not deliver promised returns. His past in Gujarat, after 2002, showed that such a worry was not fanciful.

Religious moderation in India looked robust, but what kept it that way was disputed. Hindu nationalists claimed it was the result of peaceful and moderate Hindus being in the majority. A more complete explanation was democratic India's history of moderate leaders, the strength of democratic institutions, and the benefits of having a liberal, secular constitution and the rule of law. It helped, too, that the type of Islam seen in India for the past millennium or so, the more mystical Sufi form (to which some two-thirds of Indian Muslims loosely belonged), had been closely intermingled with Hinduism. Cultural ties were strong. Members of both big religions shared many cultural practices and as long as mingling between communities continued, then understanding and moderation would be facilitated. Unfortunately, some signs suggested that, as Indians became more educated, urban, and wealthy, such mingling was in decline.

Arshad Alam, a Bihari academic at Jawaharlal Nehru University in Delhi, summed this up as Islam in India becoming more "standardized" as traditional practices were replaced by more modern ones. He saw habits in rural India, long shared by Muslims and Hindus, rapidly disappearing. "Applying vermillion on the forehead of a woman, is this Islamic?" he asked, referring to a habit usually associated with Hindus. "In Bihar there is a big debate, because it is customary for both Hindu and Muslim to apply it. Barelvis [the majority Muslim group in the area] are associated with the practice," he explained. Yet many Muslims were dropping the custom. Deobandi Muslims, who are more fundamentalist, "accuse them of adopting Hindu practice. Barelvis come under interpretative stress to conform, they are under pressure. This is happening now," he added.

Arshad also described ceremonies to mark deaths and births: "Take the singing of folk songs. One genre, in eastern Uttar Pradesh and in Bihar, is 'Sohar.' It is sung during birth, though only for the birth of a boy. The women of the locality got together, both Muslim and Hindu. It is common to both Hindu and Muslim families, but Sohar is now seen as a Hindu practice. Men told Muslim women not to do it. It was an occasion and a space to break off rigid community boundaries. Now Muslim women won't participate, so Sohar is an exclusive Hindu practice. They stop coming to Muslim houses, and Muslims don't go to theirs. The collective bonding that was there has been impacted by Islamic reform," he said, stubbing out a cigarette.

Ironically for an academic, Arshad worried that better education was shrinking the space where Muslims and Hindus could mix. As people read more—for example, on the Internet—more were defining themselves clearly by religion and as separate from neighbors of other faiths or sects. An example was how some Muslims decided to shun music. "I see Islam's role changing, but what is there to hang on to? You lose your own music, because it is 'Hindu,' but you have no music then. There is cultural anxiety in our minds, suffocation. This process will continue and increase. Everyone wants education, so the more this process will increase. Education brings more insular Islam," he said.

Migration played a role. From India—and from Bangladesh, Sri Lanka, and Pakistan—millions of young men and women, most of them Muslim, went to the Gulf, sending back tens of billions of dollars a year. That brought a great economic boon to states like Kerala, but it also began to change social habits—how some people dressed or shifting perceptions of what was considered attractive. The spread of Wahabi beliefs was one concern. Arshad pointed out that Wahabis were not necessarily more extreme than others, just as Sufis were not automatically more moderate. On the other hand, a lesson from Islamist extremism elsewhere, such as in Europe, suggested that Wahabi practices were associated with more hard-line attitudes—for example, toward non-Muslims. Arshad played down the significance of migration, but other experts saw outside influences encouraging the more inward-looking, conservative attitudes of some Muslims in India. Jamal Malik, who researched madrassas in South Asia, said migrants left for Saudi Arabia clean-shaven and many returned bearded and demanding that boys and girls be segregated in school. Such returning migrants were especially inclined to put one of their children into a madrassa, he said, and the numbers of such religious schools were growing.

In Delhi, Sultan Shahin, a middle-aged campaigner against Wahabist thought, ran a website, "New Age Islam," that he said was intended to counter sites funded by Saudis to promote hard-line views among young Muslims in India. "I thought there should be a corner of the Internet where those on the verge of converting to militancy can get a contrarian view, entirely based on the Koran," he said. He called Wahabi or Salafi Islam a "very, very poisonous ideology, getting help, support with massive petrodollars" from Saudi Arabia. "People develop a Wahabi mindset of exclusion, feeling superior, alienating themselves. It is in the air," he complained. He said that Delhi bookshops were crammed with publications that promoted ideas of isolation, and rejection of others, and that "books are either from Saudi Arabia or published here with Saudi funding. The same textbooks as are taught in Saudi Arabia. They teach that Wahabi Muslims should have no interaction with Jews, Christians, should listen to no radio or TV. Women whose grandmothers never wore a burka are today in hijab. Today men have a certain kind of beard, thinly trimmed moustache. This is Wahabi, spread by Jamaat. You see it on the roads in Delhi, Chandni Chowk, anywhere."

He saw evidence that some fellow Indian Muslims had become more hard-line. "You see it has grown phenomenally in the beards, hijabs, burkas, the way people talk. Migration has a big impact. I saw this in Kerala. So many mosques have come up, which proudly declare themselves Salafi mosques. That was very surprising for me, because Wahabi or Salafi belief used to be so minuscule. Now so many are willing to identify as Salafi. It used to be one or two people who would come to the mosques one hundred years ago when it [Salafi or Wahabi thought] came to India. Saudis propagated Wahabism, but they had little money. Now so many are willing to identify themselves," he said.

Others worried about the influence of the migrants to the Gulf who returned home to South Asia. Armed police guarded the book-lined home in Delhi of Taslima Nasrin, a liberal Bangladeshi writer in exile.

An outspoken critic of radical Islam, Nasrin had won awards and honorary degrees from foreign universities, the European Parliament, and others. An atheist who trained as a doctor, she had campaigned since the 1980s against fanatics first in Bangladesh and then, after claiming asylum, in India. Several radical Islamist leaders called for her to be killed. (Many liberals, Hindus, bloggers, and anti-extremist figures inside Bangladesh were murdered by Islamist fanatics in 2015 and 2016.) She said she was the subject of three fatwas issued by clerics in Bangladesh, and five more in India. In 2007 an Indian Muslim cleric offered 500,000 rupees for her assassination. Her books were publicly burnt.

Nasrin claimed that many Muslims in South Asia (in Bangladesh, especially) were getting "more fundamentalist" by the year, referring to a surge in mosque-building, women who felt obliged to wear the burka, and attacks on girls' schools since the 1990s. She campaigned against the "brainwash center, the madrassa," and was worried by the business activities of Islamist groups involved in banks, schools, and hospitals in Bangladesh. She said that money flowing from richer Islamic countries, notably the Gulf, encouraged radical, hostile interpretations of Islam across South Asia.

M. J. Akbar, one of India's wittiest journalists, who joined politics as a rare Muslim supporter of Modi and eventually became a minister of foreign affairs, also warned of the spread of fundamentalist Islam in India. "Go to see the headquarters of the Tablighi Jamaat," he advised. "The Tablighi Jamaat movement is the largest organization of Muslim mobilization in South Asia. Its purpose is not to convert Hindus or to interfere or intercede, its purpose is far more insidious: to turn Muslims into Wahabis. They preach distance. Their beards, you know, are knee-jerk beards. Missionaries are at the Nizamuddin station every morning, and they can get a 1-million-strong congregation at the drop of a skull cap," he said, exaggerating. He complained that a close friend had joined the Tablighi Jamaat. The two used to gamble and drink together in Bombay, he said, but "now he has a skull cap and his beard is at least three-feet long. He is only interested in purifying Islam, going from village to village." Akbar called the Tablighi movement and other fundamentalists "Wahabis of a type. They emerge from despair, the collapse of Muslim empire."[1]

The Delhi headquarters of the Tablighi Jamaat was in a large, white, domed building in Nizamuddin, a relatively prosperous and central neighborhood. Alleys nearby were stuffed with bookshops, butchers' counters, food stalls, as well as traders who sold skull caps, rose petals, blankets, and sandals. Inside the building was gloomy with all the charm of an underground carpark. Heaps of sandals and cheap shoes lay at the entrance. At the end of a long, bustling hall, a tiny office was lit by a single fluorescent light. The place looked worn. Books were tied up in bags of cloth, papers piled in tin trunks. A man sat cross-legged behind a low wooden desk with hinges made of thin brass. We sat on a threadbare carpet and drank sweet, milky chai from tiny square cups.

A member of the movement, a pharmacist from Bradford in northern England, pointed out rows of other young men who had gathered to eat and pray. Many were foreign visitors, and he identified "Sri Lankans, Bengalis, Canadians, everyone." Devout, he spoke of the duty of *dawah,* inviting others to practice Islam in a pure way. He said his group organized large gatherings for new adherents every year (notably in Bangladesh), promoted a strict dress code and the virtues of fasting, and made daily "five-times prayer compulsory, like stopping at a red light." Extra keen, he opted for a sixth session of prayer in the middle of the night. Asked what he thought of Sufi Muslims who prayed at a shrine next door, he dismissed them as "totally unIslamic" because they listened to music and, he said, prostrated themselves on the grave of a saint. It was also wrong to reach out to Shia Muslims, he added. He complained that in India and elsewhere "Islam had got tainted with idolatry" and said Muslims must dress in ways that assert their religion, and make clear their differences from non-Muslims. Women were segregated away from men. The place was dour and joyless. Even if the devout were not necessarily extremist, the message I heard seemed to confirm fears expressed by Arshad, Akbar, and others that such groups were encouraging division, not integration.

Swapping the gloom of the Tablighis' hall for a Sufi shrine next door, a place of light, color, and noisy alleys, I felt as if I was leaving a drab corner of the Gulf and falling back into lively, intense but welcoming India again. Men chatted at the tomb of the Sufi saint. They were mostly clean-shaven, and took turns scattering rose petals from tin plates. Some laid silk cloths over the supposed body of the saint. Several soldiers with a banner posed for a photo in front of the tomb. People wore bright clothes, and incense burned in the courtyard. There were women, too, and a few oil lamps lit for blessings.

It was hard to believe that the austere Tablighi Jamaat could ever appeal to a large number of Indian Muslims, but their sway was growing somewhat. The Tablighis had only had a foothold in India for a century or so, but they drew on a school of thought established at a campus in the late nineteenth century a few hours' drive north of Delhi. The Darul Uloom Deoband was the site of the most important madrassa in South Asia, set in a small town, busy with marigold sellers and car-repair businesses, and where buffaloes were herded through the streets. A grey mist hung over shops selling cellphones and an "Indo-America school of English language." Founded in 1866, the Deoband madrassa was the source of the broad "Deobandi" strand of Islam that was followed, for example, by the Taliban in Afghanistan and Pakistan. Its sprawling campus had a passing similarity to an Oxford college, with dormitories and libraries arranged around quadrangles and courtyards. It was home to 4,500 students. A spokesman said another 4,000 Deobandi madrassas, loosely affiliated with this one, existed across India—though he denied any connection with Deobandis abroad, let alone the Taliban.

The madrassa was set up in reaction to British colonial rule—and the uprising against the British a decade earlier—in the belief that Muslims would make progress only after educating themselves. The Deobandis also responded against Sufis, wanting to create a clearer gap between Muslims and non-Muslims. The spokesman said the Deobandis promoted "purification," living by the word of the Koran. The head of the madrassa, Abdul Qasim Nomani Mohtamim, with a white beard and white skullcap, suggested that Indian Muslims, as elsewhere, "are getting more religious," for which he praised groups such as the Tablighi Jamaat and madrassas. "The number of mosques is rising. Those who follow the tenets, who get beard, ensure their appearance, we see more people like that," he said. He agreed, "to an extent," that those who labor in the Gulf bring back more fundamentalist values. He denied that the Deoband accepted Saudi donations, though he suggested other Islamic groups might. "The Deoband movement is effective and strong," he said. "The Tablighi Jamaat has offices all over the world. In thought they are Deobandi. You can see the influence. People accept this form of thought."

Others saw evidence of religious hardening. The government of Kerala had long claimed that Muslim extremism was rising, especially after young fanatics in 2010 amputated the hand of a college professor, saying he had insulted the Prophet. A politician in Lucknow, Uttar Pradesh, whose party drew mostly Muslim votes, once said that "in the last twenty years we have seen a revival of the Muslim faith, or how to use it for political benefit." In Kashmir, a special case, surveys suggested that youngsters were becoming more religiously observant. A predominantly Sufi Muslim area, in the past decade or two it saw the rise of Wahabi-style practice. Some older Muslim friends in Delhi and elsewhere spoke of their sons, who were keener than they ever had been to keep a fast for Ramadan, memorize the Koran, or attend mosque.

But did these changes amount to general radicalization within one of the largest Muslim populations in the world? The most striking detail about Islam in India remained the moderation that looked widespread and well established, rather like in Indonesia, and in striking contrast to Pakistan or Bangladesh. Nor was there much evidence of Islam becoming an effective rallying issue for political ends. Indian law forbids explicit appeals to religion at elections. Congress had long cornered the Muslim vote, making it difficult for rival parties to emerge and define themselves as Muslim. Perhaps that could change, given Congress's steady decline. It is possible that Muslim voters will grow more conscious of their religion, and less trusting of Congress, in the face of Hindu nationalism under Modi. But efforts to develop strong Muslim parties saw only limited success.

A party called the All India Majlis-e-Ittehadul Muslimeen, popular in Hyderabad, made occasional forays to other states to try and muster support from Muslim voters. Another outfit claimed to be truly a pan-Indian Muslim movement, called the Popular Front of India. Its leader, P. Koya, in a scruffy corner of south Delhi, was hardly a firebrand. He was more left wing than religious, and more bothered about confronting "neo-liberal" capitalism than spiritual affairs. His group, founded in 2006, was accused of extremism by the Kerala government, which said it promoted conversions to Islam and associated with the banned Indian Mujahideen. He denied it.

Videos online did show a disturbing side of the Popular Front, its supporters marching in big, military-style parades—the Muslim equivalent of the paramilitary, Hindu nationalist RSS. "We want a pan-India Muslim organization," P. Koya said, and "some kind of religiosity is slowly getting strengthened." But he did not welcome foreign influences. He, too, lamented the influence of the Gulf, and "the Salafi mosques [that] have slowly made in-roads into the community." He believed that the "influence of Gulf countries is very damaging for the Muslims," and said Saudis supported Salafis in India, who served as a propaganda front. He worried about divisions, saying three rival Wahabi sects competed for followers in Kerala, drawing money, respectively, from Saudi Arabia, Kuwait, and elsewhere in the Gulf. He estimated that Kerala alone had twenty thousand madrassas, perhaps a quarter of them Salafi or Wahabi. In Delhi, he counted five rival Salafi groups active, which he said reflected divisions among the clergy back in Saudi Arabia.

Signs of religious hardening were still modest. Yet the perennial risk was that politicians would whip up ill-feeling for the sake of electoral gain. In September 2013, in villages scattered around a town called Muzaffarnagar, clashes between Hindu (notably of the Jat group) and Muslim neighbors turned deadly. As I drove along narrow roads between sugarcane fields, a few days after the worst bloodletting, the consequences were clear. At one madrassa around one thousand men, women, and children had taken shelter, some of the more than forty thousand Muslims who had been chased from their homes. Rakisha Begum, in her thirties and dressed in yellow, said she escaped her village, Kutba, where "our house was set on fire and eight people were killed." "Girls were molested, dragged about. People were cut in pieces, they used axes. We were so scared, they came inside the houses and killed. It was very sudden." By tradition, Hindu Jat landowners dominated the village whereas Muslims tended to work the fields as laborers. But in recent years more Muslims had been getting better-off and buying land, too. She blamed a village leader, a Hindu, for ordering the attackers "to kill Muslims." "The killers were Jats and they were from the village, they had swords and axes. We know who did it. But there was no tension before this, we lived happily as Hindus and Muslims," she said. Her former neighbors, she said, cut one of her children's ears with a knife.

A young man, Mohammad Usman, with a bandaged head, said he was shot as he drank tea at home. "We threw bricks at the attackers, they started firing," he said, adding that his uncle was killed: "He was trying to escape and they cut his head with a sword and shot him." Usman said relations between Jats and Muslims "were previously very good," and Muslims had even voted for a Jat to become the village headman. A clothes seller, Mohammad Akbar, said the village mosque and madrassa were attacked, and members of his extended family were killed. The village of some four thousand people had around seven hundred Muslims—roughly the same proportion as in India as a whole. He repeated that "there was no tension before between Hindus and Muslims."

The killings were part of wider clashes between Jats and Muslims that month, sparked by a fight and then the murders of young men, over a woman. It was disturbing to hear how quickly an apparently calm and stable community turned to murder. Underlying tensions no doubt existed: the Jat landowners worried that Muslim farmworkers were getting too wealthy and influential, as many had bought or built decent houses and were becoming landowners. More significant, however, was the fact that a big election was looming.

The village itself was reached along a pot-holed road that passed through the sugarcane fields where some of the killings had occurred. Peacocks and white egrets appeared from otherwise abandoned fields. The village was spookily quiet: most doors were bolted and windows shuttered. A few dogs slept in the road, and in a doorway a man lay on a *charpoy*. Larger homes had murals, some had painted peacocks. At one house a couple of men were willing to chat and a crowd eventually gathered. The men first denied any violence, then said all the Muslim residents had fled after burning their own houses as a ruse to get compensation. Harbir Singh, who owned a large house with cows in his courtyard, said "nothing has happened" and claimed that his various Muslim employees had all been treated well, that "relations were nice. We gave them gifts at Diwali and they gave us sweets at Eid." Yet the men also explained that they had locked down the village, fearing that Muslim men might attack through the fields.

The charred ruins of a small house with yellow walls had a blackened satellite dish on the roof, a toilet in a tiny outside shed. A neighbor in his twenties sniggered as he surveyed the damage, saying every Muslim home had been full with "fifteen or sixteen members" and "they burnt their own home for compensation." He added that Muslims "are so lazy, they sell their land, their debts are so high, they cannot pay interest on it, so they seek compensation." He pointed out the nearby mosque. It had burn marks, evidence of petrol bombs, though the damage was slight. "Attackers from outside tried to burn this," he said, implausibly. "They came from the fields, they wanted to create tension here. The Hindus wanted to live peacefully."

At least sixty-two people died around Muzaffarnagar late in 2013. Years later, tens of thousands of people remained displaced. Many believed that politicians had deliberately whipped up the violence, in time for campaigning for the general election that began a few months later. These events helped to unite the majority Jats into a strong voting bloc. Politicians—notably Amit Shah, Modi's close ally—crudely exploited the situation. Though it was mostly Muslims who were displaced or killed, Jats also felt that they had been victims. In the campaign Shah urged Jats to take "revenge" at the ballot box.

For some analysts this was proof of a readiness by the BJP, under Modi, to use a "plan B"—religious division to form blocks of Hindu voters, especially in semi-rural areas of big northern and central states such as Uttar Pradesh, Bihar, and Haryana. That would constitute a huge risk. Nobody could be sure that a spark of violence in one area, such as happened in Muzaffarnagar, would not spread and cause a wider fire of religious confrontation. The moderate middle serves India well—not hard-line movements on the Muslim side, such as the Tablighi Jamaat, nor intolerant and hard-line movements, the Hindutva believers, among Hindu nationalists. The highest-ranking politicians, notably Modi, had to discourage such fires and not fan intolerance.

Like India's Hindu and other populations, its large Muslim population was still most distinguished by moderation, despite these creeping anxieties. In general, India had much to offer the world in terms of how it avoided tension, or conflict, but it still had to deal more effectively with confrontation, as had happened in Gujarat or Muzaffarnagar, and with the long-running sore in Kashmir. India has done well to keep various religions mingling, and it should remain an inspiration to other countries struggling to cope with migration and to find tolerance of different practices and belief—assuming that it can sustain moderation beyond the first seventy years of independence, and assuming that tensions in neighboring countries do not spill over the borders. But remaining an inspiration also requires leaders who are set on preserving the idea of India as a tolerant, secular, and liberal place—not ones who are merely ready to exploit division to win elections.

LIBERALS UNDER PRESSURE

RINAGAR, KASHMIR'S CAPITAL, WAS WRAPPED IN THE SMELL OF bonfires and fallen leaves. The air was crisp, cold, Himalayan. On the streets, young men pelted rocks at paramilitary police, as they had for several months. Inside, in the modest offices of Shaukhat Shah, the atmosphere was more relaxed. The way this middle-aged figure, with a wispy grey beard, told things, many of the city's problems could be solved if he were just allowed to build a university. He appeared earnest and had a habit of tapping his head as he spoke. He seemed as gentle in his demeanor as his deputy, beside him, was surly, even aggressive.

Shah said he sympathized with the anger of youngsters outside, but not their methods. This was the third successive year of violent protests against Indian rule, part of a cycle of years of protest that would be followed by years of relative calm, then tension again. Men ran through alleys and hurled broken bricks. In Delhi, talk was of Pakistan-backed troublemakers in Kashmir who provoked anti-Indian sentiment, and of Islamist extremists, perhaps al Qaeda, trying to make the Kashmir valley ungovernable. In "mainland India" those who expressed sympathy for Kashmiri protesters were called unpatriotic. Arundhati Roy, an author, faced a sedition charge and then a mob of right-wing thugs who attacked her home in Delhi. Her crime: she had dared to suggest that Kashmir was not an integral part of India.

Shah was in an awkward spot, he said, because he was a moderate. He opposed stone-throwing: this was not Gaza during its Intifada. He discussed pervasive graffiti in Srinagar—messages that told India to go home and called for *azadi,* freedom, for Kashmir. He worried that youngsters who achieved nothing with spray paint and rocks would turn to bombs or guns. "Now we fear, we have seen boys pelting stones, getting bullets in their chests, so an apprehension comes that they may rethink of opening the old method," he said. But was his own group really moderate? It ran more than seven hundred mosques in Kashmir, spreading an austere set of values imported from the Gulf, discouraging intermingling with other religions. "We have been fighting the hardcore ideology. We have made them nonexistent. But the blame game comes from Delhi," he said, denying any clash of religious practice. In the madrassas attached to his mosques instruction was in English, he said, and youngsters learned computer skills, among other modern things. He had won an award for communal harmony and no one should accuse his organization of being "hard core," he said.

Suspicion existed because Shah's movement was Wahabi Muslim and he called himself "fundamentalist," though he meant that he believed in the fundamentals of Islam, not extremism. His group, Jamiat Ahl-e-Hadith, was heavily influenced by—and possibly funded from—Saudi Arabia. For many Kashmiris, mostly drawn from the more mystical and easy-going strand of Sufi Islam, the arrival of austere Wahabism could be unnerving. Kashmiris were used to worshipping at intricately decorated shrines, not mosques. Sufi practices of worshipping saints, burning incense, and singing were rooted in South Asian culture. The stricter Wahabi style of religion, drawn from the deserts of Arabia, felt alien, and could appear intolerant, potentially threatening. Adding to a sense of unease, Wahabi extremists committed some of the worst sectarian killings over the border, only a few miles away in Pakistan, where Sufis—along with Shia and Ahmadi Muslims, Hindus, and Christians—were too often the victims of hard-line Sunni-Deobandi outfits.

Yet, sipping tea with Shah, our shoeless feet almost touching, I found it hard to consider him a threat. He said that in his planned university, female and male students would learn science, so that youngsters could find meaning in study and jobs later. Some 110 youths had been shot dead that year by police—he said Kashmiris needed peaceful ways to grow and educate themselves. He chatted about cultural changes, whether people had become more conservative in their dress and habits. He tapped his head again, admitting "there is just a little, little component of cultural shifting." In the past one would rarely see Kashmiri women in the full, black body covering, but this had become more popular—was even considered modern—because it was imported from the Gulf. In the past some young Kashmiri women would wear jeans and T-shirts, but this was now a rarer sight. The area was more conservative than much of India—just as much of Pakistan and Afghanistan were socially more conservative than they had been, for example, in the 1970s. When local religious leaders decreed that an all-girl Kashmiri rock band should not perform, it was hard to know whether to be more impressed by the band's existence or dispirited by the ban.

A few months later a bomb exploded beside the mosque Shah attended. He was the target and died instantly. A Pakistani-backed terrorist group, with its own Wahabi ties, probably carried out his murder, perhaps believing he had been too willing to work with Indian authorities. But other possible culprits existed. A Kashmiri group opposed to the spread of Wahabis might have acted, or possibly somebody inside his own outfit had a grudge. An agent of the Indian state might have decided to be rid of him. Most likely the Pakistani group was indeed to blame, but in Kashmir a finger of guilt could be pointed in any of several plausible directions.

More confrontational figures existed, such as a leader of the stone-pelters, Shakeel Ahmad Bakshi. To pick up Bakshi for an interview, my driver and I almost had to literally scoop him up from the busy roadside, as we barely stopped the car. He was on the run from police, and had spent over fourteen of his forty or so years in jail. He crouched, wedged low on the back seat. Passing police roadblocks, Bakshi covered his face with his hands. At the house of a sympathizer, sitting cross-legged and shoeless, he was soon almost shouting. As the head of the Islamic Students League in Kashmir he regularly harangued crowds, calling for Kashmiri independence, conjuring a vision of a sort of inde-pendent Islamic Switzerland in the Himalayas, if only Indian oppres-sors would leave.

His was a hopeless dream. Neither India nor Pakistan would accept it: India would not withdraw; Pakistan, in reality, would never tolerate a truly independent Kashmir, especially if that meant giving up its own part. More reasonable were Kashmiri demands for India to be a less malign ruler, for repression and abuse to end, allowing autonomy as granted by the constitution. "I've been beaten so badly by police, my nails torn out in central Srinagar police station," said Bakshi, lifting his hands. "Sex abuses take place in prison, even of small boys who were ar-rested. But nobody cares, and this is a so-called democracy." He blamed the West for somehow forcing India to mistreat Kashmiri Muslims, but stopped short of calling for the use of guns or bombs.

Examples of repression by the state were easy to find. Leaving Sri-nagar for the nearby countryside, I caught sight of houses that had tim-ber frames, pointed roofs, and stacks of hay in open lofts—not the slum dwellings or mud homes of the plains of north India. To a European, the alpine landscape looked familiar, but that was not true of the great bunches of shockingly red chillies packed under the eaves of roofs. Sev-eral roadblocks guarded the road to a town, Palhallan, where police had recently swept through, furious after the murder of a colleague. The win-dows of many houses were smashed. At one modestly prosperous home, a grey-haired couple said uniformed men had barged in one morning shortly before, swinging wooden *lathis,* batons, through their windows, hitting furniture and the television. They broke the husband's leg when he protested, beat the wife, and hurled the family's religious books, including the Koran, to the floor. His leg was in a cast; her arms were bruised a sickly purple. It was a short-sighted form of keeping control, enraging local families. This was also, apparently, collective punishment for those who sympathized with young men who crossed to Pakistan to train as militants. It was hard to expect moderation to grow there.

Intolerance in Kashmir did not come out of the blue. When Pakistani-backed forces had tried to seize Kashmir from India outright, just after independence, the scene had been set for perennial confrontation. Kashmiri independence leaders had long been jailed. The central government had crudely rigged elections in the 1980s. Then in the 1990s, Kashmir's minority population of Pandits, Kashmiri Hindus, had been forced by intimidation and threats to flee. Many of their splendid, crumbling homes still stood empty in old Srinagar. But by the 2010s protests had their own ebb and flow. Kashmiris for a time supported anti-India demonstrations, but then tired of curfews and got frustrated over lost business when violence kept tourists away. Whoever held office in Delhi had an unchanging policy: to leave most of the work to intelligence and security agencies. Indian officials assumed that if enough generations passed, and enough people were locked up, Kashmiris would eventually reconcile themselves to being Indian. That got easier to imagine as Pakistan's fortunes fell and India's economic prospects rose. (And the worse the international perception of Pakistan became as a promoter of terrorism, the less outsiders would take seriously its complaints about problems in Kashmir.) Syed Ali Geelani, an elderly leader of the Kashmiri separatists, the All Parties Hurryiat Conference, dutifully condemned India as "an occupying imperialist power." But even he weighed his hostility carefully and spent winters in Delhi, where he got good medical care.

India, however, could have done far more to ease the problems in Kashmir and in other troubled parts of the country. The constitution promised all its people freedom of expression, of belief, and more, but this seemed to apply mostly among the more educated and urban parts of the country's population. The reality for many people in villages, or remote forests, was different. It was in town that one felt India's liberal constitution the most. Under the more Anglophile influence of Congress leaders, from Jawaharlal Nehru and before, India had mostly celebrated its democratic freedoms, letting newspapers write what they liked and, later, allowing free expression on social media and television. But even there, glaring exceptions existed. FM radio broadcasts were tightly controlled. The first amendment to India's liberal constitution, in 1951, put limits on free speech, after Nehru objected to critics of his rule. The worst abuse came during the twenty-one months of the Emergency, in 1975–1977, under the dictatorial Indira Gandhi, when democracy was suspended and government in effect took control of the judiciary, suspended civil liberties, and locked up—and in some cases tortured—thousands of activists and opponents without trial.

Congress later tried to shut down discussion of the dark days of the Emergency and repression by Indira Gandhi, as its leaders projected the idea of India as an increasingly moderate, liberal place. In fact, by the 2000s there were examples of great social progress and moderation, in striking contrast to the more repressive and fundamentalist Pakistan next door. In 2009 the Delhi high court decriminalized homosexuality, and gay pride marches were held each year in larger cities. Members of the Gandhi dynasty spoke in favor of that. (Unfortunately, in 2013, the Supreme Court reversed the decision.) The interests and rights of forest-dwellers, tribal groups, and other minorities were frequently debated, though their representatives complained of ill-treatment. There were also problems such as dubious official efforts to block websites critical of Sonia Gandhi, plus a tendency to charge critics of the government with sedition: once in Tamil Nadu, 8,400 people who had protested against a nuclear power plant were all put on sedition charges. Some in Congress also became hostile toward Salman Rushdie, hoping to whip up electoral support from Muslims—

for example, when Rushdie, ridiculously, was barred from a big literary festival in Jaipur. But Congress ministers, such as Manish Tewari, also laudably spoke up for freedom of expression, liberal values, and individuals' "right to offend." And even if journalists could be fawning, herd-like, or deferential, especially toward Sonia and Rahul Gandhi, or toward the owner of Reliance, Mukesh Ambani, generally the press was free. For the most part, commentators could criticize those in power without worry.

That did not change fundamentally after Modi came to office. But liberals spoke of a creeping intolerance from those with power. India long had (loosely enforced) legal restrictions on what one could eat or drink, for example. In Gujarat alcohol was mostly banned, and in Maharashtra its sale was at times restricted. As for beef, at least twenty of India's thirty-six states and territories by 2016 had bans (most long-standing) on cow slaughter, because many Hindus consider the animal sacred. In reality, however, buying beef or alcohol was often not very difficult, and even many Hindus rated the meat as a cheap and tasty source of protein. Dalits, those lowest in the caste pecking order, had long eaten beef.

But under Modi, Hindu nationalists—in office and beyond—became ever more intolerant of others' culture and beliefs, including what they ate and drank. Influenced by the RSS, whose members, like Modi, were often strict vegetarians and eschewed alcohol, some ministers in central or state governments became crude cultural bullies. Modi got to power backed by *sanghis,* those linked to the RSS, some of whom felt they had won a license to press their values on others. Modi's least intolerant (and perhaps least confident) supporters online, known as *bhakts,* were often abusive, threatening those seen as critical of their movement or who disagreed with their views. Such trolls were also, occasionally, inventive in adopting or dreaming up terms to attack liberals or anyone who did not fawn sufficiently. Those whom they disliked were abused as *libtards, sickular sepoys,* or *presstitutes* (terms that also appeared in American social media). In their world, the word *liberal* was already a term of abuse. I often drew anger or scorn for writing as a liberal or saying things critical of the Hindu nationalist right. Indian critics suffered far more vitriol.

Some politicians pandered to the hard Hindu right. Modi's home minister, Rajnath Singh, called for a nationwide, outright ban on cow slaughter. The minister responsible for minorities told beef-eaters they should move to Pakistan. In 2015 in Maharashtra state the Bharatiya Janata Party government tried to make it illegal to possess beef, as if it were a narcotic, though a court later overruled that. In the same state—to pander to Jain voters, who oppose the killing of any living thing—the ruling party called for a temporary ban on eating (or at least buying) meat on days Jains considered sacred.

Intrusions on personal lives spread in the first years after Modi came to national office. In Haryana, lawmakers from the BJP said those convicted of slaughtering cows should be punished as severely as murderers. The national education ministry seemed to suggest that college canteens should segregate vegetarian and nonvegetarian students. Members of the Hindu right showed an ongoing bovine obsession. The Indian government held a dozen or so patents related to cow urine, and the ruling party touted the supposed medicinal benefits of drinking it—mixing it into energy drinks, or into chocolate. A BJP lawmaker in Karnataka threatened to behead the state's chief minister, and to use his head to play football, because his rival said he would continue to eat beef. Haryana state, in 2016, announced plans for a university for cow studies.

From a distance, this looked comical. Yet the cultural turn also had nasty consequences. Some Hindus felt emboldened to intimidate and threaten non-Hindus, especially after one of Modi's ministers called non-Hindus "bastards" at an election rally in Delhi, late in 2014. The next year, a Muslim man in a village in Uttar Pradesh was lynched in front of his family after his Hindu neighbors accused him of storing and eating beef. He was murdered ahead of a sensitive election in nearby Bihar, where the BJP tried to pander to religious and caste groups. Modi, shamefully, long failed to speak about or condemn the killing, even as it drew intense media attention and public debate—an example of his ambiguity of silence. Silence from the prime minister influenced outcomes, just as critics said his early inactivity had allowed the 2002 violence in Gujarat. Modi's government was sincere in wanting to modernize India and its economy, to make it more open, yet he paradoxically also encouraged those on the Hindu right whose attitudes were nativist, inward- and backward-looking, insecure, and hostile to others' beliefs.

Would-be authoritarianism at times descended into farce. A year into office, Modi's ministers ridiculously tried to prevent adults from seeing online porn. Puritanical officials ordered telecom companies to block 857 explicit websites after a complainant said they threatened social decency, as "nothing can more efficiently destroy a person, fizzle their mind, evaporate their future, eliminate their potential or destroy society like pornography."[1] Officials and ruling politicians should have told the complainant to buzz off, but instead ministers ordered the companies to close the sites. Mockery followed, even from some on the Hindu right, at the ludicrous sight of officials trying to police the personal, online morality of hundreds of millions of people. (It was bizarre, too, considering that India gave the world the Kama Sutra and celebrated erotic sculptures—for example, at the wonderful Hindu and Jain temples at Khajuraho.) It was futile to block selected porn sites, especially when many online knew how to bypass Indian servers. Eventually the red-faced telecoms minister, Ravi Shankar Prasad, admitted defeat, while he denied "with contempt" that India had "a Talibani government, as being said by some of the critics. Our government supports free media, respects communication on social media and has respected freedom of communication always."[2]

The incidents showed Modi's government had an illiberal tendency to meddle in personal lives. Too many politicians wanted to say what was acceptable for adults to eat or drink, to watch, or to read. Censorship was not new, but seemed to be growing worse by the 2010s. For decades it had been illegal to distribute maps that contradicted official (but fictional) claims that India controlled all of Kashmir, for example. An urban myth suggested that a customs shed in Delhi was filled with confiscated, foreign globes, though I never could find it. Those—such as my publication—who dared to distribute accurate maps had long risked serious charges, but in 2016 Modi's government vowed to get really tough on map deviants, proposing fines of "100 crore rupees" (about $15 million) or seven-year jail terms for offenders. The plans had an air of bluster, perhaps covering up for a lack of any other ideas about how to solve problems on the ground in Kashmir.

More censorship concerned religion. Politicians used it to pander to favored caste or religious groups, as Congress had done toward Muslims by being hostile to Salman Rushdie. "Community-based mobilization around hurt sentiments is as old as Indian democracy," pointed out Pratap Bhanu Mehta, an insightful political commentator. Modi as chief minister of Gujarat had been a keen censor. In 2011, he banned a biography of Mahatma Gandhi by a former chief editor of the *New York Times*, Joseph Lelyveld. Modi claimed that Lelyveld's "writing is perverse in nature. It has hurt the sentiments of those with capacity for sane and logical thinking" and "deserves to be despised." He told Lelyveld to apologize for the "abnormal and outrageous mentality in his book" and said all of India should ban it. Modi, or his officials, had obviously not read the book, which was excellent. They were upset after an excited review had emphasized its speculation on Gandhi's sexual inclinations as a young man.

Under Modi, some feared that religious intolerance was rising. Statistics to measure such trends were questionable, but reports suggested there was more communal violence before state elections in states like Bihar, Haryana, and Delhi, after 2014. If true, that was perhaps—nobody could prove it either way—because perpetrators felt a license to act after Modi's minister called non-Hindus bastards, or after the head of the RSS said all Indians were truly Hindus. It was possible those responsible saw political gain from violence. A series of unexplained attacks on churches in Delhi added to anxiety among Christians and drew grumbles from overseas, including America.

No prime minister could respond to every incident, but Modi seemed to be lamentably slow at times, keeping silent where responsible leaders would have quickly condemned violence or intimidation. I asked him why he failed to speak sooner, to discourage his aggressive, extremist followers. He denied any fault: "I do speak quite a lot on these issues. Maybe not in the exact words that people want to hear it in, but I am absolutely committed to the integrity of the country, to the harmonious relations in society," he said. A more honest answer would have been that he resisted speaking too early, or often, because he needed fired-up nationalist volunteers, RSS youngsters, to turn out for his party at elections. He had a line he frequently repeated, in some version or other, including when he addressed a joint session of Congress in America in 2016: "I believe for me and my party there is only one holy book—and that is the Constitution of India." After the mysterious attacks on churches in Delhi in 2015, and after being chided by Barack Obama over rising intolerance, Modi did meet a bishop and speak about moderation and respect. Others close to Modi claimed that he confronted his aggressive supporters behind closed doors.

Modi's government also appeared to be intolerant of critics. One of Manmohan Singh's worst laws, passed in 2010, put much stronger limits on foreign funding for domestic NGOs, which seem mostly intended to silence critics of nuclear power in India. Modi applied it vigorously. He cracked down on Greenpeace, which opposed coal mining and nuclear power. Some other targets looked personal, such as the harassment of Teesta Setalvad, the Gujarati who campaigned for justice over the 2002 riots and was hounded through the courts. The Ford Foundation (which had helped to fund some of Setalvad's work) was also squeezed, as hostility to NGOs grew. In June 2016 United Nations experts said they were "alarmed" that over ten thousand civil groups had seen their licenses canceled or suspended, as the NGO law was "being used more and more to silence organisations involved in advocating civil, political, economic, social, environmental or cultural priorities, which may differ from those backed by the government."[3]

Indian liberals talked of a spreading climate of intolerance. Individual campaigners had always faced risks. In Maharashtra, in 2013, hired assassins shot dead a remarkable man, Narendra Dabholkar. A rationalist skeptic against those who promoted belief in magic, astrology, superstition, religion, or other mysticism, he had formed a Committee for Eradication of Blind Faith, which eventually got 180 branches. Dabholkar and his followers confronted "godmen," or *sadhus,* saying they duped the innocent. He campaigned against ignorance, offering cash prizes—never claimed—to any godman who could fulfill claims to make a gold chain appear from thin air or turn water into petrol. Dabholkar explained science and astronomy to less educated people, trying to banish beliefs that stars and birthdates could determine human destiny. He also opposed caste discrimination. An enthusiast for mixed-caste marriages, he knew that even the most modern Indians still put a value on caste when choosing a spouse. An example came in 2015, when a gay activist got his mother to advertise in a newspaper, seeking a groom for her son. The stunt highlighted the fact that gay marriage was not permitted, though the effect was undermined when she specified a preferred caste, an "Iyer."

Gunmen on motorbikes killed Dabholkar probably because he called for a law against "black magic," to prosecute those who took money while claiming to protect the gullible, or the frightened, from bad luck or an evil eye. Others, too, were murdered for opposing the powerful. India got a welcome Right to Information law in 2005, but in the following decade nearly three hundred activists who used that law—for example, to investigate dubious ties between business leaders and politicians—were killed.

Other murders followed. In February 2015 Govind Pansare, an elderly social activist, politician, and intellectual—a Communist who also campaigned against caste prejudice—was shot dead by two men on a motorbike. Pansare had taken up Dabholkar's cause against black magic and spoken out against Hindutva movements. He was murdered and his wife wounded after he finished a morning stroll near Mumbai. A few months later assassins struck again, this time in Karnataka, a southern state. Once again, two hit men on a motorbike murdered an intellectual: M. M. Kalburgi was an outspoken scholar, a former university vice-chancellor who courted controversy by speaking out against "idol worship," upsetting many Hindu nationalists. He was shot when he answered a knock at his door. Hindu nationalist right-wingers gloated on social media, and the public mood darkened.

Nobody proved that these murders were connected, though each victim had apparently been killed for speaking out against repression and superstition. Other liberals, academics, and outspoken campaigners were naturally worried. Romila Thapar, a friend in Delhi who was one of India's foremost historians, had long been pilloried by Hindu nationalists as a "Marxist and anti-Hindu" (she was neither). She had been at the center of controversies for years, and far-right figures were enraged when the American Library of Congress appointed her to a prestigious chair. But her understanding of history was liberal, astute, and humane.

Romila said the murders of intellectuals had a chilling effect on her fellow writers and thinkers. She took more seriously the threats and abuse she had received for years, in the form of aggressive e-mails and phone calls, often several times a day. "For years, every night, in the middle of the night, the phone would ring and I would wake up and wonder who would be at the other end," she said. It was always the same far-right Hindu nationalist thugs, hurling threats and abuse at a scholar well into her eighties. Several of the e-mails, from Hindu nationalists who disliked her view of Hindu history, contained explicitly sexual abuse. Plenty of other writers, journalists, and public figures got similar threats.

Some liberals protested the changing climate by returning awards and speaking out. But legal threats, harassment, and other pressure helped to limit debate. Penguin India had agreed to recall copies of a book, *The Hindus,* by Wendy Doniger, a respected American academic and Sanskrit scholar who had offended Hindu nationalists by writing about Hinduism using a psychoanalytical approach. Penguin backed down after a four-year legal challenge, just before Modi came to office. The openness of India is undoubtedly one of India's great strengths, but it is extremely rare to hear the prime minister speak up for freedom of expression or support diversity of opinion. It is too soon to judge whether the public space for liberal debate is being reduced, but critics believe it is becoming harder to speak out. It would be a tragedy if they are proved right.

All this, however, does not suggest a great unraveling of Indian society. Concerns about the "Nation," or the idea of India, the topic of the concluding section of this book, are up for debate. The first seven decades after independence have seen a broadly accepted understanding (broadly accepted at least by the elite in India) that the constitution, drawn up with individual rights mostly in mind, sets forth an explicitly secular understanding of democracy. Although Hindus easily constitute the majority of Indians, composing around 80 percent of the population, the nation is defined primarily as a secular place, where freedoms of belief, expression, and faith are the highest of all values. The rise of Hindu nationalism, the particular narrative of Narendra Modi's growing clout in Indian politics along with that of the RSS, putative questions about the "hardening" of some parts of the large Muslim population, and concerns about intolerance all raise questions to challenge that secular idea of the Indian nation.

How liberal and secular Indian democracy remains will be connected to how stable and prosperous the country becomes, how strong and independent the rule of law can be, and how easy it is for outsiders—tourists, investors, traders, members of the Indian diaspora—to visit. The idea of India as tolerant, secular, and welcoming gives it a tremendous advantage over more authoritarian countries, and helps to keep it stable.

PARTY LIKE IT'S 2047

I NDEPENDENCE DAY, AUGUST 15, IS FOR CELEBRATION AND TAK-
ing stock. It brings speeches by political leaders, parades, patriotic
songs, and flag-raising, usually set to dark skies and the promise of
monsoon rain. Yet downpours don't spoil the mood. The day is also a
moment to reflect, in newspaper columns and lengthy television debates, assessing India's progress since shaking off colonial rule in 1947.

Imagine, then, how India will party in 2047, marking its centenary
of freedom. Long before then, India will have the world's single-largest
population and one of the largest economies. In various ways, predictions of being "Number One" will have come true. Fireworks might be
banned, because they pollute, but celebrations will be lavish. Screaming
planes will criss-cross Delhi's skies, releasing clouds of smoke in three
hues, symbolizing the Indian tricolour in saffron, white, and green.
Leaders will gather early, before the heat is too excessive, to hear the
prime minister, head of the world's largest democracy, give a traditional
address from the ramparts of the Red Fort. He, or perhaps she, will talk

of thousands of years of glorious Indian civilization, not just of one hundred years of modern history. Tens of millions of Indians around the globe will tune in. Rather than the usual twenty-one-gun salute, a hundred guns will fire, somewhat deafening those who attend.

Indians, still youthful even as the rest of the world is aging, will mark the day in typical fashion. Extended families will eat together, as enormous screens blare a Bollywood drama in which the lead actor has the surname Khan. Those with an eye on the grand ceremonies in Delhi will cheer when they spot celebrities from cricket, film, music, social media, and television. Some might even be interested in the politicians, local and foreign. Between meals, youngsters who tire of being online will rush outside to play cricket where they can find space. India's national cricket team will compete against an international rival, "the-best-of-the-rest-of-the-world," in a brief game in a huge floodlit stadium. A great deal of money will be bet on the performances of the players. Though alcohol sales are traditionally banned on Independence Day, great quantities will be consumed.

What sort of country will India be by then? Looking ahead three decades from the late 2010s is an exercise fraught with uncertainty, even if the distance is not terribly great. If you look back a similar length of time, to the late 1980s and early 1990s, it is possible to trace a distinct path, a clear enough narrative of the passing years. Great changes followed the liberalizing reforms of Narasimha Rao and the early opening up of the economy. India grew into a lower-middle-income country and began to reduce poverty for many of its people as its services industry thrived. At the same time, the steady decline of the Indian National Congress—so dominant in the years after independence—became obvious. As a regional and national political force, it lost ground especially as more powerful chief ministers, and local politicians, grew stronger. Although Congress, in coalitions, ruled India for a decade from 2004 onward, it was badly diminished. The rise of Hindu nationalism was evident in this period, too. The clout of the Bharatiya Janata Party grew alongside that of regional politicians. First in the late 1990s and then in the early 2000s, the center-right party made gains. The arrival of Narendra Modi as prime minister in 2014, with the largest electoral mandate in decades, coincided with an especially dramatic slump in Congress's fortunes. It became clearer that voters were increasingly concerned with their economic prospects, and were ready to reward—or punish—politicians according to their credibility on delivering jobs, rising incomes, and a more stable country. The rise of Modi, however, also marked a growing sense of nationalism among voters and more self-confidence among the Hindu right.

Three decades ahead, such trends are likely to continue. Liberal economic reforms, to open the economy, might have arrived more slowly than some critics demanded, but the direction of travel was clear: one by one, reforms did come. The impact of creating a single market in India, expected to begin in 2017, would be broad and long-lasting, assuming the new system could be kept simple enough. The European Union got its single market three decades earlier than India, and it helped to create and spread wealth in that continent. The same would happen in India. As the economy gradually got less isolated from the rest of the world, opening up for investment and trade, India would benefit, too. More investment in infrastructure such as better train lines, power lines, and Internet connections, plus tarred roads and new airports, would deliver concrete gains that people could appreciate directly. The benefits of this, the arrival of new technology, and the entry of more Indian businesses into global supply chains would brighten India's prospects—even if India could not quite sustain the long-term high rate of growth, let alone the high levels of job creation, that China had managed in the late twentieth century and beyond.

Progress in India would be part of keeping a broad, global, economic story improving. In the two decades before 2015, rates of global poverty fell by half, almost entirely because of rapid economic gains and improving lives in China. The subsequent decades were India's turn to cut the worst poverty almost as dramatically. In 2015, less than one-tenth of the world's population survived on less than $2 a day—a huge improvement over earlier decades. Back in 1990, one-third of the world had been that poor. India's task, in the years to 2047, would be to drain one of the largest remaining pools of absolute poverty in the world. It would be within India's grasp to do so.

India could pick another yardstick to measure progress, one century after it was rid of British rule. It could compare itself to another democracy, and how it looked with its first century of independence completed. America in 1876—like India in the early twenty-first century—was evidently on the cusp of becoming much stronger, a country of global significance, even if few would have bet just then on its eventual international dominance. It had only 45 million people (less than a quarter of Europe's size), but the population of America was growing fast as the country industrialized and drew migrants, especially from Europe. Europe remained much wealthier, with a much larger share of global GDP than America. But—again, like India—America's expansion was so rapid that its relative military and diplomatic power and the clout of its businesses abroad were rising, too. The rolling out of railways and other new infrastructure coincided with overall rapid economic growth. There were also periods of severe recession, such as in 1873. Yet the growing self-confidence of Americans in the late nineteenth century came despite economic downturns and the depth of social, political, and other problems.

In 1876 America marked its centenary with a great fair and a sense of optimism. Yet it had to shake off memories of debilitating civil war in the previous decade, while in the South, especially, race relations were dire: slavery might have ended but black Americans were denied voting and other rights by Southern states. At the same time, America was pursuing a border conflict—that is, a war of expansion—with Mexico. Its frontiers were not settled, as America also sparred with Britain over old disagreements and control of Canada. More internal conflicts raged as settlers moved into the traditional lands of Native Americans and as the US cavalry fought against native Lakota, Cheyenne, and Arapaho—for example, losing the Battle of Little Bighorn. It might be a stretch to liken these events to India's difficulties in fixing its external borders and in tackling Maoist insurrectionaries or its failure to address the needs of tribal and forest-dwelling people. But what the two countries, at their different times, did have in common was a need to settle internal weaknesses even while emerging as a stronger international actor.

America in the 1870s and beyond faced some social, political, and economic problems that Indians today might find familiar. Take crony-capitalism and its crooked political system, for example. The notorious corruption of Ulysses S. Grant's government, plus the immense inequality of American society (it was in 1873 that Mark Twain wrote of America's "Gilded Age"), were combined with public anxiety over a rush of people to the cities and a big influx of migrants. Though incomes were rising and American industrial strength was beginning to grow, such periods are typically when popular frustration becomes evident. Earlier in the century, Tocqueville had pointed out a fact about America that was equally applicable to India in the twenty-first century: "Social frustration increases as social conditions improve."

Public debates concerned social problems that Indians also know today. Some in America campaigned for the prohibition of alcohol, others for the country to be rid of child labor, all amid anger over corruption. The robber barons of the era would have seemed entirely familiar to Indians today studying many of their own billionaires with dubiously close connections to politicians. At the same time, elections—again, as in India—were marked by enthusiastic participation by voters. As for party politics, America's presidential election of November 1876 proved so rancorous that a new president could not be decided upon until the following year. By contrast, India's democracy in the twenty-first century—despite scandals and its sometimes raucous style—appeared strikingly efficient.

The hope for India is that, by mid-century, it will be more obviously on a path toward a cleaner democracy, a stronger economy, and a less corrupt political system with fewer crony-capitalists. American democracy outperformed European monarchies in the late nineteenth century and beyond. Indians should take cheer that their own democracy, however imperfect, should be able to deliver better long-term outcomes than will authoritarian systems, as in China. A key to this will be whether India's political leaders see the benefits both from modernizing the Indian state and public firms and from liberalizing reforms. India has to get on with what most other economies in the world already do.

With a properly functioning internal single market, and by removing barriers at state borders, India will generate more wealth internally. If Indian firms get more closely connected to those in other economies, if better labor laws and other rules make it easier to do business, and if good infrastructure finally is put in place, then incomes will surely rise fast. Just as vital, however, are the really basic measures needed to improve human capital. Long before 2047 India must solve its worst problems with public hygiene—specifically, by changing social attitudes for new generations, educating people, and building proper public health and sewage systems in cities and villages. Getting far more men and women to be well educated—not just basically literate but also numerate and able to use technology—will also happen. The jobs of the future will require brainwork, imagination, and creativity.

More factories will come up in India, producing smartphones, cars, pharmaceuticals, and other goods. But most new jobs will have to be created by entrepreneurs, in the digital economy, among small and niche manufacturers—more like the craftsmen of old—and especially in services. Hundreds of millions of people, by 2047, will leave behind a rural life, creating homes and lives in growing cities. New technology—for example, building on structures like the biometric system, Aadhaar—will be key to improving how government functions. India's administration will, rightly, give out much larger dollops of welfare in the future. But this must be done cleanly and well.

India can get more things right. It can learn to trust markets, to produce food far more efficiently and at scale. The state should get out of running banks that provide dodgy loans to politically favored business leaders. Gradually the economy can become more solid, able to make more from having a huge pool of young labor. Will that amount to a

Superfast achievement? Faster growth will come, as India catches up from being a lower-middle-income country to something richer, even if the economy falls short of what, potentially, might have been possible.

More economic strength should then be the basis for improvements in the three other big areas for India discussed in this book. The political system is evolving. It will improve as voters—increasingly urban, educated, and informed—show that they care increasingly about the quality of their government and the economic outcomes generated. "Identity politics," voting on the basis of caste or religion, will not disappear entirely. Ugly trends, such as a rise in nationalism and Hindu extremism, will have to be kept in check and might worsen—for example, as Indian television channels and social media stoke up such things. Politicians of a new generation, getting beyond the most feudal and old-fashioned sort of dynastic rule, will focus on how to deliver outcomes that benefit all—especially by ensuring that more jobs are created. Politicians will learn that being responsive—communicating with voters nonstop by means of various social media—is essential, but it can also be distracting, and is not a substitute for action. Because more power will be devolved from the central government, a virtuous cycle is possible: experiments that prove successful in one state should be adopted elsewhere.

Crucially, India will have to address two big issues in the coming decades. First, how much is done to improve the situation of women by mid-century will be a litmus test for wider progress. As education standards rise and more flexible ideas of paid work in a digital economy emerge, the situation for many women should improve. If far more women get formal jobs, and thus economic power, then some of the worst inequality in India will decline. If the clout of women rises, then their power socially and inside the family will increase, too. Discrimination against girls should also decline, as families with fewer children should be better able to afford education, good food, and proper medical care for all of their offspring. Rising education, the decline of dowries, and growing social pressure should also discourage parents from aborting female fetuses. But social preferences will take generations to change entirely.

The second big issue that will become a mainstream political matter, and an urgent priority for politicians, is the environment. Visible pollution—such as smog and poisoned rivers—will get much worse in the years to come, while, at the same time, scientists will become ever more adept at setting out the consequences of all this for human health. Panic over smog in Delhi, late in 2016, when the government was forced to close hundreds of schools because of deadly air, was an early sign that the pollution problem would have profound political consequences. Economists, too, will make clear how the widest costs from environmental degradation build up. Added to local pollution will be the ever more apparent effects of a changing climate, which will be obvious long before mid-century. India will become one of the largest, probably the single-largest, producer of carbon emissions. It will have to find ways to respond. A large and rising proportion of Indian energy will have to come from carbon-free sources, such as solar, wind, hydro, and nuclear. Better-maintained reservoirs and more irrigation across India are the most obvious means for the country to cope with less predictable monsoons. Though India's broad political prospects are complicated and challenging, a Primetime period in the democracy is indeed possible in the coming decades.

Abroad, India will also, gradually, begin to match greater diplomatic (and military) prowess to its rising economic clout. As a stable, hopefully peaceful democracy, India can offer moral authority abroad—more so than authoritarian rivals. As America and its allies demonstrated from the nineteenth century onward, democracies build more robust international structures and longer-lasting coalitions than authoritarian and repressive powers manage to do. Given India's youthful population, plus a somewhat better-equipped army and navy than before, its influence is likely to creep up over the coming decades. Once those with personal memories of Partition are no longer alive, and the benefits of peace are more evident to both India and Pakistan, it should become easier to imagine resolving the border conflict. Much will depend, however, on the stance of Pakistan's army and how it expects to justify its oversized say in Pakistan's economy and political system. Resolving the situation in Kashmir is imaginable, if India's authorities learn to be less repressive and allow more autonomy for those who run the territory and if factions in Pakistan's army stop supporting cross-border terrorists. More trade between the countries should create big economic incentives to maintain peace. Probably most important, if civilian rule becomes the norm in Pakistan (despite strong army influence there), the cross-border relationship will improve.

Similarly, with China, increased stability is possible as India's economic weight increases and as China sees more to gain from warm relations with another big Asian power, rather than confrontation. That might not, however, mean a resolution of the disputed border. An enormous breadth of areas exists where conflict could arise—from Himalayan mountains, to islands in the Bay of Bengal or the South China Sea, and on to relationships with third countries. No doubt internal progress in China, as its population ages and growth slows, will have great influence on relations with other countries.

It might help to concentrate China's mind that India and America, having improved relations steadily in the early twenty-first century, will probably become closer still. This process is not simply destined to continue, and the fact that the two countries are democracies, are English-speaking (mostly), and share other characteristics does not automatically create warmer ties. Mutual interests, in the economic, diplomatic, and military spheres, will have to reinforce the growing relationship.

At the time of writing, in 2016, uncertainty about America's international role is high, given doubts about president-elect Trump and his understanding of foreign affairs or commitment to traditional alliances. His early enthusiastic statements toward India suggest that continued warming of this relationship is possible, and some similarities in personality between Trump and Modi could suggest the same. Both leaders are nationalist, fond of performing before large rallies of adoring fans as well as on social media; both came to office with a history of showing hostility toward Muslims and foreigners; and both whipped up support among voters who liked talk, however simplistic, of making their respective country "great" and favoring a "strongman" in the highest office.

On the other hand, Trump's more isolationist stance, his hostility toward American companies that create jobs abroad, his anti-trade views, and his promises to reduce immigration all have the potential to directly threaten Indian interests. The role of European countries, especially Britain, in helping to bind closer relations might also prove important. The enormous, successful Indian diaspora in America could play a big part in consolidating those ties. Thus for the Ultimate aspect of this book, or foreign policy, India has the chance to take great strides toward playing a much bigger global role by mid-century, even if its recognition by others as a "great power" might remain elusive for years yet.

Finally, by 2047 it is possible to hope that tensions will decline between Hindus, Muslims, Sikhs, Christians, and others inside India— the Nation aspect of this book. Unfortunately, a risk also exists that irresponsible politicians might stoke up division within Indian society for the sake of obtaining power. Hindu nationalism and the RSS organization, which marks its own centenary in 2025, have apparently grown stronger in the twenty-first century. At the same time, there is evidence suggesting some Indian Muslims are growing less willing to mingle with non-Muslims than before. These trends can be contained. They do not mean that the Indian public as a whole, as it gets more urban, literate, and influenced by mass communication, will turn its back on secularism and long traditions of tolerance that serve India well. But it will be essential for political leaders to keep explaining and supporting the benefits of a secular, liberal, and tolerant society—one where freedom of expression, of belief, and other values are treasured.

Is all that likely by 2047? Nobody—neither parrot-wielding astrologers nor foreign journalists—can make a forecast with certainty. But Indians who are youthful, numerous, and diverse do the most to grab an enormous opportunity over the next generation. By mid-century India has the potential to flourish. Given a chance to grow into more of a Superfast, Primetime, Ultimate Nation—let India take it.

ACKNOWLEDGMENTS

THIS IS NOT MY BOOK ALONE. OVER THE COURSE OF YEARS OF living in, and traveling to, India and the rest of South Asia, I have learned enormously from others. Interviewees were often remarkably willing to share their time and ideas. The majority of quotations in this book are from such interviews. The generosity of hosts of dinners and parties, academics, researchers, drivers, diplomats, colleagues, attendees at conferences, fellow journalists, friends, and family—all helped to give more than a glimpse of India and the region. Those who welcomed us as residents in Delhi for some of the most enjoyable years of our lives, provided me with material and ideas, and brought me to make judgments, that informed this book. I am indebted to all. Friends in India, and elsewhere, have helped shed light on a changing country, whether over bottles of Kingfisher beer on the election trail in Uttar Pradesh, debating Indian politics at a conference in Sweden, discussing books at literature festivals or on beaches in Goa, sharing a walk on a pilgrim's route in Kashmir, or strolling up a supposedly leopard-infested hill in Nepal.

At *The Economist* Indrani Bhattacharya helped to interpret India for us from our first day, worked with me in researching, preparing, and checking stories for five years, then read and helped to fact-check drafts of this book. Her advice and corrections have been, as always, invaluable, though any mistakes remain mine alone. Others at *The Economist,* notably Dominic Ziegler and Simon Long, both veteran Asia hands and great company, were engaged and supportive throughout my time in India. I am grateful to them, and to many others at the publication, as well as to stringers in India and the wider South Asian region.

Much of my grasp of India and its neighbors comes from reading and reviewing others' books, research reports, and articles. My shelves are stuffed with thoughtful assessments of India and its neighbors, on their histories and on current affairs. I have not included a bibliography, nor—to avoid too many tedious footnotes—have I referenced all the books. One of the great pleasures of reporting from South Asia is the chance to learn from others' work.

For helping to get this book completed, and offering reliably excellent advice, I am grateful to my editors (and their many colleagues) at different publishers. It has been a pleasure to work with Clive Priddle, Sandra Beris, and Christine Arden at Public Affairs, as well as with Andrew Franklin and Cecily Gayford at Profile Books. At Hachette India, Thomas Abraham also read the manuscript and offered many helpful suggestions. As ever, Will Lippincott has been a wonderful and energetic agent, helping to shepherd this book from its first ideas until the last.

More than anyone, my love and gratitude go to my family. My dad, Glyn Roberts, read and commented on early passages of the book in the final months of his life. My sons, Edvard and Magnus, came wide-eyed to live in Delhi as four-year-olds, and thrived while there. Their observations of India, in our many travels and adventures together, were often astute and revealing. Anne, my wife, and I began discussing this book long before a single word had been written, and she has since read over drafts, offering detailed and thoughtful advice. To her my love and appreciation are greatest. Thank you.

NOTES

2. ARGUMENTATIVE INDIANS

1. Jagdish Bhagwati and Arvind Panagariya, letter published in *The Economist,* July 12, 2013, http://econ.st/1br4eXe.

2. As quoted in the *Financial Times,* April 17, 2014, "Lunch with FT: Jagdish Bhagwati," https://www.ft.com/content/f3a22bc8-c3db-11e3-a8e0–00144feabdc0; for the original article, see "Why Amartya Sen Is Wrong: Jagdish Bhagwati," *Mint,* July 23, 2013, http://www.livemint.com/Opinion/9Qzg05zypjEUbioqK9N1UM /Why-Amartya-Sen-is-wrong.html.

3. Amartya Sen, letter published in *The Economist,* July 20, 2013, http://www .economist.com/news/letters/21581963-amartya-sen-defence-spending-britain -egypt-immigration-france-gdp-sailing.

5. TECH DREAMS AND SILVER BULLETS

1. Dina Nath Batra, *Tejomay Bharat* (Gujarat State School Textbook Board, 2014), pp. 60, 64, 92–93; as reported in the *Indian Express* newspaper, July 27, 2014, http://indianexpress.com/article/india/gujarat/science-lesson-from-gujarat-stem -cells-in-mahabharata-cars-in-veda/.

2. Rajat Gupta et al., "From Poverty to Empowerment: India's Imperative for Jobs, Growth, and Effective Basic Services," February 2014, p. 2, www.mckinsey .com/global-themes/asia-pacific/indias-path-from-poverty-to-empowerment.

3. Study by the Planning Commission, 2009, available online at http://times ofindia.indiatimes.com/india/Rajiv-was-right-Montek-says-only-16p-of-Re-reaches -poor/articleshow/5121893.cms.

6. WEAKER FAMILIES, STRONGER DEMOCRACY?

1. Interview with the author, as published in *The Economist,* August 21, 2015, http://www.economist.com/news/asia/21661825-legislators-are-unacknowledged -poets-world-honeybees-and-souls.

2. *A Journey—Poems by Narendra Modi,* translated from Gujarati by Ravi Mantha (Rupa Publications, 2014).

3. Speech by Rahul Gandhi, as reported by the Press Trust of India, January 20, 2013.

4. Quotes in the rest of this chapter are from interviews with the author between November 2011 and 2014.

7. SEASONS OF SCAMS

1. Amarjit Singh Dulat, with Aditya Sinha, *Kashmir: The Vajpayee Years* (Harper Collins, 2015).

8. ELECTIONS NEVER END, BUT THEY IMPROVE

1. "India (Government Policy)," House of Commons Debate, Vol. 434, March 6, 1947, available online at http://hansard.millbanksystems.com/commons/1947 /mar/06/india-government-policy.

2. Interview with the author, 2012.

3. Milan Vaishnav and Reedy Swanson, "Does Good Economics Make for Good Politics? Evidence from Indian States," *India Review* 14, no. 3 (September 2015): 279–311.

4. Quotes from Vaishnav interviews with the author, 2015.

5. As recorded by the author, at the event, November 23, 2013.

6. Interview with the author, 2014.

9. INDIA'S WOMEN, INDIA'S MEN

1. Veena Venugopal, *The Mother-in-Law: The Other Woman in Your Marriage* (Penguin, 2014).

2. Speech given in Haryana state, January 22, 2015, as reported by Reuters, http://uk.reuters.com/article/uk-india-girls-idUKKBN0KV0ZW20150122.

3. Jonathan Woertzel et al., *How Advancing Women's Equality Can Add $12 Trillion to Global Growth* (McKinsey Global Institute, September 2015), p. 35.

10. TACKLING THE TRAGEDY OF THE COMMONS

1. World Health Organization, Ambient (Outdoor) Air Pollution in Cities Database, with data from almost 1,600 cities in 91 countries, available online at http://www.who.int/phe/health_topics/outdoorair/databases/cities-2014/en/.

2. "Study on Ambient Air Quality, Respiratory Symptoms and Lung Function of Children in Delhi," Central Pollution Control Board, Ministry of Environment & Forests, October 2012, http://www.cpcb.nic.in/upload/NewItems/NewItem_191 _StudyAirQuality.pdf.

3. Michael Greenstone and Anant Sudarshan et al., "Lower Pollution, Longer Lives: Life Expectancy Gains If India Reduced Particulate Matter Pollution," *Economic and Political Weekly* 50, no. 8 (February 2015), http://www.epw.in/journal /2015/8/special-articles/lower-pollution-longer-lives.html.

11. LIFTING AN OLD CURSE FROM PAKISTAN

1. Tanvi Madan, "Trump, India, and the Known Unknowns," Brookings, November 2, 2016, https://www.brookings.edu/blog/order-from-chaos/2016/11/02/trump -india-and-the-known-unknowns/.

2. Interview with the author, 2011.

3. Interview with the author, 2014.

12. A SHADOW CAST FROM THE EAST

1. Masood Kahn, as quoted in *The Economist*, "Sweet as Can Be?," May 11, 2011, http://www.economist.com/node/18682839.

2. Participant speaking at conference titled "China and India: Towards Cooperation Between the Giants of Asia," hosted by The Lee Kuan Yew School of Public Policy, Singapore, April 2012.

13. AMERICA CALLS

1. Richard Verma, speaking at East-West Center, Hawaii, in September 2015; text as e-mailed to the author by the ambassador's office. The transcript, published by *Huffington Post*, is available online at http://www.huffingtonpost.com/eastwest-center /ambassador-rich-verma-on_b_8161782.html.

2. Interview with the author, 2015; Sanjoy Chakravorty, Devesh Kapur, and Nirvikar Singh, *The Other One Percent: Indians in America* (Oxford University Press, 2016).

3. Chakravorty, Kapur, and Singh, *The Other One Percent: Indians in America,* p. 84.

14. HINDUTVA NATION?

1. "The Man Who Thought Gandhi a Sissy," *The Economist*, December 19, 2014, http://www.economist.com/news/christmas-specials/21636599-controversial -mentor-hindu-right-man-who-thought-gandhi-sissy?spc=scode&spv=xm&ah =9d7f7ab945510a56fa6d37c30b6f1709; original quotations taken from Savarkar's writings, as published on http://www.savarkar.org/en/veer-savarkar.

2. Dhananjay Keer, *Veer Savarkar* (Popular Prakashan, 1988).

3. "The Man Who Thought Gandhi a Sissy."

4. Ibid.

5. Ibid.

6. Ashis Nandy, "Obituary of a Culture," Seminar, May 2002, http://www.india -seminar.com/2002/513/513%20ashis%20nandy.htm.

15. WHY GUJARAT, 2002, STILL MATTERS

1. Much has been published on the events in Gujarat in 2002. Ramachandra Guha, in *India After Gandhi: The History of the World's Largest Democracy* (Macmillan, 2007), describes the "collusion" of the Gujarat administration in the violence, suggesting that "graceless" statements issued by the chief minister, Modi, had "in effect justified the killings." More recent volumes include the much-debated *Gujarat Files: Anatomy of a Cover Up* (self-published, 2016), by an investigative journalist, Rana Ayyub, and *The Fiction of Fact-Finding: Modi and Godhra,* by Manoj Mitta (Harper India, 2014). *Tehelka* magazine conducted impressive investigative research, notably its edition of November 7, 2007, "The Truth: Gujarat 2002," which included secretly recorded footage of participants in the riots later boasting of their actions. (The videos are available online, at *www.tehelka.com.*) International organizations, such as Human Rights Watch and Amnesty International, have also published several reports on the events in 2002. On February 4, 2012, Human Rights Watch issued a statement, complaining that "authorities in India's Gujarat state are subverting justice, protecting perpetrators, and intimidating those promoting accountability 10 years after the anti-Muslim riots that killed nearly 2,000 people" (https://www.hrw.org/news/2012/02/24/india-decade-gujarat-justice-incomplete).

2. *On Their Watch: Mass Violence and State Apathy in India—Examining the Record,* edited by Surabhi Chopra and Prita Jha (Three Essays Collective, October 2014), http://www.threeessays.com/books/on-their-watch/.

16. THE POWER OF MINGLING

1. Interview with the author, 2014.

17. LIBERALS UNDER PRESSURE

1. "How India Tried to Ban Porn and Failed," August 5, 2016, *The Economist,* http://www.economist.com/blogs/economist-explains/2015/08/economist-explains-2.

2. Ibid.

3. "UN Rights Experts Urge India to Repeal Law Restricting NGO's Access to Crucial Foreign Funding," United Nations Human Rights Office of the High Commissioner, Press Release, June 16, 2016, http://www.ohchr.org/EN/NewsEvents/Pages/DisplayNews.aspx?NewsID=20112&LangID=E.

INDEX

Kumari, Ranjana, 147–148
Kumbh Mela (Hindu festival), 70–71

labor force
  biometrics improving performance, 86
  decaying railways, 6
  India's growth in population and human capital, 59–60, 285
  India's unhelpful work culture, 67–69
  lack of growth under Singh, 44–45
  role of telecommunications in, 9–10
  women's representation in, 149
  young population, 59–60
labor laws, 69
labor unions, 17–18, 52
Laws of Manu, 157
legal system, corruption crippling, 116
Li Keqiang, 201
liberalism
  conservative elements in Kashmir, 267–269
  creeping intolerance under Modi, 275–276
  democratic freedoms under Congress, 271–272
  growing intolerance under Modi, 271–273
  long-term optimism for increased tolerance, 289–290
  violence against religious skeptics, 277–278
  See also violence

Mahasabha (extreme-right organization), 227
Mahindra, Anand, 35, 94–95
Maino, Edvige Antonia Albina. See Gandhi, Sonia
Mallya, Vijay, 112
Mangalyaan orbiter, 74–77
manufacturing industry, 29–30
  balancing environmental quality and, 160
  Chinese investment in, 199–200
  energy sector contribution, 64–68
  global and regional economies, 61–62
  lack of growth under Singh, 44–45
  low-cost technology, 77–78
  Modi's promises of economic success, 34–35
  small-scale and large-scale, 66–70
  specialist manufacturing, 66–67
Mao Zedong, 191
maritime interests, India's, 201
marriage
  changing role of women in, 143–145
  dowry payments, 138–139
  Modi's, 230–231
  mothers-in-law controlling daughters-in-law, 142–143
  premarital investigations, 139–141
  sanitation as contingency for, 156
  trafficking in brides, 146
Mars program, 74–78
Marxist politics, 124–125, 191. *See also* China
Mayawati, Kumari, 111–112
media
  attacks on journalists, 184
  elections as national entertainment, 121–122
  elites' control of, 119
  Modi's role in the Gujarat massacres, 248
  recent growth and spread, 8–9
medicine: production line surgery, 76
Mehta, Pratap Bhanu, 275
Menon, Amarnath, 126–127
Menon, Shivshankar, 179–180, 216
middle class: changing voting behavior, 134

migration: effect on Indian tolerance
and moderation, 256–259
military
Afghanistan, 182–183
Bangladesh secession, 99–100
China–India relations, 191–192,
197–200
China's advantage over India, 193–194
China's presence in South Asia, 196
India–Pakistan relations, 184
India's acquisition of British
equipment, 206
India's growth as a power, 208–209
Pakistani army's political control,
181, 186–187
promoting India's naval power,
201–203
US provision of equipment, 210
US–India concerns over the ascension
of China, 216–217
Mishra, Vishwambhar Nath, 153
mobility, social and geographic, 4–7,
9–10
Modi, Kamuben, 230–231
Modi, Narendra, 11
addressing violence against girls and
women, 149
background and family, 223–225
cash welfare program, 85–86
centralization of power, 55–56
China–India relations, 195,
199–201
Congress's political decline, 282
creeping intolerance under, 275–277
criticism of Singh's administration,
47–49
demonetization program, 49–52
diaspora, 212–213, 215–216
dynastic politics, 96, 103–104, 107
economic policy and growth, 24–25,
55–57, 72–73
effect of economic growth on
elections, 131–132

encouraging religious divisions,
254–255
family, 229–230
family and private life, 230–231
growing intolerance under, 272–273
Hindu nationalism, 223–224,
226–228, 233–234
improving air quality, 160
inauguration, 167–168
India–Pakistan relations, 168–169,
174, 176–181, 187
India's Buddhist heritage, 189–190
infrastructure improvements, 88
lavish campaign spending, 130
legislation inhibiting business growth,
66
limited political and economic gains,
55
official trip to China, 200
political cost of Gujarat killings,
247–248
political influence of the RSS,
233–235
political manipulation of religious
factions, 265
popular approval, 237
promise to clean the Ganges, 153–154
railway modernization, 18
religious violence, 237–247, 274–275
role of India's identity in the election
of, 222
technology, 78–81, 83
US foreign policy under Donald
Trump, 176
US–India relations, 207, 211,
217–218
money laundering, 117
Mongolia, 195
monsoons, 161–162
mothers-in-law, 140–145
mountaineering, corruption in, 114
Mughals, 97, 172
Mujahideen, 254, 262

violence *(continued)*
  Hindu nationalism, 101, 226–227,
    235, 237–247, 263–264
  India's multi-religious democracy,
    253–254
  Pakistan–India relations, 185–186
Vivekananda Express, 5–7, 10–13, 16,
    18–19

Wahabi Islam, 251–252, 256–259,
    261–262, 267–268
wealth, 60–61, 93–95, 104–106,
    111–112
welfare spending, 56, 85, 134

WikiLeaks, 111, 127, 248
Wipro firm, 83–84
women and girls
  India's political and social future,
    286–287
  infanticide, 136–137
  investment in public health and
    education, 22, 25
  marriage customs, 138–146
  Modi's private life, 230–231
  rape and murder Delhi 2012,
    146–147
  safety concerns for female tourists, 71
World Trade Organization (WTO), 211